THEODORE BEZA'S
DOCTRINE OF PREDESTINATION

BIBLIOTHECA

HUMANISTICA & REFORMATORICA

VOLUME XII

THEODORE BEZA'S
DOCTRINE
OF PREDESTINATION

by

JOHN S. BRAY

NIEUWKOOP
B. DE GRAAF
1975

To Eleanor,

Julia, and Libby

© B. DE GRAAF, NIEUWKOOP 1975

ISBN 90 6004 334 0

TABLE OF CONTENTS

PREFACE

A work of this type reflects such dependence upon a host of friends and scholars that it would be impossible to acknowledge all of them. My debt to many scholars has already been formally acknowledged in the Bibliography and footnotes, but I would like to take this opportunity to express my gratitude to those whose contributions appear to me to be the greatest.

I owe a word of thanks to Professor Robert M. Kingdon, University of Wisconsin, who first suggested that I undertake this study. An earlier version of this work was subjected to sound criticism by Professors Philip Dawson, Carl N. Degler, and Lewis W. Spitz of Stanford University. My friend Brian Armstrong has made a number of helpful suggestions. I appreciate the critical observations rendered by Richard A. Muller concerning the relationship of Theodore Beza to the rise of Protestant scholasticism. A special debt of gratitude is owed to Dr. Spitz whose scholarly insight and humane understanding made him an ideal mentor and served as a continual inspiration to me.

Some of the research for this monograph was done at the University of Strasbourg and at Geneva. I owe a great debt to Dr. Peter Fraenkel, Director of the Institut d'Histoire de la Réformation, for his friendship and encouragement that made my stay at Geneva so memorable.

Lyle E. Seymour and Eddie M. Elliott, both of Wayne State College, did much to facilitate the completion of this work. Gary Hudson went far beyond the call of duty in locating library matérials that pertained to my research. His diligence and enthusiasm will always be remembered. Katherine Corcoran did an outstanding job of typing the final draft of this manuscript.

But words cannot express the gratitude that I feel toward my wife, Eleanor, whose patience and cooperation made the completion of this work possible.

INTRODUCTION

THE PROBLEM

Theodore Beza was a crucial figure in the development of Calvinism. It was Beza who served as spokesman at the Colloquy of Poissy, was sent as emissary to the Court of French Navarre, and ministered as chaplain to the Prince of Condé. It was his responsibility to establish the tone and the character of the new Academy in which so many Calvinist pastors would be trained. As the Rector of the Academy and as the successor to Calvin as Professor of Theology, Beza was viewed as the outstanding Calvinist dogmatician. It was a surprise to no one when Beza was elected as Moderator of the Venerable Pastors of Geneva when Calvin died in 1564.

Beza viewed himself as Calvin's heir and sought to maintain the purity of his master's theology. His post as Moderator of the Company of Pastors gave him added leverage in the theological developments at Geneva. As Calvin's successor in Geneva, Beza wielded more influence than any other single person — even though he strove to minimize the cult of personality. It would be very difficult to envisage significant changes in the development of Calvinistic theology without Beza being involved at some point in the process.

But in spite of Beza's resolve to be true to the thought of Calvin, there is clear evidence that in some areas Beza did, in fact, alter the practice and the teaching of Calvin. The alterations by Beza are especially striking in the field of church government. Calvin himself was ambiguous concerning the form of church government advocated in the New Testament. He did not feel that question lent itself to any easy solution. But Beza was adamant in his insistence that the only appropriate form of church government was representative government, and he led the battle against episcopacy. As a result of his crucial role, a presbyterian form of government was assured for the Reformed Church.[1]

The fact of Beza's activity in the field of church government would give rise to the possibility that he might have become involved in other areas in which he also had a hand in altering the Calvinist development. In recent years a growing number of scholars have argued that Beza did deviate from Calvin's thought.[2]

[1] For a detailed analysis of this question see Robert M. Kingdon, *Geneva and the Consolidation of the French Protestant Movement, 1564–1572* (Madison, 1967), pp. 37–148.
[2] The following studies depict Beza as a transformer of Calvin's theology: David C. Steinmetz, *Reformers in the Wings* (Philadelphia, 1971), pp. 168–169; Carl Bangs, *Arminius: A Study in the Dutch Reformation* (Nashville and New York, 1971), pp. 64–80; John W. Beardslee (ed.), *Reformed Dogmatics* (New York, 1965), pp. 19–20; Brian Armstrong, *Calvinism and the Amyraut Heresy* (Madison, 1969), pp. 37–42, 136–137, 198–199; Edward

This monograph will focus upon the role that Theodore Beza played in the gradual transformation of Calvin's biblically oriented theology into a new type of scholasticism. Predestination became the keystone of the theological structure erected by scholasticism and, for that reason, we will concentrate upon Beza's doctrine of predestination.[3]

Scholasticism is one of the most tenacious movements encountered by the historian.[4] There is now good evidence that the Renaissance and the Reformation were not characterized by an abandonment of Aristotle and of scholasticism; rather, scholasticism continued as a strong movement from the fourteenth century through the early part of the seventeenth century.[5] Kristeller has summarized the situation in the following words:

> Simultaneously with humanism, Italian Aristotelianism developed steadily through the fourteenth century under the influence of Paris and Oxford, became more independent and more productive through the fifteenth century, and attained its greatest development during the sixteenth and seventeenth centuries, in such comparatively well known thinkers as Pomponazzi, Zabarella, and Cremonini.[6]

A. Dowey, Jr., *The Knowledge of God in Calvin's Theology* (New York, 1952), p. 218; François Laplanche, *Orthodoxie et Prédication* (Paris, 1965), p. 25; Ernst Bizer, *Frühorthodoxie und Rationalismus* (Zürich, 1963), pp. 5–15; Karl Barth, *Church Dogmatics*, trans. Geoffrey W. Bromiley *et al.* (Edinburgh, 1957), II/2, pp. 335–340; Johannes Dantine, 'Das christologische Problem im Rahmen der Prädestinationslehre von Theodor Beza,' *Zeitschrift für Kirchengeschichte*, LXXVII (1966), pp. 81–96; Dantine, 'Les Tabelles sur la doctrine de la prédestination par Théodore de Bèze,' *Revue de Théologie et de Philosophie*, XVI (1966), pp. 365–377; Basil Hall, 'Calvin against the Calvinists,' *John Calvin: A Collection of Distinguished Essays*, ed. Gervase E. Duffield (Grand Rapids, 1966), pp. 19–37; Basil Hall, 'The Calvin Legend,' *John Calvin*, ed. Gervase E. Duffield (Grand Rapids, 1966), pp. 1–18; Pontien Polman, *L'Elément historique dans la controverse religieuse de XVIe siècle* (Gembloux, 1932), p. 127; Walter Kickel, *Vernunft und Offenbarung bei Theodor Beza* (Neukirchen, 1967), *passim.*

---

3 See Johannes Dantine, 'Les Tabelles sur la doctrine de la prédestination par Théodore de Bèze,' *Revue de Théologie et de Philosophie*, XVI (1966), 365.

4 The ensuing discussion concerning the rise and the nature of Protestant scholasticism draws heavily upon Brian G. Armstrong, *Calvinism and the Amyraut Heresy: Protestant Scholasticism and Humanism in Seventeenth-Century France* (Madison, 1969).

5 For representative studies reflecting the newer position see Ernst Cassirer, *The Individual and the Cosmos in Renaissance Philosophy*, trans. Mario Domandi (New York, 1963); Umberto Pirotti, 'Aristotelian Philosophy and the Popularization of Learning: Benedetto Varchi and Renaissance Aristotelianism,' *The Late Italian Renaissance*, ed. Eric Cochrane (New York, 1970), pp. 168–208; Paul O. Kristeller, *Renaissance Thought* (New York, 1961), pp. 24–47, 92–118; Kristeller, *Renaissance Thought II* (New York, 1965), pp. 102–118; Kristeller, *The School of Padua and the Emergence of Modern Science* (Padua, 1961); Ernst Cassirer *et al.*, eds., *The Renaissance Philosophy of Man* (Chicago, 1948), pp. 257–381; Paul O. Kristeller, *Eight Philosophers of the Italian Renaissance* (Stanford, 1964); F.C. Copleston, *A History of Philosophy* (Garden City, 1963), III/ii, p. 153.

6 Kristeller, *Renaissance Thought*, p. 36.

Throughout the seventeenth century Aristotle persisted as the major intellectual influence at Cambridge and Harvard.[7] However the Aristotle of the sixteenth and seventeenth centuries was essentially that of Renaissance professors at Padua rather than that of the medieval commentators.[8]

During the sixteenth and the seventeenth centuries some of the Protestant theologians came increasingly under the influence of scholasticism and began to employ a scholastic methodology and terminology in their theologizing. This Protestant reversion to scholasticism became known as Protestant scholasticism or as Protestant orthodoxy.[9] It penetrated both the Lutheran and the Reformed traditions.[10]

However, it would be a mistake to conceive of late sixteenth and seventeenth century Protestant theologians as having divided into two tight camps, one scholastic and the other marked by humanism. In practice the lines were exceedingly blurred. As Kristeller has observed, 'all kinds of adjustments and combinations between humanism and scholasticism were possible and were succesfully accomplished.'[11]

7 William T. Costello, *The Scholastic Curriculum at Early Seventeenth Century Cambridge* (Cambridge, 1958); Samuel Eliot Morison, *Harvard College in the Seventeenth Century* (Cambridge, 1936), 2 vols.

8 John P. Donnelly, 'Peter Martyr on Fallen Man: A Protestant Scholastic View' (Unpublished Ph. D. dissertation, Department of History, University of Wisconsin, 1972), p. 32. The impact of this Italian Aristotelianism was emphasized by Emil Weber in his work *Die Philosophische Scholastik des deutschen Protestantismus in Zeitalter der Orthodoxie* (Leipzig, 1907).

9 The term itself is very broad and is frequently used to refer to much of seventeenth century Protestant theology. Charles Beard used the term as early as 1882 in *The Reformation of the 16th Century* (Ann Arbor, 1962), pp. 262–299; see Armstrong, *op. cit.*, p. 31 n. 84.

10 A rather large body of literature has developed concerning Protestant scholasticism. Two of the better recent studies for Lutheranism are Robert Scharlemann, *Aquinas and Gerhard: Theological Controversy and Construction in Medieval and Protestant Scholasticism* (New Haven, 1964) and Robert D. Preus, *The Theology of Post Reformation Lutheranism; A Study of Theological Prolegomena* (St. Louis, 1970). Another volume on Lutheran orthodoxy that merits special mention is Robert D. Preus, *The Inspiration of Scripture: A Study of the Theology of the 17th Century Lutheran Dogmaticians* (Mankato, Minn., 1955). A statement of Luther's position on predestination, which may serve as a valuable touchstone in the analysis of Lutheran scholasticism, has been presented by Gerhard Rost, *Der Prädestinationsgedanke in der Theologie Martin Luthers* (Berlin, 1966). For a recent translation of a major work from the era of Lutheran scholasticism see Martin Chemnitz, *The Two Natures in Christ*, trans. Jacob Preus (St. Louis, 1970). A fine, brief summary of Reformed developments may be found in Introduction to John W. Beardslee III, ed. and trans., *Reformed Dogmatics* (New York, 1965), pp. 3–25. For other helpful studies see Ernst Bizer, *Frühorthodoxie und Rationalismus* (Zurich, 1963); Otto Gründler, *Die Gotteslehre Girolamo Zanchis* (Neukirchen, 1965); Ernst Troeltsch, *Vernunft und Offenbarung bei Johann Gerhard und Melanchthon* (Göttingen, 1891); Walther Zeller, ed., *Der Protestantismus des 17. Jahrhunderts* (Marburg, 1963); Paul Dibon, *La Philosophie néerlandaise au siècle d'or: L'Enseignement philosophique dans les universités a l'epoque précartésienne (1575–1650)* (Paris, 1954); Max Wundt, *Die Deutsche Schulmetaphysik des 17. Jahrhunderts* (Tübingen, 1939). A monograph that deals with Calvin, Bucer, and the other orthodox dogmaticians but that, inexplicably, pays scant attention to Beza is Jürgen Moltmann, *Prädestination und Perseveranz: Geschichte und Bedeutung der reformierten Lehre 'de perseverantia sanctorum'* (Neukirchen, 1961).

11 Kristeller, *Renaissance Thought*, p. 116.

Although the move toward Protestant scholasticism began during the lifetime of the magisterial reformers, it did not impinge upon the area of metaphysical speculation until the end of the sixteenth century.[12] It was with the revival of interest in metaphysics in the seventeenth century that scholasticism really began to take hold.[13] By the seventeenth century the orthodox theologians within the Reformed camp were so committed to scholasticism that they made virtually no references to Calvin, and it appears that the thought of Calvin lacked normative value for them.[14] The high esteem in which scholasticism was held may be seen in a rule passed at the French national synod of Alais (1620) which stipulated that every Reformed academy would have a professor of theology whose task would be to expound the commonplaces 'as succinctly as possible, in a scholastic manner, in order that the students may be profited as much as possible and that they may be enabled to apply themselves most forcefully to disputes and metaphysical distinctions.'[15]

The Protestant return to scholasticism is even more startling in light of the very negative attitude toward this movement in the thought of Luther and Calvin. Luther's denunciation of scholastic method is well known and may be seen clearly in his 1520 *Disputation against Scholastic Theology*.[16] John Calvin had undergone humanistic training and shared Luther's hostility toward scholasticism.[17]

It is difficult to formulate a precise definition of Protestant scholasticism, and one encounters few attempts at such a definition in the extant literature.[18] Thus it appears wise to follow the lead of Armstrong and to point to certain 'basic tendencies' that marked scholasticism, rather than to attempt a precise definition in the traditional sense of the term.[19]

Six basic tendencies are to be found in virtually all the works that one would ordinarily label as reflecting Protestant scholasticism. The first tendency is an approach to religious truth which stresses the need to discover basic assumptions or principles on which one may build a logical system of belief that would be capable of rational defense. This approach usually assumed some form of syllogistic reasoning.[20] Although this *apriori*, synthetic bias was to be found in both

12 Scharlemann, *op. cit.*, p. 3; Armstrong, *op. cit.*, pp. 129–131.
13 Scharlemann, *op. cit.*, p. 22; Armstrong, *op. cit.*, pp. 131–132.
14 François Laplanche, *Orthodoxie et prédication: L'oeuvre d'Amyraut et la querelle de la grâce universelle* (Paris, 1965), p. 273.
15 Jean Aymon, *Tous les synodes nationaux des églises réformées de France* (The Hague, 1710), II, p. 210, cited in Armstrong, *op. cit.*, p. 135.
16 The original text of the *Disputation* may be found in *D. Martin Luthers Werke Kritische Gesammtausgabe* (Weimar, 1883), I, 222–228. For a clear statement of Luther's theological position and its transformation see Jaroslav Pelikan, *From Luther to Kierkegaard* (St. Louis, 1950).
17 Quirinus Breen, *John Calvin: A Study in French Humanism* (New York, 1968); Alexandre Ganoczy, *Le jeune Calvin: Genèse et evolution de sa vocation réformatrice* (Wiesbaden, 1966).
18 For a discussion of the difficulties in defining Protestant scholasticism see Bengt Hägglund, *History of Theology*, trans. Gene L. Lund (St. Louis, 1968), pp. 299–300.
19 Armstrong, *op. cit.*, p. 32.
20 *Ibid.*, pp. 121–122, 166; Edward A. Dowey, Jr., *Knowledge of God in Calvin's Theology* (New York, 1965).

Lutheran and Reformed scholasticism, it was more clear-cut and obvious in orthodox Calvinism.[21]

On the theological level, especially in the Reformed camp, this first tendency expressed itself in an emphasis upon predestination as the starting point from which a theological system could be built. This synthetic, deductive starting point explains why some scholars came to view predestination as the *Centraldogma* of Calvinism.[22] The divine decrees became the starting point for orthodox Calvinism and led both Beza and Zanchi to place the doctrine of predestination under the doctrine of God.[23] This quest for a logical starting point also explains the conflict between the infra- and the supra-lapsarians.[24]

A second tendency of Protestant scholasticism has been alluded to above, a heavy dependence upon the methodology and philosophy of Aristotle. The new interest in Aristotle dovetailed with the revival of metaphysics in the seventeenth century and was very pronounced among both Lutherans and Calvinists.[25] Aristotelianism was reflected in a new admiration among some Protestants for Thomas Aquinas.[26] It has been traditional for scholars to trace the rebirth of Aristotelianism within Lutheranism to the figure of Melanchton, but this generalization has been seriously questioned within recent years.[27] Nevertheless, the impact of Aristotelianism upon Lutheranism is sufficiently clear to enable Basil Hall to speak of 'Flacius Illyricus and his aristotelianizing successors' who 'distorted the original insights and emphases of Luther.'[28]

The impact of Aristotle may also be clearly seen in Reformed scholasticism. A prime example may be found in the seventeenth century figure of Pierre du Moulin, who, in his work *Elementa logicae* (Leyden, 1596), not only repeated the categories of Aristotle but even used the examples utilized by Aristotle to illustrate the categories.[29]

But one need not go to the seventeenth century to trace the impact of Aristotle upon Reformed theology. Indeed, the course was well set even before the death of Calvin and may be seen in the work of Girolamo Zanchi, Theodore

21 Jürgen Moltmann, 'Prädestination und Heilsgeschichte bei Moyse Amyraut,' *Zeitschrift für Kirchengeschichte* LXV (1954), 287. For analyses of the differences between Lutheran and Reformed orthodoxy see Scharlemann, *op. cit.*, pp. 7—8; Paul Althaus, *Die Prinzipien der deutschen reformierten Dogmatik im Zeitalter der aristotelischen Scholastik* (Leipzig, 1914).
22 This position was popularized in the two-volume work by Alexander Schweitzer, *Die Protestantischen Centraldogmen* (Zurich, 1853—1856).
23 , Gründler, *op. cit.*, p. 112; Heinrich Heppe, *Die Dogmatik der evangelisch-reformierten Kirche*, ed. and rev. by Ernst Bizer (Neukirchen, 1958), p. 119.
24 Armstrong, *op. cit.*, pp. 136—137.
25 Scharlemann, *op. cit.*, pp. 3, 22; Beardslee, *op. cit.*, p. 12; Armstrong, *op. cit.*, p. 32; Basil Hall, 'The Calvin Legend,' *John Calvin: A Collection of Distinguished Essays*, ed. Gervase E. Duffield (Grand Rapids, 1966), p. 2 n. 2.
26 Armstrong, *op. cit.*, p. 188.
27 Paul Schwarzenau, *Der Wandel im theologischen Ansatz bei Melanchton von 1525—1535* (Gütersloh, 1956); see also Scharlemann, *op. cit.*, pp. 22—28.
28 Hall, *loc. cit.*, p 2 n. 2.
29 Armstrong, *op. cit.*, pp. 83—84.

Beza, and Peter Martyr Vermigli.[30] In each of these instances it would appear that the strongest source of Aristotelianism was from Italian influences, rather than through Melanchthon as Althaus had assumed.[31]

A third tendency of Protestant scholasticism was closely related to the first two: a stress upon the role of reason and logic in religion. In practice this meant the elevation of reason to a status equal to that of revelation and, consequently, less of an emphasis upon Scripture as the formative element in one's theology. It was the custom of the orthodox, even when they were exercising great confidence in man's ability to grasp the divine mind, to pay lip service to the fact of their own intellectual limitations. However, by the time of du Moulin there are virtually no acknowledgements of the difficulty of probing the mind of God on the part of the orthodox.[32] Furthermore, their works are increasingly dominated by the need for logical consistency — a passion missing from the thought of Calvin.[33] The quest for logical consistency has also been viewed by some scholars as one of the basic factors responsible for the theological formulations known as supralapsarianism and limited atonement (or, as some would prefer to label the last doctrine, specific atonement).[34]

Another mark of orthodoxy was a strong interest in speculative, metaphysical thought which tended to focus upon questions relating to the will of God.[35] During the sixteenth century scholasticism did not exhibit a marked interest in metaphysics, but by the middle of the seventeenth century a chair of metaphysics could be found in virtually every Reformed academy.[36]

A fifth tendency in scholasticism was an interpretation of Scripture which tended to define Scripture in an unhistorical fashion as a body of propositions, once and for all delivered by God, the purpose of which was to provide an

---

30 These figures have been selected as representative of an early shift to an increasingly Aristotelian approach to theology because du Moulin himself cited them as being harbingers of his theological style when he was attacked by Amyraut in the name of Calvin; see Armstrong, *op. cit.*, pp. 87, 158. At this point no more will be said of the impact of Aristotle upon Beza, for the question will be considered in some detail below.
31 Armstrong, *op. cit.*, p. 128; Althaus, *op. cit.*, p. 12. The impact of Aristotle upon Zanchi is a major consideration in Gründler, *op. cit., passim.*, and in Bizer, *Frühorthodoxie und Rationalismus*, pp. 50–60. The issue is not as clear-cut with reference to Martyr. Two major works have considered the question of Aristotelianism in Martyr; Joseph C. McLelland, *The Visible Words of God; An Exposition of the Sacramental Theology of Peter Martyr Vermigli* (Grand Rapids, 1957); Philip McNair, *Peter Martyr in Italy* (Oxford, 1967). A summary of the most significant conclusions found in these above-cited studies of Zanchi and Martyr may be found in Armstrong, *op. cit.*, pp. 128–132, 136–138. An excellent study of the impact of Aristotle upon Martyr is the dissertation by John P. Donnelly that has already been cited. The broad question of the relationship between Aristotelian philosophy and Christian theology is discussed in Walter Kickel, *Vernunft und Offenbarung bei Theodore Beza* (Neukirchen, 1967), pp. 61–68.
32 Armstrong, *op. cit.*, p. 194.
33 Dowey, *op. cit.*, p. 241; Armstrong, *op. cit.*, pp. 137, 183–185.
34 Armstrong, *op. cit.*, pp. 136–138.
35 Beardslee, *op. cit.*, pp. 18–19; Scharlemann, *op. cit.*, pp. 3, 22; Armstrong, *op. cit.*, pp. 137, 163.
36 Armstrong, *op. cit.*, pp. 131–132.

14

inerrant, infallible base upon which a solid philosophy could be constructed.[37] To Amyraut and his friends this meant 'that a faulty apriori methodology had produced in orthodoxy a barrier to honest historico-exegetical research.'[38]

Finally, a sixth tendency found in Protestant scholasticism was a new concept of faith which differed markedly from that held by the magisterial reformers. For Calvin and Luther faith was a cardinal doctrine that held a prominent place in their theology.[39] However, in scholasticism faith became simply another doctrine, not necessarily more significant than other doctrines, and given no prominence in the order of discussion.[40]

Gründler, in his analysis of Zanchi, has shown an even more significant shift in the doctrine of faith: the object of faith has become, for Zanchi, the truth of the Scripture, rather than a personal bond with Christ through the Holy Spirit. 'In unequivocal terms faith, or the act of faith, is described as assent to the propositions of the entire body of Scripture as the true Word of God.'[41] This became an accepted interpretation of faith in the ranks of the orthodox.[42]

Furthermore, Zanchi's doctrine of faith involves a different understanding of the nature of faith. Faith has become, for Zanchi, 'a virtue or power freely infused by the Father.'[43] Gründler has drawn the conclusion that 'there can be no doubt that Zanchi's view represents a conscious and clear return to the Thomistic understanding of faith as an infused habit and virtue, a supernatural quality by which we believe.'[44]

A giant leap has been taken to move from the theological world of John Calvin to the mind-set of the Protestant scholastics, as described above.[45] The key to understanding Calvin's theology is to view him as one who desired to be a theologian of the Word; his concern was with Scripture, rather than with dogmatics.[46] For this reason Calvin refused to distort and to twist the obvious meaning of Scripture in order to harmonize it or to bring it into accord with reason. For Calvin there were sharp restrictions upon man's ability to prove rationally the essence of God. Indeed, Calvin taught that in a very basic sense all of our

---

37 Dowey, *op. cit.*, p. 241; Armstrong, *op. cit.*, pp. 120–121.
38 Armstrong, *op. cit.*, p. 166.
39 Dowey, *op. cit.*, pp. 151–204.
40 A ready instance of this may be found in Wollebius' *Compendium Theologiae Christianae* (trans. by Beardslee in *Reformed Dogmatics*, pp. 29–262), in which faith is discussed after the doctrines of God, christology, ecclesiology, and the sacraments.
41 Gründler, *op. cit.*, p. 49.
42 Armstrong, *op. cit.*, p. 139.
43 Gründler, *op. cit.*, p. 48.
44 *Ibid.*, p. 58. However it should be noted that serious questions have been raised recently about Gründler's interpretation of Zanchius. For an example of one type of criticism see Norman Shepherd, 'Zanchius on Saving Faith,' *The Westminster Theological Journal*, XXXVI (1973), pp. 31–47.
45 The statements immediately below concerning Calvin's theology will be discussed at length and documented in Chapter II of this study.
46 Dowey, *op. cit.*, p. 3. For a fine exposition of Calvin's theology see Gilbert Rist, 'Modernité de la méthode théologique de Calvin,' *Revue de Théologie et Philosophie*, no. 1 (1968), pp. 19–33.

knowledge of God is of an accommodated character. Hence, the quest for a rational, logically consistent theology would be inherently futile.[47] Nor does one find in Calvin speculative statements regarding the order of the decrees or the extent of the atonement.

Calvin also differs from the scholastics concerning the matter of faith. For Calvin the only appropriate object for faith is the person of Christ himself. Faith represents the commitment of the total man, rather than a matter of intellectual assent to propositions concerning either Christ or the Scriptures. Even the written Word is useless to us apart from the enlightening work of the Holy Spirit.[48] Armstrong has done a fine job of capturing the genius of Calvin's theology.

> His theology then is an expression of faith and complete trust in God, written by a man of faith to encourage and aid the faithful of God. As such the rational dimension is clearly subordinated to the religious. In this program theology is designed not to meet the demands of a rationally acceptable and defensible system but to assist the faithful in understanding God's revelation. If man's reason is offended by any of this revelation Calvin always answers that we are not to debate with God but to worship him, to submit ourselves in obedience to what God has deemed necessary that we know.[49]

The disparity that one finds between the theology of Calvin and Luther, on the one hand, and the Protestant scholastics, on the other hand, forces upon one's consciousness the question of how to explain such a drastic shift in theology. Simply to cite the revival of interest in Aristotle and metaphysics does not explain why Protestantism should respond positively to the new thirst for Aristotle.

There is no scholarly consensus concerning the reasons for the rise of Protestant scholasticism.[50] Although individual scholars have stressed a variety of factors, the interpretations may be placed within two categories. The first was initiated by George Hornius (*Historia philosophica*, 1654) who stressed the polemical function of the new scholasticism. Hornius viewed Roman Catholicism as the object of the polemic. Later scholars agreed with Hornius' polemic interpretation of Protestant scholasticism but differed with him concerning the object of that polemic. Thus Emil Weber demonstrated that many times the new scholasticism was employed as a weapon in intra-Protestant theological conflicts as well as in the conflicts with the Jesuits.[51] The contemporary scholar John Beardslee has agreed with Hornius concerning the impetus provided for Protestant scholasticism by the threat from a revived Catholicism. 'To carry on an imminent struggle, one must be armed with

---

47 Dowey, *op. cit.*, pp. 3–17; Armstrong, *op. cit.*, pp. 163, 188–191, 194.
48 Rist, *loc. cit.*, pp. 24–28.
49 Armstrong, *op. cit.*, pp. 34–35.
50 A brief summary of interpretations may be found in Scharlemann, *op. cit.*, pp. 13–18.
51 The most significant works by Weber that analyze this question are *Die analytische Methode der Lutherische Orthodoxie* (Naumburg, 1907), *Der Einfluss der protestantischen Schulphilosophie auf die orthodox-Lutherische Dogmatik* (Leipzig, 1908), and *Die philosophische Scholastik des deutschen Protestantismus im Zeitalter der Orthodoxie* (Leipzig, 1907).

the weapons already available. And these weapons were provided by a scholastic methodology and a set presuppositions inherited from the late Middle Ages.'[52] However, he freely acknowledged that there were also other factors to which at least Reformed scholasticism responded.[53]

The second type of interpretation has had as its most illustrious spokesman Ernst Troeltsch, though one should note that his conclusions were anticipated to some degree by the work of Dietrich Tiedemann (*Geist der spekulativen Philosophie*, 1791–1797) and Wilhelm Gass (*Geschichte der protestantischen Dogmatik*, 1854).[54] In his work *Vernunft und Offenbarung bei Gerhard und Melanchthon* (Göttingen, 1891) Troeltsch argued that the development of scholasticism was a natural development based upon principles inherent within Protestantism. The study of Troeltsch had focused upon Lutheranism, but Paul Althaus expanded the analysis and applied it to Calvinism as well.[55] A good deal of contemporary scholarship has built upon the position of Troeltsch and may be seen in the work of Bizer, Kickel, and Peterson.[56]

Even if one views the two schools of interpretation which have been described above as complementary rather than as contradictory in their explanations of the origins of Protestant scholasticism, it remains the case that we do not have a totally satisfactory explanation of its origins. Nor will we attempt to present one here.

Rather our goal will be to study the figure of Theodore Beza in an attempt to see whether it is true, as a number of scholars have argued, that Beza was the crucial figure in the transformation of Calvin's theology into a rigid scholasticism.[57] Amyraut had insisted that Beza had employed a *'méthode particulière,'* and many scholars have agreed with Amyraut's accusation.[58]

The problem, then, will be to determine to what degree it is accurate to cast Beza in the role of a Protestant scholastic who was, to large measure, responsible for the transformation of Calvin's theology. Because of the importance ascribed to the doctrine of God by the scholastics, particular attention will be given to Beza's doctrine of predestination.

THE METHOD TO BE EMPLOYED

The body of this monograph will be divided into six chapters. Chapter I, "A Brief Biography of Beza,' will trace the early development of Beza, his labors as a

52 Beardslee, *op. cit.*, p. 8.
53 *Ibid.*, pp. 9–10.
54 Scharlemann, *op. cit.*, pp. 14–15.
55 Paul Althaus, *Die Prinzipien der deutschen reformierten Dogmatik im Zeitalter der aristotelischen Scholastik* (Leipzig, 1914). But note the modifications of Althaus suggested by Armstrong, *op. cit.*, p. 128.
56 The basic works of Bizer and Kickel have been cited above. The most significant work by Peter Petersen is *Geschichte der aristotelischen Philosophie im protestantischen Deutschland* (Leipzig, 1921).
57 Laplanche, *op. cit.*, p. 25; Armstrong, *op. cit.*, p. 129.
58 Amyraut, *Defense de la doctrine de Calvin* (Saumur, 1644), p. 206, cited in Armstrong, *op. cit.*, p. 159.

young reformer, and his role as successor to Calvin. The chapter will be concluded by an analysis of Beza as scholar and as theologian. In addition to the standard biographies of Beza, this chapter will also draw upon the correspondence of Beza and recent specialized works which have focused upon specific aspects of the Calvinist dimension of the Reformation.

Chapter II will attempt to establish the historical context for Beza's thought. The bulk of this chapter will be devoted to an explanation of Calvin's doctrine of predestination in the light of recent research. Although the exposition of Calvin may appear to be somewhat lengthy, it will be crucial to later portions of this study in which Beza's thought will be compared and contrasted with that of Calvin. Chapter II will also contain a brief description of some of the differences between Calvin and some of his successors who viewed themselves as the heirs of Calvin but, nonetheless, were not faithful to certain basic elements in his theology. The chapter will conclude with a short resume of Beza's work as an active combatant in the predestination controversies.

Chapters III-V will expound Beza's doctrine of predestination. Chapter III, 'The Position of Predestination in Beza's Theology,' will analyze the systemic significance of predestination for Beza. The structure of his most significant theological works will be scrutinized, and the location of predestination within them will be studied in a search for clues to tell us what significance the doctrine held for Beza. Was predestination a central dogma for Beza, or did he view it as a secondary issue? Chapter IV will fix upon the fact, the cause, the ground, the goal, and the means of election. The second part of the chapter will trace the actual execution of the divine decree according to Beza. Chapter V will treat the marks of election, the extent of the atonement, and the decree of reprobation.

Chapter VI, which will build upon the previous three chapters, will focus upon the question of the degree to which Beza's doctrine of predestination was the product of rationalism and whether or not it represented a stage in the development of Protestant scholasticism. The chapter will conclude with an analysis of the rationalistic influences to which Beza had been exposed.

The last chapter of this monograph will be devoted to summarizing the basic conclusions of the entire study.

THE STATUS OF BEZA IN CONTEMPORARY SCHOLARSHIP

One of the major problems that one encounters in attempting to understand the historical significance of Theodore Beza is the dearth of studies that are historically informed and theologically sensitive. The biographies tend to minimize Beza's theological significance. The theological monographs all too often ignore the historical context of his thought.

This distinction between historical and theological treatments of Beza may be seen in the earliest studies of his life which almost ignore his theological works and thought.[59] This pattern was perpetuated in the nineteenth century by the four

59 Jerome Bolsec, *Histoire de la vie, moeurs, doctrine et deportements de Théodore de Bèze* (Paris, 1582); Jacob Laingaeus, *De vita et moribus Th. Bezae omnium haereticorum nostri*

major biographers of Beza: Schlosser, Baum, Heppe, and Baird.[60] Today even our finest contemporary biography of Beza by Paul Geisendorf is marred by the same inattention to the theological dimensions of Beza's significance.[61] The only work which attempts to place Beza's theological significance within a solid historical context is the very short study by Clavier which, unfortunately, is based almost totally upon secondary works.[62]

Until quite recently the only perceptive theological study of Beza was the brilliant work by Hans Weber.[63] Fortunately, Weber's monograph has been supplemented in recent years by the critical study of Walter Kickel, who criticized Weber's work on the grounds that it was so comprehensive that it provided a minimum of helpful insights into specific aspects of Beza's theology.[64] Kickel's approach is much more incisive than that of Weber, but Kickel's methodology is so heavily theological and philosophical that he comes dangerously close to treating Beza's theology as an exercise in philosophical development rather than as the product of a number of dynamic forces in a given historical context. The paucity of theological monographs focusing upon Beza is attributed by Kickel to the inaccessibility of Beza's theological writings, to the highly repetitive quality of his works which reflects their polemic and apologetic purpose, and to the general assumption on the part of many theologians and historians that Beza is, after all, only a perpetuator of Calvin's thought and hardly worthy of individual attention.[65]

Jill Raitt has enriched our understanding of Beza with the publication of her splendid, little volume: *The Eucharistic Theology of Theodore Beza.*[66] The value of Raitt's study is twofold. First, it greatly amplifies our understanding of the Genevan eucharistic theology which taught the real, spiritual presence of Christ

temporis facile princiois (Parisii, 1585); Antoine de la raye, *brej discours de la vie et mort de M. Th. de Bèze* (Geneve, 1610).

60 Friedrich Christophe Schlosser, *Leben des Th. de Beza* (Heidelberg, 1809); Johann Wilhelm Baum, *Theodor Beza, nach handschriftlichen Quellen dargestellt* (Leipzig, 1843–52); Heinrich Heppe, *Theodor Beza. Leben und ausgewählte Schriften* (Elberfeld, 1861); Henry M. Baird, *Theodor Beza* (New York and London, 1899).

61 Paul F. Geisendorf, *Théodore de Bèze* (Geneva and Paris, 1949).

62 Henri Clavier, *Théodore de Bèze. Un aperçu de sa vie aventureuse, de ses travaux, de sa personnalité* (Cahors, 1960).

63 Hans Emil Weber, *Reformation, Orthodoxie und Rationalismus.* Beiträge zur Forderung Christlicher Theologie, vols. 37 and 51 (Gütersloh, 1937 and 1951).

64 Walter Kickel, *Vernunft und Offenbarung bei Theodor Beza. Zum Problem des Verhältnisses von Theologie, Philosophie und Staat.* Beiträge zur Geschichte und Lehre der Reformierten Kirche, vol. 25 (Neukirchener, 1967).

65 *Ibid.,* pp. 8–9.

66 Jill Raitt, *The Eucharistic Theology of Theodore Beza: Development of the Reformed Doctrine.* A.A.R. Studies in Religion, n. 4 (Chambersburg, Pennsylvania, 1972). This monograph is a revision of Chapters IV–V of Raitt's dissertation 'The Conversion of the Elements in Reformed Eucharistic Theology with Special Reference to Theodore Beza' (Unpublished Ph.D. dissertation, Divinity School, University of Chicago, 1970). A shortened revision of Chapter VII of the same dissertation appeared in the *Journal of Ecumenical Studies,* Vol. 8 (1971), pp. 581–604 under the title 'Roman Catholic New Wine in Reformed Old Bottles? The Conversion of the Elements in the Eucharistic Doctrines of Theodore Beza and Edward Schillebeeckx.'

while denying both the Roman Catholic and the Lutheran positions. The Genevans argued that the liturgical elements were changed in a spiritual, mystical fashion by the Holy Spirit when they were used in the appropriate sacred context. As a consequence, Christ was present in a real, spiritual sense while the bread and wine retained their nature as food and drink. A second value of this work is the light that it throws upon the assertion of some scholars that Beza was the crucial figure responsible for transforming the biblically oriented theology of Calvin into the Reformed scholasticism of the seventeenth century.

Raitt's modest, cautious conclusions are a refreshing change from the exaggerated positions taken by a number of Beza scholars. She concludes that Beza's eucharistic theology was essentially the same as Calvin's. But Beza's controversies with Roman Catholics and with Lutherans forced him to develop greater precision in formulating his eucharistic theology. In his quest for greater precision, Beza turned increasingly to the terminology and method of the scholastics. May one then conclude that Beza was responsible for seventeenth-century scholasticism? Not so, according to Raitt, unless one is willing to assume that for Beza method is of equal weight with content. Raitt argues that the doctrinal position of Beza stands between that of Calvin and seventeenth-century orthodoxy. Beza's emphasis upon what he termed the 'mystical' in his eucharistic formulation is one of the reasons for Raitt placing him closer to Calvin than to Wollebius, the Reformed scholastic. Raitt refuses to commit herself on the question of whether Beza was responsible for seventeenth-century scholasticism.

Fortunately, the world of scholarship has recently received two crucial tools which will undoubtedly open many new avenues of Beza research. The first was the appearance in 1960 of a complete bibliography of Beza's theological, literary, historical, and legal works by Frédéric Gardy and Alain Dufour.[67] The second was the appearance in 1960 of the first volume of Beza's correspondence under the editorship of Henri Meylan and Alain Dufour.[68] With the aid of these two instruments scholars are now aware of the location of Beza's major works, and his correspondence — much of which has been in unpublished form until now — will be increasingly accessible to them. Thus there is every reason to believe that our understanding of Beza will be significantly enlarged and corrected in the years to come.

A revival of interest in Beza's thought may be seen clearly in the field of political theory. In a sense, his political ideas have never ceased to fascinate

---

67 Frédéric Gardy and Alain Dufour, *Bibliographie des oeuvres théologiques, littéraires historiques et juridiques de Théodore de Bèze*. Travaux d'Humanisme et Renaissance, vol. 41 (Geneva, 1960).
68 Theodore Beza, *Correspondance de Théodore de Bèze*. Collected by Hippolyte Aubert. Edited by Fernand Aubert, Henri Meylan, Alain Dufour, Arnaud Tripet, and Alexandre de Henseler. Six vols. to date: vol. I (1539—1555), vol. II (1556—1558), vol. III (1559—1561), vol. IV (1562—1563), vol. V (1564), vol. VI (1565). Travaux d'Humanisme et Renaissance, vols. 40, 49, 61, 74, 96, and 113 (Geneva, 1960). (Hereinafter cited as Meylan, *Correspondance*.)

scholars.[69] But the heightened attention given to Beza may be seen in the recent appearance of new editions of his major work concerning political theory, *De jure magistratuum*.[70] In recent years a number of periodical articles have stressed the vital connection between the political and the theological concepts of Beza.[71] It appears that future research concerning Beza will stress the interrelations between the diverse facets of his thought and life.

It may be helpful to the reader if, at this juncture, I indicate the basic conclusions toward which this monograph moves. Although Beza's doctrine of predestination did depart from Calvin's teaching at certain basic points, I do not agree with Bizer, Kickel, and, to a lesser degree, Dantine, who tend to view Beza as a Protestant scholastic. Many of the emphases found in scholasticism are absent from Beza's work.

Hence my research concerning Beza's doctrine of predestination has led me to the same basic conclusions that Raitt reached in her analysis of his eucharistic theology. Beza is best viewed as a transitional figure who bridged the gulf between the biblical-Christocentric position of Calvin and the scholasticism of those who followed him. Whether Beza's position was closer to that of Calvin or of the seventeenth-century scholastics is yet to be demonstrated.

69 As instances of the continued interest in the political theory of Beza see Alfred Cartier, 'Les idées politiques de Theodore de Bèze d'après le traité: "Du droit des magistrats sur leurs sujets," ' *Bull. de la Soc. d'Hist. et d'Arch. de Genève*, II (1900), 187–206; Paul F.-M. Mealy, *Origine des idées politiques libérales en France. Les publicistes de la Réforme sous François II et Charles IX* (Paris, 1903), pp. 203–220; Emile Doumergue, 'Les théories politiques de Théodore de Bèze,' in *Troisième centenaire de la mort de Th. de Bèze* (Genève, 1903), pp. 12–16; Charles Mercier, 'Les théories politiques des calvinistes en France au cours des guerres de religion,' *Bulletin de la Société de l'histoire du protestantisme français*, LXXXIII (1934), pp. 243–248; A. Picard, *Théodore de Bèze, ses idées sur le droit d'insurrection et son rôle pendant la première guerre de religion* (Cahors, 1906).

70 For the most recent edition of this work see Robert M. Kingdon's critical edition: Théodore de Bèze, *Du droit des Magistrats* (Geneva, 1970). A rather full abridged translation of this work has been provided by Julian H. Franklin, *Constitutionalism and Resistance in the Sixteenth Century. Three Treatises by Hotman, Beza, & Mornay* (New York, 1969). A complete, literal translation based upon the Latin edition of 1595 has been done by Henri-Louis Gonin: Theodore Beza, *Concerning the Rights of Rulers over their Subjects and the Duty of Subjects Towards Their Rulers* (Capetown, Pretoria, 1956). The best critical Latin edition, based on the text of 1580, is that by Klaus Sturm: Theodor Beza, *De jure magistratuum* (Neukirchen-Vluyn, 1965).

71 See the following works: Robert M. Kingdon, 'The First Expression of Theodore Beza's Political Ideas,' *Archiv für Reformationsgeschichte*, LV (1955), 88–100; Kingdon, 'Les idées politiques de Bèze d'après son traitté de l'autorité du magistrat en la punition des hérétiques,' *Bibliothèque d'humanisme et Renaissance*, XXII (1960), 566–569; Irmgard Hoss, 'Zur Genesis der Widerstandlehre Bezas,' *Archiv für Reformationsgeschichte*, LIV (1963), 198–213; A.A. van Schelven, 'Beza's "De jure magistratum in subditos," ' *Archiv für Reformationsgeschichte*, LIV (1954), 62–83.

CHAPTER I

A BRIEF BIOGRAPHY OF BEZA
THE EARLY LIFE AND WORK OF BEZA

The controversies which surround Theodore Beza extend even to his name, which, in the opinion of some scholars, was originally Dieudonné de Bèze.[1] He was born on June 24, 1519, in the Burgundian town of Vezelay.[2] He came from a minor noble family and received an education appropriate for one of his social rank.[3] Although Beza's social standing would later provide him with a valuable entree to aristocratic circles during his activities for the Reformed cause, it has also been suggested that the same background would predispose him to oppose religious groups of lower-class origins.[4] The young Beza was very prone to illness and was finally taken to Paris by his uncle Nicolas to recover from a particularly severe illness. His uncle also offered to instruct Beza and provided him with the elements of an excellent education.[5]

One of the most important episodes in the life of Beza took place when he left Paris in December 1528 to continue his education in Orléans at the house of Melchior Wolmar. When the nine-year-old Beza arrived at Orléans, Wolmar already enjoyed the reputation of being an outstanding Christian humanist with very strong Lutheran sympathies. By 1528 Wolmar had studied under Lefèvre d'Étaples and Guillaume Budé at Paris and was a recognized master of Greek and Latin. It was under the influence of Wolmar that Beza was guided into humanism, the evangelical drive for reform, and, in all probability, the Reformation itself. Beza never ceased to refer to himself as a follower of his master, Wolmar.[6] A few days after his conversion in 1548 Beza wrote to Wolmar and thanked him for having been his spiritual father who had initiated him into the faith.[7] When Wolmar was called to Bourges by Marguerite of Navarre to become her Greek instructor in 1530, Beza accompanied him and continued to study with him. The atmosphere at Bourges was marked by an intellectual freedom and ferment which focused upon the residence of Wolmar and was aided by the liberal protection

---

1 Paul F. Geisendorf, *Théodore de Bèze* (Geneva and Paris, 1949), p. 6; see also Johann Wilhelm Baum, *Theodor Beza, nach handschriftlichen Quellen dargestellt* (Leipzig, 1843–52) and Heinrich Heppe, *Theodor Beza. Leben und ausgewählte Schriften* (Elberfeld, 1861).
2 Geisendorf, *op. cit.*, p. 6.
3 *Ibid.*, p. 5.
4 Robert M. Kingdon, *Geneva and the Consolidation of the French Protestant Movement, 1564–1572* (Madison, 1967), pp. 18–19. (Hereinafter cited as *Geneva*.)
5 Geisendorf, *op. cit.*, pp. 8–9.
6 *Ibid.*, p. 10.
7 Eugene Choisy, 'Beza,' *Realencyklopädie für protestantische Theologie und Kirche*, ed. J.J. Herzog, II (1897), p. 678.

22

provided by the Queen. While heretics were being condemned to the stake at Paris and Bordeaux such outstanding evangelicals as Jean Chaponneau and Jean Michel were preaching freely at Bourges and influencing the masses of students who had come there to study law under the guidance of the illustrious Alciat. Once again, because of Wolmar's influence, Beza was immersed in a society dominated by humanism and evangelical doctrine. This idyllic atmosphere was shattered by the affair of the Placards in 1534 which caused Francis I to attack the evangelicals. Marguerite lacked the stuff to become a heroine, and Wolmar decided it was to his advantage to leave Bourges for Lyons on May 1, 1535. By this time Beza's father was thoroughly disturbed by the impact that the heretic Wolmar was having upon his son and he refused Theodore permission to accompany Wolmar from Bourges.[8]

The patience of Pierre de Bèze was exhausted by the varied intellectual interests of Theodore, and he ordered his son to Orléans to study law, but, once again, Beza's thirst for humanism drove him into the company of virtually every humanist in Orléans. Though he did apply himself to the study of law and eventually took his license in 1539, Beza refused to abandon his love of poetry and continued to compose it in the presence of his humanist friends Jean Dampierre, Louis Vaillant, Jean Truchy, and Maclot Pompon.[9] His Latin poems were done in the style of Ovid, Catullus, and Tibullus and were enthusiastically received by his friends.[10]

After receiving his license in law on August 11, 1539, Beza went to Paris to begin a career in law as his father had requested.[11] But even while practicing law and supporting himself from the proceeds of two ecclesiastical benefices, Beza continued to compose poetry.[12] In 1548 his poetic labors bore fruit with the publication of his *Iuvenilia* by Conrad Badius.[13] This slender volume of poems contained elegies, epitaphs, epigrams, and sylvae, all of which were written in a spirit of dry, witty mockery which delighted his friends and provided him with an immediate if limited degree of literary fame.[14] A number of poems in the *Iuvenilia* were marked by a spirit of licentiousness, but this should not be interpreted, as it has by some, to mean that Beza's religious desires had chilled.[15] Henri Meylan has argued against this interpretation by pointing to the *Iuvenilia* itself and by demonstrating that it contains many passages which place Beza in the footsteps of

8 Geisendorf, *op. cit.*, pp. 11–12.
9 *Ibid.*, pp. 12–14.
10 Choisy, 'Beza,' p. 678. For a description and criticism of these poems see Geisendorf, *op. cit.*, pp. 16–22. Beza's work up to 1547 has been described by Eugénie Droz in 'Notes sur Théodore de Bèze,' *Bibliothèque d'Humanisme et Renaissance*, XXIV (1962), 402–412, 585–594.
11 Geisendorf, *op. cit.*, p. 14.
12 *Ibid.*, p. 15.
13 Gardy, *op. cit.*, pp. 1–17; Geisendorf, *op. cit.*, pp. 18, 280, 394. See also Théodore de Bèze, *Un premier recueil de Poesies Latines de Théodore de Bèze*, ed. Fernand Aubert, Jacques Boussard, and Henri Meylan (Geneva, 1954); Alexandre Marchand, *Les Juveniles de Théodore de Bèze* (Paris, 1879).
14 Geisendorf, *op. cit.*, pp. 16–18; Droz, 'Notes,' 602. For a striking study of the high regard that other humanists had for Beza see Natalie Z. Davis, 'Peletier and Beza Part Company,' *Studies in the Renaissance*, XI (1964), 188–222.
15 Geisendorf, *op. cit.*, p. 25.

Erasmus — one who loved the world but was also moved by deep religious motivation.[16] There is the additional evidence that Beza made it a point to listen to the Lutheran sermons of Claude d'Espence.[17] The position of Beza was similar to that of many of his contemporaries: on the one hand he had a deep appreciation for the ideas of the Reformation, but, on the other hand, he was so drawn to the attractions of Parisian life that he did not make a public commitment to those ideas. Natalie Davis has suggested that Beza's conversion was also postponed because of his close friendship with Peletier, a friendship that 'showed French humanism and literary life to Beza, not at its frivolous and imitative worst, but at its best.'[18]

Beza's evangelical crisis was hastened by a very severe illness and by his decision to marry Claudine Desnoz (or Denosse).[19] As a result of his evangelical decision, Beza left France in October, 1548, and abandoned his family, friends, literary fame, and fortune.[20] Beza arrived in Geneva on October 23 or 24, 1548, and, in keeping with his promise to Claudine, shortly thereafter had their clandestine marriage blessed in the church. The flight to Geneva was interpreted by the French authorities as the final confirmation of Beza's evangelical sympathies, and the Parlement of Paris acted swiftly. On April 3, 1549, Beza was banished by the Parlement on three grounds: he was a heretic, he had sold his benefices, and he had fled to Geneva. This was followed by further actions on May 31, 1550, which confiscated all of Beza's possessions and condemned him to be burned at the stake.[21]

It would appear that Calvin played no role in Beza's conversion. The crucial influence was Wolmar to whom Beza had sent a letter shortly after his conversion acknowledging that Wolmar was his 'spiritual father.'[22]

The Protestant reformer who was probably the most influential in Beza's conversion was Bullinger, whose work was studied by Beza when he was a student with Wolmar at Bourges in 1535.[23] Beza remained united with Bullinger all of his

16 Henri Meylan, 'La conversion de Bèze ou les longues hesitations d'un humaniste chrétien,' *Geneva*, VII (1959), 104.
17 Meylan, *Correspondance*, I, pp. 63–65.
18 Davis, 196.
19 The centrality of Beza's marriage as a motivating force for his conversion has been explored and demonstrated by a number of scholars; see Hippolyte Aubert, 'La conversion de Théodore de Bèze à la Réforme. Théodore de Bèze et sa famille d'après des extraits de la correspondance de Bèze,' *Bulletin de la Société de l'Histoire protestant français*, LIII (1904), 533–548; Meylan, 'La conversion de Bèze,' *Geneva*, VII (1959), 103–125; Françis Molard, 'Quand Théodore de Bèze a-t-il rompu avec l'Eglise romaine?,' *Bulletin de la Société des sciences historiques et naturelles de l'Yonne*, 1888, 201–204.
20 Beza recounted his confused emotional state at the time and the factors which led him to his decisions in a letter sent to Wolmar as a preface to Beza's work, *Confessio christianae fidei* . . . (1560). This has been reproduced in Meylan, *Correspondance*, III, pp. 43–49.
21 Geisendorf, *op. cit.*, pp. 29–30.
22 This letter has been reproduced in Meylan, *Correspondance*, III, pp. 43–49.
23 Meylan, *Correspondance*, I, 63–65.

24

life and addressed him as 'my father,' even when the latter did not return the warmth.[24]

Though Beza had rejected the doctrine of transubstantiation as early as 1535, he remained outwardly attached to the Roman Church. Meylan suggests that this was because of Beza's unwillingness to relinquish the income that he was receiving from his two ecclesiastical benefices. Beza, himself, hinted at this in his letter to Capponi concerning the Italian Spiritualists at Lyon. He argued that the officials who were involved in the Eucharistic conflict should be forced to state their positions as clearly as possible. They had to be decisive in their teaching in order to avoid the sin of theological ambiguity for the purpose of material gain. Toward the end of the letter Beza alluded to his own youth in which he was tempted by the same materialistic impulse.[25] Thus after his conversion Beza stressed the need for theological clarity and consistency as the prerequisite for a stable Christian life. According to Ritschl this may be an explanation for the emphasis that Beza placed upon predestination: it had such great implications for one's practical Christian life.[26]

THE REFORMER

Now that Beza had been converted and had joined the Calvinist cause, a new chapter opened in his life. He had forsaken the income from his benefices, all of his remaining goods in France had been confiscated, and he himself had been condemned to death. His most pressing problem was to find employment. Initially he had hoped to establish a printing firm with his good friend Crespin, a well-known humanist who would become the historian of the Huguenot martyrs, but in November, 1549, he accepted the post of Professor of Greek at the new Academy of Lausanne, where he remained for nine years.[27]

Beza's teaching was well received at Lausanne, and he found himself devoting an increasing portion of his time to teaching theology to the large number of student refugees from France. He became a familiar figure within the circle of humanists and Reformed theologians.

24 Henri Meylan, 'Bèze et les Italiens de Lyon,' *Bibliothèque d'Humanisme et Renaissance,* XIV (1952), 248. Beza's close dependence upon Bullinger is best seen in his letter to Bullinger on August 18, 1568, and Bullinger's response of August 24, 1568. This correspondence has been published by Hippolyte Aubert in his article 'La conversion de Théodore de Bèze à la Réforme,' *Bulletin de la Société de l'Histoire,* LIII (1904), 533–548. Dantine has argued that Beza was converted to Bullinger's understanding of the eucharist while studying his work *De origine erroris in negotio Eucharistiae ac missae* with Wolmar; see Johannes Dantine, 'Die prädestinations lehre bei Calvin und Beza' (Unpublished doctoral dissertation, Faculty of Theology, Göttingen University, 1965), p. 19.
25 Henri Meylan, 'Bèze et les Italiens de Lyon,' *Bibliothèque d'Humanisme et Renaissance,* XIV (1952), 235–249.
26 Otto Ritschl, *Dogmengeschichte des Protestantismus* (Leipzig, 1908f.), III, 296f.
27 The best summary of Beza's days at Lausanne is to be found in Geisendorf, *op. cit.,* pp. 33–70. That is the source from which the following factual data have been taken unless indicated to the contrary.

During the nine years at Lausanne Beza produced a steady flow of scholarly works, both literary and theological. This included such items as *Zographie Cochleae* (1549),[28] *Epistola Passavantii* (1553),[29] and *Abraham sacrifiant* (1550).[30] Beza also completed the translation into French verse of the Psalms which had been started by Clement Marot but was cut short by his death.[31] Even though this turned out to be a popular work, the consensus of critical opinion was that Beza's translations suffered when compared to those of Marot.[32] The most significant theological works that Beza produced at Lausanne were the *Réponse à la confession du duc de Northumberland* (1554),[33] *De Haereticis* (1554),[34] *Tabula Praedestinationis* (1555)[35] his Latin translation of the Greek New Testament (1556),[36] *De la predestination, contre Castellion* (1558),[37] *De Coena Domini plana et perspicus tractatio* (1559),[38] and his *Confession de la foi chretienne* (1559).[39]

28 This was originally printed under the title of *Brevis et utilis Zographia Joannis Cochleae* and has been reprinted in Meylan, *Correspondance*, I, pp. 49–55. See also Gardy, *op. cit.*, pp. 17–18; Geisendorf, *op. cit.*, pp. 46–47.

29 Gardy, *op. cit.*, pp. 34–40. See also Geisendorf, *op. cit.*, 48–51; Charles Bost, 'Théodore de Bèze et Rabelais, le Passavant,' *Revue du XVIe siècle*, XIX (1932–1933), 282–290.

30 Gardy, *op. cit.*, pp. 18–32. See also Geisendorf, *op. cit.*, pp. 51–54; Raymond Lebrègue, *La tragédie religieuse en France; Les Débuts, 1514–1573* (Paris, 1929), pp. 293–318, 507–513. A helpful critical edition of *Abraham Sacrifiant* is that edited by Keith Cameron, Kathleen M. Hall, and Francis Higman and produced by the Droz Press of Geneva in 1967.

31 Geisendorf, *op. cit.*, pp. 54–63.

32 Marc Monnier, *Genève et ses poètes* (Paris, 1874), p. 95; Virgile Rossel, *Histoire littéraire de la Suisse romande* (Neuchâtel, 1903), p. 97; Emmanuel-Oretin Douen, *Clément Marot et le psautier huguenot* (Paris, 1878), I, p. 573.

33 Gardy, *op. cit.*, pp. 40–41.

34 This was originally published with the title *De haereticis a civili magistratu puniendis libellus adversus Martini Belii farraginem et novorum academicorum sectum Theodoro Beza Vezlii auctore*. See Gardy, *op. cit.*, pp. 44–47; Geisendorf, *op. cit.*, p. 65; Heppe, *op. cit.*, p. 371. This was the first work in which Beza expressed his political ideas; see Robert Kingdon, 'The First Expression of Theodore Beza's Political Ideas,' *Archiv für Reformationsgeschichte*, XLVI (1955), 88–100.

35 Gardy, *op. cit.*, pp. 47–53; Geisendorf, *op. cit.*, pp. 74–75. This work is crucial for our purposes and is discussed in detail below.

36 The title of this work was *Novum D.N. Jesu Christi Testamentum. Latine jam olim a veteri interprete, nunc denuo a Theodoro Beza versum: cum ejusdem annotationibus, in quibus ratio interpretationis redditur*. See Geisendorf, *op. cit.*, p. 70; Clavier, *op. cit.*, p. 41 n.; John Calvin, *Joannis Calvini opera quae supersunt omnia* (59 vols.; Corpus Reformatorum, vols. 29–50; Brunswick, 1863–1900), XVII, p. 233 n.

37 The original title of this work was *Ad sycophantarum quorumdam calumnias quibus unicum salutis nostrae fundamentum, id est aeternam Dei predestinationem evertere nituntur responsio Theodori Bezae Vezelii*. However, in later editions the expression 'Sycophanta' was replaced by the name of Sebastien Castellion. See Gardy, *op. cit.*, pp. 55–58; Geisendorf, *op. cit.*, p. 68.

38 Geisendorf, *op. cit.*, p. 113; Gardy, *op. cit.*, pp. 59–60.

39 The first edition of this work bore the title *Confession de la foy chrestienne, contenant la confirmation d'icelle, et la refutation des superstitions contraires*. See Geisendorf, *op. cit.*, p. 78; Gardy, *op. cit.*, pp. 60–80. A fine modernized text of this confession with introduction and notes has been prepared by Michel Réveillaud. The eucharistic theology of the confession has been explored by Jill Raitt: *The Eucharistic Theology of Theodore Beza: Development of the Reformed Doctrine* (Chambersburg, Pennsylvania, 1972), pp 10–30.

As Beza's fame grew in Lausanne, he was pressed into the role of diplomat for the Calvinist cause. In the years 1557 and 1558 he traveled to Germany three times in order to uphold the position of the Waldensians and the Huguenots, and he was quite active as an ecumenical protestant who sought to harmonize the theological differences between the Lutheran and the Reformed interpretations of the Eucharist. But his efforts were in vain as the theological debates degenerated into polemics. Beza's defense of the doctrine of predestination also created problems. At the same time the situation in Lausanne was becoming increasingly tense as the radical reformer Viret battled the Magistrates of Bern who exercised political power in the Vaud. At first Beza tried to mediate between Viret and Bern, but, increasingly, he was identified with the cause of Viret and also became the object of Bern's wrath. By 1558 things were so bad in Lausanne that Beza resigned his post rather than to be deposed and happily accepted the call to go to Geneva as minister and Professor of Greek.[40]

When Beza arrived in Geneva in 1558 the city was governed by the friends and allies of Calvin. The major battles were over: the Libertines had been eliminated as a threat to Calvin, his theological opponents had fled the scene, the Council was filled with Calvin's friends, and Geneva was filled with enough French refugees to assure Calvin control of the city.[41]

Beza was extremely well received in Geneva. In less than a year he was Professor of Greek, Pastor, and finally, Rector of the new Academy when it opened its doors.[42]

The new institution was an immediate success. When Calvin died the Academy had an enrollment of fifteen hundred students: twelve hundred in the elementary and secondary department and three hundred in the advanced department. The higher section of the Genevan Academy became the model for academies and seminaries that were established throughout Europe and served to create a Calvinist elite in many European countries.[43]

There is no question concerning the crucial role that Calvin played in establishing the Academy. It was Calvin who had pressed for the founding of the Academy; he, rather than Beza, drew up the Academy's constitution, the *Leges Academicae*, which he presented to the Small Council on May 22, 1559; and Calvin was responsible for developing the general pattern and outline of the Academy.[44]

Calvin was the creator of the Academy, but, as Charles Borgeaud has demonstrated, Beza determined the spirit of the Academy and was responsible for its fame.[45] His influence may be seen in the selection of the original faculty members, several of whom had been his companions at the Academy of Lausanne.[46] A

40 Geisendorf, *op. cit.*, pp. 81–103.
41 *Ibid.*, p. 105.
42 *Ibid.*, p. 107.
43 Emile G. Léonard, *A History of Protestantism*, ed. H.H. Rowley, trans. Joyce M.H. Reid (London, 1965), I, p. 346.
44 Geisendorf, *op. cit.*, p. 108.
45 Charles Borgeaud, *Histoire de l'Université de Genève* (Genève, 1900), I, 'La part de Bèze,' pp. 313–330.
46 Geisendorf, *op. cit.*, pp. 108–109; Léonard, *op. cit.*, I, pp. 345–346.

gigantic step in determining the character of the Academy was taken when Beza insisted that Aristotle be included in the curriculum, an action that was parallelled in Lutheranism by the work of Melanchthon at Wittenberg.[47] Beza's impact was also magnified by his genial personality, which the students found to be a refreshing change from the ruggedness and the rigidity of the ageing Calvin.[48] Though Beza was actively involved in politics and overwhelmed by the responsibilities of teaching, administration, writing theological tracts, maintaining an extensive correspondence, and counselling, for the remainder of his life he strove to set aside his best hours for the work of the Academy.[49]

But in spite of Beza's desire to focus his energies upon the Academy, by October of 1559 he found himself once more traveling through Germany and France in the hope of improving the worsening plight of the French Protestants. This journey was made by him with the knowledge that the sentence of capital punishment continued to hang over his head. The trip drained Beza's energy and even endangered his life, but accomplished little for the Reformed cause.[50] More succesful was his trip to Nerac in 1560 when one of his goals was to visit the Court of French Navarre with the purpose of warning its leaders of a plot against the French crown.[51]

By 1561 Beza was so highly regarded as a spokesman for the Reformed cause that he was requested by the French Protestants to represent their views at the Colloquy of Poissy which was called by Catherine de'Medici and opened on September 9, 1561.[52] The goal of the Colloquy was to end the religious disunity that had divided France. There were some who requested that Calvin represent

47 On December I, 1570, Beza wrote a letter to Ramus in which he insisted upon the importance of Aristotle to the Genevan curriculum. This letter is quoted by Borgeaud, *op. cit.*, I, pp. 113–114. Yet one must be careful not to overstate the case *vis-a-vis* Beza introducing Aristotle to the Academy. The *Rules of the Academy* that had been drawn up by Calvin listed Aristotle as one of those authorities whose work might be drawn upon in Dialectics and in Rhetoric. But Calvin did not require the study of Aristotle.
48 See Alain Dufour, 'Les mythe de Genève au temps de Calvin,' *Schweizer. Zeitschrift für Geschichte*, 1959, 489–518, cited by Emile G. Léonard, *A History of Protestantism*, ed. H.H. Rowley, trans. R.M. Bethell (London, 1967), II, p. 4.
49 Geisendorf, *op. cit.*, p. 108.
50 N. Weiss, 'Le proces de Beze au Parlement de Paris,' *Bulletin de l'Histoire du Protestantisme Français*, XXXVII (1888), 530–537.
51 This has been demonstrated by Alain Dufour, 'L'affaire de Maligny (Lyon, 4–5 septembre 1560) vue à travers la correspondance de Calvin et de Beze,' *Cahiers d'histoire publiés par les universités de Clermont-Lyon-Grenoble*, VIII (1963), 269–280.
52 For general studies of the Colloquy see Donald G. Nugent, 'The Colloquy of Possy: A Study in Sixteenth Century Ecumenism' (Unpublished Ph.D. dissertation, Department of History, University of Iowa, 1965); H.O. Evennett, *The Cardinal of Lorraine and the Council of Trent* (Cambridge, 1930), pp. 283–394; Alain Dufour 'Le Colloque de Poissy,' *Mélanges d'histoire du xvie siècle offerts à Henri Meylan* (Lausanne, 1970), pp. 129ff.; J. Carbonnier, 'Le Colloque de Poissy,' *Foi et Vie*, new series, LX (1961), n. 4–5, pp. 43–52. An extensive treatment of Beza's role at the Colloquy has been provided by Geisendorf, *op. cit.*, pp. 125–166. The eucharistic theology of Poissy has been explored by Raitt, *op. cit.*, pp. 31–35. Maruyama (*op. cit.*, pp. 63–97) has analyzed the ecclesiology of the Colloquy and provides a number of additional bibliographical leads. A very helpful bibliographical footnote is by Leonard, *op. cit.*, II, p. 107, n. 1.

Geneva at the Colloquy, but the consensus was for Beza. Nugent has caught the nuances of this decision very well.

Actually Calvin was never seriously considered. The City Council of Geneva was unwilling to risk the loss of the commander-in-chief, and forbade his going. The danger was not only to Calvin, but from him. Apart from his chronically poor health, he was known to be choleric and uncompromising, and thus his presence might militate against concord and even irritate the Queen. Thus, the Admiral considered his coming inadvisable. Beza, on the other hand, was a skillful diplomat and a polished orator, and, as a noblemen, would be equal to the exacting demands of court protocol. While he was, at bottom, as firm in the faith as Calvin, he was more conciliatory on matters of form. As such, he was a fine complement to Calvin and a becoming choice.[53]

, Beza was the chief spokesman for the Reformed cause at Poissy, and, as Raitt has observed, 'Poissy was a brilliant peak in the life of Beza . . . he represented the doctrine of the Reformed Churches before the King of France, the Queen Mother, the whole French court, and the French princes of the Roman Catholic Church, plus papal delegates . . .'[54] Although Beza, accompanied by Peter Martyr Vermigli at the second session, made a very strong impression at Poissy and was invited to continue the discussions at Saint-Germain, all negotiations halted abruptly with the massacre at Vassy, in Champagne, on March 1, 1562.[55]

The massacre of Vassy marked the beginning of what some have referred to as the Wars of Religion. As the word spread through France that Duke Henry had massacred the Huguenots at Vassy, the Huguenots began to arm themselves for war.[56] Beza was in Paris when word reached him about the massacre. He fled to the court of Condé at Orléans where he argued that the Huguenots should present a complaint to the Queen Mother rather than engage in military reprisals.[57] As the war clouds thickened the activism of Beza was seen once again as he attached himself to Condé as chaplain and also served as his secretary. During most of the first war Beza was in France on the side of the Huguenots. He left only after the war was terminated by the Edict of Amboise on March 19, 1563.[58] It was now time for Beza to return to Geneva. Much work awaited him, and he would be needed to assume the labors of Calvin who would die on May 27, 1564.

It was a surprise to no one when Beza was elected moderator, on June 2, 1564, one week after Calvin's death.[59] In the political arena Beza had been Calvin's

53 Nugent, *op. cit.*, pp. 72–73. The entire matter is considered in Geisendorf, *op. cit.*, pp. 128–129.
54 Raitt, *op. cit.*, p. 8.
55 Geisendorf, *op. cit.*, pp. 167–190.
56 *Ibid.*, p. 190.
57 Meylan, *Correspondance*, IV, p. 255.
58 Geisendorf, *op. cit.*, pp. 191–225.
59 Robert M. Kingdon and Jean-François Bergier, eds. *Registres de la Compagnie des Pasteurs de Genève au temps de Calvin* (3 vols.; Geneva, 1962, 1964, 1969), II, pp. 102–104. (Hereinafter cited *R.C.P.*) The best summary of Beza as Calvin's successor is to be found in Geisendorf, *op. cit.*, pp. 245–281; see also Eugène Choisy. *L'état chrétien calviniste à Genève au temps de Théodore de Bèze* (Geneva, 1902); Herman de Vries, *Geneve Pépiniere du Cal-*

right-hand man and had served the Reformed cause well as diplomat, spokesman at the Colloquy of Poissy, emissary to the Court of French Navarre, and chaplain to the Prince of Condé. His political credentials were beyond reproach.

Nor were Beza's intellectual gifts and accomplishments lacking. Kingdon has summarized it well:

> Beza's formal qualifications for intellectual eminence were, if anything, superior to Calvin's. His reputation as an elegant Latin stylist was deservedly high. Montaigne regarded him as one of the greatest Latin poets of the century. His knowledge of Greek was thorough and constantly useful, in his translations of Scripture, his teaching, and his scholarly publications. Linguistic competence of this sort was of prime importance to anyone making his way as a sixteenth-century intellectual. Beza was also thoroughly acquainted with the contents of the writings of antiquity. He saw to it that the new Academy of Geneva had a thoroughly classical foundation to its curriculum.[60]

One of the greatest differences between Calvin and Beza was that of personality. Beza, with his background as a member of the lesser nobility, maintained an easy and fluidity of manner which was never attained by 'the intense and somewhat more awkward Calvin.'[61] He moved freely in aristocratic circles and, unlike Calvin, was on very good terms with the Huguenot military leaders. After 1571 he served Henri of Navarre as his Genevan agent.[62] It may have been this aristocratic background which provided Beza with the confidence to assume a political stance which Monter has labeled as 'slightly imprudent.'[63]

But one thing is clear: in the struggles between church and state in Geneva Beza consistently sided with the members of the Small Council, whose social positions were similar to his own, rather than with his fellow ministers.[64] He accepted the decree of the magistrates, that he give them advice and information from a bench at the foot of the council, rather than from the table itself, and he refused to make entries in the official minutes or to correct diplomatic dispatches as had Calvin.[65] In short, after the death of Calvin there was a progressive reassertion of authority by the civil magistrates over the church in Geneva, a reassertion that was hastened by the retirement of Beza as moderator in 1580 and by the outbreak of war in 1589.[66] But at the same time one must acknowledge, as has Choisy, that

---

vinisme Hollandais. Vol. 1: *Les Etudiants des Pays-Bas à Genève au Temps de Théodore de Bèze* (Fribourg, 1918), pp. 19–24.

60 Kingdon, *Geneva*, p. 18.
61 *Ibid.*, p. 18.
62 E. William Monter, *Calvin's Geneva* (New York, 1967), p. 211. This slender volume, based upon Monter's research in the Genevan archives, is a storehouse of valuable information.
63 *Ibid.*, p. 210.
64 The most helpful study in this area is that by Eugène Choisy, *L'état chrétien calviniste à Genève au temps de Théodore de Bèze* (Geneva, 1902); see also Kingdon, *Geneva*, p. 19.
65 Geisendorf, *op. cit.*, p. 249.
66 The early stages of this reassertion have been traced by Kingdon, *Geneva*, pp. 13–29.

the church in Geneva was never subject to the tight control exercised over the other Swiss Protestant churches by their magistrates.[67]

As successor to Calvin, Beza continued Calvin's struggle against the cult of personality. In Beza's mind no single man should ever be allowed to head the church. Thus Beza led the battle against episcopacy and argued for a representative form of church government. Kingdon has demonstrated the crucial role that Beza played in assuring a presbyterian form of government for the Reformed Church, even though Calvin, himself, was ambiguous concerning the form of church government advocated in the New Testament.[68]

This is one of the points at which Beza deviated from Calvin's theology according to a number of scholars.[69] Basil Hall, for example, views Beza's doctrinaire presbyterianism as a distortion that upset the 'balance of Calvin's theology.'[70] Patrick Collinson labels Beza and his Puritan followers 'neo-Calvinists' because of their elevation of presbyterianism to the rank of dogma.[71]

But the question is not as simple as these scholars assume. Few scholars would agree with Pannier in asserting that Clavin viewed episcopacy as an integral part of his theology and sought to establish it as the only acceptable church form.[72] On the contrary, Calvin seems to have shared the attitude of Bullinger and Peter Martyr that it was best for the Elizabethan Reformers to seek reform through the episcopalian system rather than to try to change the system itself.[73] In any case, Calvin argued that in Scripture the terms bishop and presbyter were used synonymously. The administrative functions that came to be associated with the office of the bishop were 'introduced by human agreement to meet the needs of the times.'[74] Initially Beza exhibited an irenic spirit concerning episcopacy. His statements on the ministry in his early work, *Confession de la foi* (1559), represented the same position as that expressed in the last edition of Calvin's *Institutes.* But with the passage of time Beza moved increasingly in the direction

---

67 Choisy, *op. cit.*, pp. 412, 451 ff.; see also Geisendorf, *op. cit.*, p. 323 n. 5. The resent study by Maruyama (*op. cit.*, pp. 422–428) provides a helpful analysis of Beza's understanding of the relationship between the ecclesiastical and the civil government. He has noted a development in Beza's understanding that may be described 'as a development from optimism, to realism, from political thinking to theological thinking and, above all, from a humanist position to that of a Reformer' (p. 422). Maruyama also faults Kickel for basing his understanding of Beza's doctrine of church-state relations almost entirely upon Beza's early theological work, *De haereticis*, and ignoring such other important works as the *Tractatus pius et moderatus* (1590); see Maruyama, *op. cit.*, p. 216 n. 74.
68 Kingdon, *Geneva*, pp. 37–148.
69 The following discussion concerning episcopacy draws heavily upon Maruyama, *op. cit.*, pp. 303–313.
70 Basil Hall, 'Calvin against the Calvinists,' *John Calvin*, ed. Gervase E. Duffield (Grand Rapids, 1966), pp. 19–37.
71 Patrick Collinson, *The Elizabethan Puritan Movement* (Berkeley and Los Angeles, 1967), p. 109.
72 Jacques Pannier, *Calvin et l'épiscopat: l'épiscopat élément organique de l'Eglise dans le Calvinisme intégral* (Strasbourg and Paris, 1927).
73 Maruyama, *op. cit.*, pp. 304–305; Alexandre Ganoczy, *Calvin, Théologien de l'Eglise et du ministère* (Paris, 1964), pp. 386–396; John T. McNeill, 'The Doctrine of the Ministry in Reformed Theology,' *Church History*, XII (1943), 78–86.
74 Calvin, *Institutes*, IV, 4, 4.

of presbyterianism. This shift reflected Beza's reconsideration of the biblical data and also a change in the historical circumstances.[75]

Beza's fears of personality and of episcopacy extended as well to his own post as moderator of the Company of Pastors. Even though Calvin had been responsible for appointing Beza moderator a few months before his death, shortly after Calvin's death Beza requested that there be a new election and that the appointment be made on an annual basis in order to avoid establishing a preeminence of some members of the Company.[76]

On numerous occasions Beza requested that the office of moderator be limited to a specific tenure, rather than be a lifetime appointment, but the magistrates refused to heed his plea. Finally, in March, 1580, they agreed to a new formula whereby the moderator would be changed every week. This new formula reflected their fear of episcopacy and their desire to bring Geneva in line with the practices of the Bernese and French Reformed Churches.[77] Beza stepped down as moderator after they had agreed to the new formula.[78]

But Beza's first love was the Academy, and it was to it that he continued to direct his energy, even after he had given up preaching in 1598.[79] The basic impact of Beza upon the Academy was to liberalize and to secularize it with the aid of the magistrates. It was Beza who did away with the statement of faith, the Formula Confessionis fidei, which Calvin had established, and had required that students sign. In June, 1576, the title of the confession was changed to 'Sommaire de la doctrine chrétienne, laquelle est enseignée en l'Eschole de Genève,' and it was only imposed upon the professors and regents in order to guarantee the orthodoxy of teaching. This was in sharp contrast to Germany where all professors and all candidates for the doctorate in all fields – even the master of dancing – had to sign the Formula of Concord until the end of the seventeenth century.[80] The relaxation of doctrinal discipline at the Academy began immediately after the death of Calvin and was reflected in the doctrinal subscriptions demanded of the students.

From the beginning students had abstained from signing on in the Rector's Book so as not to have to put their signature to the Calvinist Confession of Faith: this was particularly the case for the Lutherans. Between 1566 and 1572, students were admitted on the strength of a mere brief declaration. From 1572 to 1576, no names were inscribed although the Academy was flourishing: then the Company of Pastors suppressed the obligation on the grounds that 'it does not seem reasonable to press a man's conscience to sign what is not yet under-

---

75 Maruyama, op. cit., pp. 306–313.
76 R.C.P., II, pp. 102–103: Maruyama, op. cit., pp. 221 ff.
77 Olivier Labarthe, 'La changement du mode de presidence de la Compagnie des Pasteurs de Genève (1578–1580),' Zeitschrift für schweizerische Kirchengeschichte, LXVII (1972), 160–186.
78 Geisendorf, op. cit., pp. 321–322.
79 Monter, op. cit., p. 212. The finest work on this topic is that by Charles Borgeaud, Histoire de l'Université de Genève (Genève, 1900), I, 'La part de Bèze,' pp. 313–330.
80 Borgeaud, op. cit., I, pp. 140–414.

stood.' A new oath, instituted in 1584, merely proscribed 'all papal superstitions together with all condemned and manifest heresies.'[81]

The new oath of 1584 was probably a reflection of the greatest structural change that Beza had made in the Academy: the establishment of the 'Scholarques' in 1581. These men were representatives of the civil authority — they were appointed by the Council — who made matriculation at the Academy a civil matter. Their supervision changed the complexion of the Academy drastically, and it became, in essence, a type of university. Calvin had been familiar with the institution of the 'seigneurs Scholarques' at Strasbourg but had deliberately excluded them from the order of things at Geneva in order to insure clerical control over the Academy. It remained for Beza, with his strong orientation toward the civil magistrates, to secularize the Academy.[82]

But this is not to say that Beza abdicated his responsibilities at the Academy, nor did he renounce his influence. Whenever a basic decision had to be made at the Academy, it was Beza to whom the principals came for advice and counsel. It was his presence which attracted a number of top scholars to the Academy.[83] Furthermore, Beza fought vigorously against the introduction of a second chair of theology.[84] When Beza did have to step down from the chair of theology, he attempted to name his own successor, but he was out-maneuvered by the craftly La Faye.[85]

Beza sought to be true to the work of Calvin, but his teaching methods led to innovations. Calvin had taught theology primarily by means of biblical exegesis, but Beza felt the need to clarify and to systematize the passages in question. As a consequence, the course content became so unwieldly that finally two courses, Scripture and Doctrine, had to be taught separately. Beza was opposed to this division but agreed to it reluctantly in 1595.[86]

At the same time the general intellectual flavor of the Academy was progressive. This was demonstrated when the law course was established in 1572. It represented a victory for the progressive French method — 'mos legendi Gallicus' — which was still repressed in Italy and Germany, rather than the old method of the bartolistes: 'mos Italicus.'[87]

As de Vries has pointed out, there was a strange dualism in Theodore Beza.[88] On the one hand, Beza viewed himself as continuing the work of Calvin and as being responsible for maintaining doctrinal purity at Geneva.[89] But, at the same time, in his personal relationships with those who appeared to take issue with his theology, he was warm, tolerant, and understanding. Even though Beza was convinced of

81 Léonard, *op. cit.*, II, p. 2 n. 4.
82 Borgeaud, *op. cit.*, I, pp. 150—152, 325, 330.
83 *Ibid.*, p. 317.
84 *Ibid.*, pp. 227—241.
85 *Ibid.*, p. 324.
86 Pontien Polman, *L'Element historique dans la controverse religieuse du XVIe siècle* (Gembloux, 1932), pp. 126—127.
87 Borgeaud, *op. cit.*, I, p. 152.
88 de Vries, *op. cit.*, I, pp. 19—33, 212—220.
89 Borgeaud, *op. cit.*, I, pp. 323—334.

the truth of Calvin's theology, he feared falling into the pattern of imposing his authority upon others.[90]

But in spite of his strong interest in the life of the Academy, Beza was never able to devote the time nor the energy to it because of his other duties, especially in the areas of diplomatic and political activity. This was particularly the case after the resumption of the wars within France in 1567 after the uneasy Peace of Amboise.[91]

The second war in France was precipitated by the Conspiracy of Meaux.[92] After a careful analysis of the role of Beza in the Conspiracy, Kingdon concluded that

> the accounts of the meetings ... make no mention of any pastors being present. While it is at least possible that those who were chaplains to such leaders as Condé and Coligny were consulted, and even more likely that they knew what was going on, I have found no evidence that they played an important part in the decisions for war.[93]

There is no evidence that Condé sought the advice of his pastors before going to war. A breech had been growing between him and the pastors for quite a while, and it was broadened by the letter from Calvin and Beza which scolded him for his amorous relations with the ladies at the court.[94] But it is surprising that Coligny did not seek such advice, for he had been moving closer to Beza during the months preceeding the war.[95]

During the first war Beza and Spifame had served as ambassadors for the Huguenots, but this role was played in the later wars by secular noblemen, rather than by the pastors. Nevertheless Beza was actively involved in the later wars and served to coordinate the contributions of the Reformed pastors. Beza's efforts focused upon two goals. 'He did what he could, within reason, to aid the official ambassadors of the Huguenot party. And he got involved deeply, in a special and highly secret private effort to recruit troops for the Huguenot armies.'[96] As a result of these war-time activities, Beza gained the reputation, even among his friends, of being a conspirator.[97] But here, once again, Beza was operating within the tradition established by Calvin, who had also been labeled a conspirator, and with some degree of justification.[98]

90 Carl Bangs, *Arminius: A Study in the Dutch Reformation* (Nashville and New York, 1971), pp. 75–77.
91 The finest summary of the place of Geneva and Beza in the French wars has been provided by Kingdon, *Geneva*, pp. 149–202. A gold mine of valuable bibliographical footnotes has been included in the account by Léonard, *op. cit.*, II, pp. 128–153.
92 Kingdon, *Geneva*, p. 162.
93 *Ibid.*, p. 165.
94 Meylan, *Correspondance*, IV, 201–202.
95 At the same time there is evidence that Coligny sought Beza's advice on the relationship between church and state, but his request was so vague and general in tone that, in all probability, Beza did not grasp the full significance of Coligny's request. See Kingdon, *Geneva*, pp. 166–170.
96 *Ibid.*, pp. 177, 190.
97 *Ibid.*, p. 195.
98 *Ibid.*, p. 190, n. 1.

Beza also served the Huguenot cause as a propagandist by distorting the news as his mentor, Bullinger, requested. He stressed the Huguenot victories, minimized their defeats, and emphasized the reports of Catholic atrocities.[99]

During the wars Beza continued his attempts to consolidate the French Reformed Church, and he was a key figure at both the Synod of La Rochelle (1571) and the Synod of Nîmes (1572).[100] The end result of these synods was to impose upon the French Church the Swiss pattern of close collaboration between State and Pastors, and to bring the French Church more in line with the theology of Geneva through the establishment of a new confession of faith – the La Rochelle Confession.[101] The Confession contained a long discussion of the word 'substance' as it was used in the subject of Communion, and appeared to some to contradict the Helvetic Confession.[102] Peter Ramus was infuriated by the Confession and quickly wrote a letter to Bullinger denouncing the innovations of the synod.[103]

The bickering concerning the La Rochelle Confession would probably have become very complex and protracted, but it was cut short by the Massacre of St. Bartholomew's Day on August 24, 1572, in which Ramus, along with many other Protestant leaders, was killed.[104] Furthermore, those who had opposed Beza on the question of congregationalism, such men as Morely, had found their greatest support from the protestant churches in the area of Paris, but these were the very churches that had been hit hardest on St. Bartholomew's Day. Thus the party of Beza won the day, but only because their opponents had been slain or frightened out of the country.[105]

The initial impact of St. Bartholomew upon the Protestant community was shock and despair. Even Beza, who was ordinarily characterized by a deep sense of trust in the Providence of God, seemed close to despair as he wrote to Bullinger of the atrocity.[106] 'Many Protestants found their faith itself shaken by the massacres. They found it hard to believe that God could permit such savage treatment of their fellow believers, if their form of Christianity was really the only true one.'[107]

Despair also resulted from discovering that those responsible for ordering the massacre were no less than the King and the Queen Mother. Up until this time the French Protestant political theorists had argued that the wars against the crown were actually only against evil advisors to the crown, but now the monarchs

---

99 *Ibid.*, p. 191.
100 Geisendorf, *op. cit.*, pp. 300–305; Léonard, *op. cit.*, II, pp. 138–141; Kingdon, *Geneva*, pp. 96–111, 194–198.
101 Kingdon, *Geneva*, pp. 194–198.
102 Léonard, *op. cit.*, II, pp. 138–140. A helpful analysis of the La Rochelle Confession has been provided by Roger Mehl: *Explication de la Confession de Foi de La Rochelle* (Paris, 1959).
103 Letter of September 1, 1571, cited by Léonard, *op. cit.*, II, p. 140.
104 *Ibid.*, p. 142. The same page contains a helpful bibliographical footnote.
105 Kingdon, *Geneva*, p. 202.
106 Extensive quotations (in translation) of these letters are to be found in Geisendorf, *op. cit.*, pp. 306–308.
107 Kingdon, *Geneva*, p. 200.

themselves had publically taken their stand against Protestantism. The result was a flurry of Huguenot political tracts advocating new theories of resistance.[108]

One of the most significant of these tracts was Beza's *De jure magistratuum*.[109] This was not the first time that Beza had dealt with the topic of political theory. In his work of 1554, *De haereticis a civili magistratu puniendis*, in which he had defended the execution of Servetus against the attacks of Castellio, he touched upon the means acceptable in the defense of the true religion. At that time he concluded that, under certain circumstances, it was permissible for inferior magistrates to resist the monarch.[110]

Another expression of Beza's political theory before the publication of his *De jure magistratuum* may be found in the *Confession de la foi* (1559) and the Latin version, *Confessio fidei*, that appeared in 1560 with significant revisions.[111] Beza's *Confession* is a summary of the Reformed faith in seven parts. Several earlier analysis of Beza's political philosophy have overlooked his discussion of political theory under Part V, 'The Church.'[112] Contrary to what one might expect after having read *De haereticis*, there is a total absence of resistance theory in the *Confession de la foi*. All resistance to the magistrates is discouraged.[113] Kingdon feels that in this work Beza has abandoned his views of 1554.[114] Part of the explanation may be tied to the fact that each of these two works has a different subject. The *De haereticis*, with its emphasis upon the need for the state to punish heretics, 'Looks at this church-state issue from the viewpoint of the magistrates and their responsibility *to* the church. On the other hand, the *Confession de la foi*

---

108 *Ibid.*, p. 201. For a useful analysis of these works see Pierre Mesnard, *L'essor de la philosophie politique au XVI^c siècle*, 2nd ed. (Paris, 1952).

109 See Gardy, *op. cit.*, pp. 162–165; Geisendorf, *op. cit.*, pp. 313–315. Some scholars have argued that the experience of St. Bartholomew had little, if any, impact upon *De jure magistratuum*; see Ralph E. Giesey, 'The Monarchomach Triumvirs: Hotman, Beza and Mornay,' *Bibliothèque d'Humanisme et Renaissance*, XXXII (1970), 41–43. A rather full abridged translation of Beza's work has been provided by Julian H. Franklin, *Constitutionalism and Resistance in the Sixteenth Century. Three Treatises by Hotman, Beza, & Mornay* (New York, 1969). A complete, literal translation based upon the Latin edition of 1595 has been done by Henri-Louis Gonin: Theodore Beza, *Concerning the Rights of Rulers over Their Subjects and the Duty of Subjects Towards Their Rulers* (Capetown, Pretoria, 1956). The best critical Latin edition, based on the text of 1580, is that by Klaus Sturm: Theodor Beza, *De jure magistratuum* (Neukirchen-Vluyn, 1965). Robert Kingdon has produced a fine French edition with notes and an Introduction: *Du droit des Magistrats* (Geneva, 1970).

110 Analyses of the political doctrine found in the *De haereticis* may be found in the following works: Robert M. Kingdon, 'The First Expression of Theodore Beza's Political Ideas,' *Archiv für Reformationsgeschichte*, LV (1955), 88–100; Kingdon, 'Les idées politiques de Bèze d'après son traitté de l'autorité du magistrat en la punition des hérétiques,' *Bibliothèque d'Humanisme et Renaissance*, XXII (1960), 566–569; Irmgard Hoss, 'Zur Genesis der Widerstandlehre Bezas,' *Archiv für Reformationsgeschichte*, LIV (1963), 198–213.

111 Gardy, *op. cit.*, pp. 60–79. This work will be discussed in more detail in Chapter III below.

112 For an explication of the political theory found in these works see Maruyama, *op. cit.*, pp. 5–31, 53–62; Kingdon, Introduction to *Du droit*, pp. viii–xii.

113 Kingdon, Introduction to *Du droit*, p. ix.

114 *Ibid.*

treats the magistrates as the church's principle members and examines this issue from the viewpoint of the church i.e. their responsibility *in* the church.'[115]

But the publication of Beza's *Confessio fidei* in 1560, which was to be a Latin version of the *Confession de la foi*, was marked by a very different attitude toward resistance. The *Confessio fidei* contains powerful arguments favoring resistance to the magistrates under certain circumstances.[116] How may one explain the shift of Beza's position from 1559 to 1560? Kingdon has suggested the importance of two factors. The first factor was the Conspiracy of Amboise. But there was another factor as well: the debate among Reformed theologians in Switzerland concerning resistance theory, particularly as that debate was fired by the work of Christopher Goodman and John Knox.[117] Kingdon has argued that Beza was probably not familiar with these two works until late in 1559 and that the *Confessio fidei* represents, in part, an attempt to come to grips with their arguments.[118]

These earlier works by Beza should put in perspective the resistance theory found in his work *De jure magistratuum* of 1574. In some of these earlier works Beza had touched upon the question of resistance to the magistrates, but in the *De jure magistratuum* Beza develops, deepens, and emphasizes the doctrine.[119] Beza asserted that only God possessed absolute power; the power of kings was bestowed upon them by virtue of a covenant made with the people. If a king violates the covenant, it is the responsibility of the magistrates to resist him, if the situation demands, to depose him. One influence which was responsible for radicalizing Beza's political theory was the massacre, but another may be traced to Francois Hotman with whom Beza had consulted.[120] And yet, as Robert Kingdon had demonstrated, Beza had always *acted* on the political theory found in the *De jure magistratuum*, but he had never before expressed it so clearly.[121]

115 Maruyama, *op. cit.*, p. 54.
116 For a summary of the resistance theory found in the *Confessio fidei* see Kingdon, Introduction to *Du droit*, pp. x–xi.
117 Kingdon refers specifically to the work *How Superior Powers Ought to be Obeyed* by Goodman and to Knox's famous work, *First Blast of the Trumpet Against the Monstrous Regiment of Women; Ibid.*, p. ix.
118 *Ibid.*, pp. ix–x.
119 See the following for helpful summaries of the *De jure magistratuum*: Alfred Cartier, 'Les idées politiques de Théodore de Bèze d'après le traité: "Du droit des magistrats sur leurs sujets," ' *Bull. de la Soc. d'Hist. et d'Arch. de Genève*, II (1900), 187–206; Paul F.-M. Mealy, *Origine des idées politiques libérales en France. Les publicistes de la Réforme sous François II et Charles IX* (Paris, 1903), pp. 203–220; Geisendorf, *op. cit.*, pp. 313–314; Choisy, *op. cit.*, pp. 495–497; Emile Doumergue, 'Les théories politiques de Théodore de Bèze' in *Troisième centenaire de la mort de Th. de Bèze* (Genève, 1903), pp. 12–16; Mesnard, *op. cit.*, pp. 315–326; Charles Mercier, 'Les théories politiques des calvinistes en France au cours des guerres de religion,' *Bulletin de la Société de l'histoire du protestantisme français*, LXXXIII (1934), pp. 243–248; A. Picard, *Théodore de Bèze, ses idées sur le droit d'insurrection et son rôle pendant la première guerre de religion* (Cahors, 1906); A.A. van Schelven, 'Beza's "De jure magistratuum in subditos," ' *Archiv für Reformationsgeschichte*, LIV (1954), 62–83; Franklin, *op. cit.*, pp. 33–39; Kingdon, Introduction to *Du droit*, pp. vii-xliii.
120 Ralph E. Giesey, 'Why and When Hotman Wrote the Francogallia,' *Bibliothèque d'Humanisme et Renaissance*, XXIX (1967), 582.
121 Kingdon, *Geneva*, pp. 188–189.

Others, such as John Knox, had argued for a radical interpretation of the right of resistance before Beza had published *De jure magistratuum.* But Beza's 'was the first clear statement, from an official Calvinist standpoint, of the proper limits to monarchical power.'[122] Elliott has argued that Beza bestowed a certain degree of respectability upon the theory of resistance by shifting the burden of resistance to the magistrates. Because of the unusual political situation in France, this was the formulation most likely to appeal to the French people.[123] At any rate, Beza's *De jure magistratuum* served as the core for the best known of all the political tracts which emerged in the sixteenth century: the *Vindiciae contra Tyrannos* which was probably published by Philippe du Plessis-Mornay in 1579.[124]

The *De jure magistratuum* was viewed with alarm by the censors of the Geneva city council. Elliott has suggested that this was because of the tension they had experienced with the French crown after allowing Hotman to publish his *Franco-Gallia* in their city.[125] Michel Roset, the leading magistrate in the city, had argued against the publication of Beza's work on the grounds that 'it would be very scandalous and might cause a lot of troubles for which the city would be blamed.'[126] Thus the work was published anonymously, probably at Heidelberg, in 1574.[127]

An era ended when Beza stepped down as Moderator in 1580. He had never experienced robust health, and in 1580 he suffered a recurrence of a severe pulmonary infection which had, in the past, immobilized him for weeks at a time. Although Beza continued as a figurehead leader in Geneva for another twenty-five years his general health worsened and he was plagued by chronic insomnia, deafness, and muscular deterioration.[128] In spite of his journey to Montbéliard in 1586 to engage in a colloquy with Jacob Andreae, he tended to withdraw increasingly from the active life.[129] Beza made out his will in 1595, taught classes until the fall of 1598, gave his last sermon in 1600, and died on October 13, 1605, at 86 years of age.

BEZA AS SCHOLAR AND THEOLOGIAN

Beza's scholarship was marked by both depth and breadth. By the time that he was elected moderator, on June 2, 1564, he had already established his credentials as a first-rate scholar. He was a renowned Latinist, was distinguished for his knowledge of Greek, and had also mastered both Hebrew and Syriac.[130]

122 J.H. Elliott, *Europe Divided, 1559—1598* (New York and Evanston, 1968), p. 222.
123 *Ibid.*, p. 223.
124 Franklin, *op. cit.*, p. 39.
125 Elliott, *op. cit.*, p. 222.
126 Geisendorf, *op. cit.*, p. 312.
127 E. Droz, 'Fausses adresses typographiques,' *Bibliothèque d'Humanisme et Renaissance,* XXIII (1961), pp. 379—384.
128 Geisendorf, *op. cit.*, pp. 321—323.
129 Leonard, *op. cit.*, II, p. 34. See also P. Pfister, *Le colloque de Montbéliard* (Geneva, 1873): A. Lods, 'Les Actes du colloque de Montbéliard, 1586. Une polemique entre Théodore de Bèze et Jacques Andreae,' *Bulletin de la Société de l'histoire de protestantisme français,* XXXXVI (1897), 192—215.
130 Kingdon, *Geneva,* p. 18; Clavier, *op. cit.*, p. 40.

His reputation as a humanist scholar was insured by the publication of his early poems in his *Iuvenilia*, and by the widespread praise which greeted his monumental *Abraham sacrifiant*. His philological gifts were also demonstrated in his works concerning the Greek and French languages.[131]

His translations of the Bible and his critical edition of the Greek New Testament were not exempt from criticism for inaccuracies, but they contributed to Beza's reputation as a scholar. Indeed, some twentieth century scholars have continued to argue for the value of Beza's biblical scholarship.[132]

There is little question concerning the significance of Beza as a political theorist. His basic ideas and their historical impact have been analyzed above.

The bulk of Beza's energy as a scholar was devoted not to historical or political works, but to the theological and doctrinal controversies in which he was involved — especially after the death of Calvin in 1564.[133] These controversies focused primarily upon Eucharistic theology, Christology, ecclesiology, and predestination.[134] In all of these controversies Beza viewed himself as the defender of Calvin and sought to clarify the positions of Calvin in order to make them more defensible.[135] Indeed, I shall argue later that Beza's drive for logical clarification contributed to his distortion of Calvin's doctrine of predestination. When he dealt with controversial theological issues Beza's literary style lost its sparkle as he ponderously refuted his enemies, point by point. But his tracts were so thorough and overwhelming in their force that other leaders in the Reformed community were continually beseeching him to refute various theological errors and foes.[136] Consequently, Beza's controversial tracts did much to form and shape Reformed theology.

Beza also had a tremendous impact upon posterity through his confessions of faith — especially the *Confession de la foi chrétienne* of 1559.[137] This impact was deepened with the publication in two parts of his *Quaestiones et responsiones* (1570–1576)[138] and the appearance in 1575 of his *Petit catéchisme*.[139] His leader-

---

131 The most important works were *Alphabetum Graecum* (Geneve, 1554), see Gardy, *op. cit.*, pp. 41–44; and Geisendorf, *op. cit.*, p. 64 n. 1; *Grammaire Grecque* (1568), see Gardy, *op. cit.*, pp. 136–137; and *De francicae linguae recta pronuntiatione tractatus* (Genevae, 1584), see Geisendorf, *op. cit.*, p. 335.
132 A summary of opinions may be found in Clavier, *op. cit.*, pp. 60–63, notes 56–63.
133 The major theological works of Beza have been collected in the *Tractationes theologicae*, 3 vols., 1570–1582. Volume I contains sixteen works written from 1554 to 1565. Volume II was published in 1573 (Geisendorf was mistaken in affixing the date 1572) and includes twelve works written since 1570, ten by Beza and two by other authors. Volume III contains thirteen works. See Geisendorf, *op. cit.*, pp. 330–331 and Gardy, *op. cit.*, pp. 144–147.
134 A skillful discussion of the major theological works of Beza during this period integrating them into their historical context has been given by Geisendorf, *op. cit.*, pp. 347–389.
135 Beza's genius for clarification may be seen in his letter to the Vidam of Chartes, Jean de Ferrière, which is a beautiful summary of Reformed eucharistic theology; see Meylan, *Correspondance*, V, pp. 30–33.
136 These requests stud the correspondence between Beza and other reformers.
137 Walter Hollweg, *Neue Untersuchungen zur Geschichte und Lehre des Heidelberger Katechismus* (Neukirchen, 1961), pp. 86–123.
138 Gardy, *op. cit.*, pp. 148–157; Geisendorf, *op. cit.*, p. 280.
139 Gardy, *op. cit.*, pp. 167–170.

ship in the Reformed community was reinforced by his attempts to harmonize all of the Reformed confessions. This was reflected in the publication in 1581 of the *Harmonia confessionum fidei* . . ., of which Beza was probably the chief author.[140]

But what of Beza's relationship to humanism; is it appropriate to view him as a humanist? At this point we shall accept the concept of Renaissance humanism advocated by Paul Kristeller.[141] The Renaissance humanists continued the rhetorical tradition of medieval Italy and added to it the concept that the greatest models for eloquence were to be found in Greek and Roman literature.[142] They sought to produce cultured, well-rounded men who apply their intelligence to the solution of societal problems. Their primary interest was in practical ethics, rather than in logic, metaphysics, or systems of truth.

Thus it is a mistake to associate Renaissance humanists with a philosophical school of thought or to assume that they were philosophers who opposed the philosophy of Scholasticism. Most of the works of the humanists had nothing at all to do with philosophy. They were generally content to leave the study of philosophy to the other strains in Renaissance thought which Kristeller has dubbed the Platonic and Aristotelian.[143]

One may be very much under the influence of humanism with its stress upon eloquence, the sources, and ethics, while, at the same time, accepting some of the tenets of Scholasticism. This was precisely the position of Theodore Beza, and it explains some of the tensions in his theological method. Beza was attracted by the glitter of humanism and found great delight in such humanist activities as translating documents, composing poetry, and doing philological research, but the pressure of his labors and his desire for clarity led him increasingly to formulate theological answers in scholastic form.

It is clear that Beza felt no compulsion to forsake all humanistic activity after his conversion to the Reformed cause. The humanist interest in history left a strong impact upon Beza and was reflected in his concern that the true history of the reformation not be lost to posterity. This was the reason Beza gave for the publication of his *Icones* in 1580.[144] The *Icones* contained pictures of pre-reformers and protestant reformers accompanied by biographical notes in Latin. Beza requested that the notes also be done in French.[145] There is some scholarly disagreement concerning the authorship of the *Vie de J. Calvin* (1564), but the weight of opinion is that the first edition of this historical work was written by Beza and that subsequent editions were heavily dependent upon Beza.[146]

---

140 See Geisendorf, *op. cit.*, pp. 337–338, and Gardy, *op. cit.*, pp. 184–185.
141 Paul O. Kristeller, *Renaissance Thought: The Classic, Scholastic and Humanist Strains* (New York, 1961), and *Renaissance Thought II: Papers on Humanism and the Arts* (New York, 1965).
142 Kristeller, *Renaissance Thought II*, p. 4. See also the helpful article by Hanna Gray, 'Renaissance Humanism: The Pursuit of Eloquence,' *Journal of the History of Ideas*, XXIV (1963), 497–514.
143 Kristeller, *Renaissance Thought*, p. 100.
144 *Icones, id est verae imagines virorum doctrina simul et pietate illustrium . . . Theodoro Beza auctore* (Genevae, 1580). See Gardy, *op. cit.*, pp. 180–184.
145 Geisendorf, *op. cit.*, pp. 333–334.
146 Gardy, *op. cit.*, pp. 104–126; Geisendorf, *op. cit.*, pp. 264–266.

Perhaps the most significant historical work to which Beza contributed was the *Histoire ecclésiastique des églises réformées au royaume de France* . . . (1580).[147] This massive three-volume work of more than 2200 pages has served as one of our most important sources for the history of this period. Beza, himself, always spoke of it in his correspondence as an anonymous work, but apparently Beza provided most of the materials and supervised the actual composition of the book.[148] The *Histoire ecclésiastique*, the *Icones*, and the *Vie de J. Calvin* demonstrate the significant contributions of Beza to the field of historical scholarship.

Beza also continued to pursue the philological and linguistic activities that had consumed him before his conversion. Reference has already been made to his works concerning the Greek and French languages and also his translation into French verse of the Psalms. His most important contribution in the field of translation was his revision of the Geneva Bible in 1588. This revised edition had a profound influence upon Reformed circles for years.[149] Beza also received wide acclaim for his Latin translation of the New Testament. This work, begun at the suggestion of Calvin, consumed five years of his life (1552–56).[150] In addition to his translations, Beza also made a major contribution to philological and linguistic science by his establishment of a Greek text of the New Testament.[151] His text, first published in 1565, utilized the Greek texts of Erasmus, Robert Estienne, Tremellius, and others. But, in addition to these standard texts, Beza also drew upon two famous codices now known as the Codex Bezae (Cantabrigiensis) and the Codex Claromontanus.[152]

In spite of his excellent humanistic credentials, Beza's work as a translator and textual critic of the New Testament has been subjected to severe criticism on the grounds that his readings were too timid and traditional, and, more importantly, that he used the biblical text to justify his own confessional position.[153] The sting of this criticism is not removed by Douen's observation that every confessional group

147 Although these volumes bear the imprint of J. Rémy of Antwerp, it has been shown that they were actually published by J. de Laon in Geneva. See Eugénie Droz, 'L'imprimeur de L'Histoire ecclésiastique (1580),' *Bibliothèque d'Humanisme et Renaissance*, XXII (1960), 371–376.

148 A detailed analysis of the authorship of the *Histoire ecclésiastique* has been provided by Geisendorf, *op. cit.*, pp. 340–345; see also Gardy, *op. cit.*, p. 222.

149 Geisendorf, *op. cit.*, p. 339; S.L. Greenslade (ed.), *The Cambridge History of the Bible*, Vol. III: *The West from the Reformation to the Present Day* (Cambridge, 1963), pp. 119–121.

150 The title of this work was *Novum D.N. Jesu Christi Testamentum. Latine jam olim a veteri interprete, nunc denuo a Theodoro Beza versum: cum ejusdem annotationibus, in quibus ratio interpretationis redditur.* See Geisendorf, *op. cit.*, p. 70; Clavier, *op. cit.*, p. 41 n. 57; John Calvin, *Joannis Calvini opera quae supersunt omnia* (59 vols.; Corpus Reformatorum, vols. 29–50; Brunswick, 1863–1900), XVII, p. 233; Maruyama, *op. cit.*, p. 233.

151 *Iesv Christi D.N. Novum testamentum, siue Nouum foedus. Cuius Graeco textui respondant interpretationes duae; Vna, vetus: altera, noua, Theodori Bezae, deligenter ab eo recognita. Eivsdem Th. Bezae Annotationes, quas itidem hac secunda editione recognauit, & accessione non parua locupletauit.* (Genevae, Heniricus Stephanus, 1565).

152 For a discussion of Beza's use of the Greek texts see Greenslade, *op. cit.*, III, p. 62; Maruyama, *op. cit.*, pp. 233–235.

153 Greenslade, *op. cit.*, III, pp. 83, 91; Maruyama, *op. cit.*, pp. 235–236.

at that time utilized textual criticism as a form of confessional apologetics.[154]

It is clear that many of Beza's humanistic interests continued after his conversion, but the critical question was his basic attitude toward humanism. Were humanistic activities justified *per se*, or was their value instrumental? There can be little question about Beza's view of humanism after his conversion, for his attitude was thoroughly consistent. His understanding of the relationship between humanism and theology was not altered by time nor by circumstance. Perhaps his clearest statements are to be found in the sermons that he preached toward the end of his life.[155] In them Beza clearly acknowledged that humanism is a gift from God, and that it should be used for his glory – not to call attention to the humanist. Humanistic knowledge is not an end in itself, but it is to be used as an aid to Christian theology. The common sense and practicality stressed by the humanists should also help man to overcome the practical problems that plague his life. Errors and excess come from humanism when the humanist violates the divine boundaries of his discipline and devotes himself to vain speculation or to self-glorification.

The qualified approval which Beza gave to humanism in his late sermons is also found in the first humanistic work that he produced after his conversion – *Abraham sacrifiant*. In a foreword Beza categorized and criticized other writers of his day. The first group followed the tradition of Petrarch, as understood by Beza, by allowing themselves to fall madly in love and by being inappropriately concerned about immortality. A second group of writers, among whom Beza included himself, wrote witty, ambiguous epigrams. A third group contained members who devoted themselves to attacking everything without replacing the attacked values and institutions with more desirable alternatives. Lastly, a fourth group viewed as their purpose in life the enrichment of language by the addition of Greek and Latin words.[156] Beza rejected all of these literary variants, including the second group in which some of his work placed him, and he contrasted with them *Abraham sacrifiant* as an example of humanism in the service of theology.

The message of *Abraham sacrifiant* was clear: As Abraham had been willing to sacrifice his beloved son, even so should Beza be willing to sacrifice his promising future as a humanist. The glitter of humanism was that of fool's gold.[157] The publication of *Abraham sacrifiant* was a devastating blow to a number of Beza's former humanist friends – especially Peletier.[158]

Some critics have viewed *Abraham sacrifiant*, with its mixture of classical and biblical motifs, as a new literary form from which the Protestant biblical drama

154 O. Douan, 'Notes sur les alterations catholiques et protestantes du Nouveau Testament traduit en français . . .,' *Revue de Théologie* (Third Series), VI (1868), pp. 1–24, 97–117, 137–153; cited in Maruyama, *op. cit.*, p. 236.
155 See especially his *Sermons sur l'Histoire de la Résurrection de nostre Seigneur Jesus Christ* (Geneve, 1593), p. 211, and his *Sermons sur l'Histoire de la Passion et Sepulture de nostre Seigneur Jesus Christ* (Geneve, 1593), pp. 313 f.
156 These remarks may be found on pp. 47–48 of the critical edition of *Abraham sacrifiant* by Cameron, Hall and Higman.
157 For a reprint of the 1550 edition of the preface to *Abraham sacrifiant* see Meylan, *Correspondance*, I, 200–202.
158 Davis, *loc. cit.*, 213–215.

would proceed.[159] It is clearly based on an Old Testament story, but, at the same time, it is modeled after the Greek tragedy without copying all of the characteristics of the pagan theater.[160] Beza took a biblical plot and enhanced it 'with classical touches such as a prologue imitated from Roman comedy, laments reminiscent again of the plot of *Iphigenia in Aulis*, and a chorus which was used ... to separate the play's diverse "acts." '[161] At the same time *Abraham sacrifiant* has such a strong theological orientation to the moral and psychological questions that plague Abraham, that Emile Faguet has labeled it as a Calvinistic pamphlet.[162] The following observations by Stone capture well the delicate blending of Beza's humanistic and theological interests as reflected in *Abraham sacrifiant*:

> The polemical nature of *Abraham sacrifian* ... is no less present. The cantique sung by Abraham and Sara ends with a censure of idolatry and a prayer for vengeance (vv. 165–76). Satan's description of the clergy (vv. 231 ff) as well as his monk's clothing readily reveal Beze's militant Protestantism. Finally, though an excellent humanist, Beza makes it very clear that he has placed his pen at the disposition of magnifying 'la bonté de Dieu' and disparages the wordly poetry of self-glorification written by his contemporaries as well as any style or orthography which is not in keeping with common usage.[163]

In short, *Abraham sacrifiant* has become a sermon for Beza in which he utilizes, in a very selective fashion, those classical and humanistic techniques which maximize the theological impact of his message. The techniques are humanistic to a large degree, but the content is Reformed.

Thus for Beza humanism was used instrumentally. He would employ humanistic techniques and methodology to the degree that they were compatible with his goals as a Reformed statesman, theologian, and educator.

---

159 Fritz Holl, *Das Politische und Religiöse Tendenzdrama des 16. Jahrhunderts in Frankreich* (Leipzig, 1903), p. 318.
160 Lebègue, *op. cit.*, p. 318.
161 Donald Stone, Jr., ed., *Four Renaissance Tragedies* (Cambridge, Mass., 1966), p. xix.
162 Emile Faguet, *La Tragédie française au XVIᵉ siècle* (Paris, 1883), p. 98.
163 Stone, *op. cit.*, p. xix.

CHAPTER II

BEZA'S THEOLOGY IN ITS HISTORICAL SETTING

The purpose of this chapter will be to establish some historical touchstones that will enable us to understand the theology of Beza more adequately within a given historical context. We shall look first at Calvin's doctrine of predestination, for, whatever else may be the case, it is generally agreed by scholars that Beza thought he was being faithful to the work and to the thought of Calvin.[1] We have already indicated some of the ways in which Beza differed from Calvin; whether or not there are differences in their doctrines of predestination remains to be seen. After a rapid survey of Calvin's doctrine of predestination, we shall make a few observations concerning the differences between Calvin and some of those groups which chose to label themselves as 'Calvinists.' Finally, we shall sketch the role of Beza as a combatant in the predestination controversies. With the conclusion of this chapter, we should be in a position to study the theory of predestination held by Beza.[2]

CALVIN'S DOCTRINE OF PREDESTINATION

The flood of writings about Calvin is, itself, sufficient to keep many at great distance from him. This effect is aggravated by the tendency of many scholars to use Calvin as a weapon when they dispute theological points.[3] This is a basic reason for the diverse interpretations of Calvin. There is also a tendency for Calvin scholarship to be influenced by current theological concerns.[4]

1 See Borgeaud, *Histoire de l'Université de Genève* (Geneva, 1900), I, pp. 228, 324; Geisendorf, *Théodore de Bèze* (Geneva, 1949), p. 261; Kingdon, *Geneva*, p. 18; and Monter, *Calvin's Geneva* (New York, 1967), pp. 210–214.
2 In citing the works of Calvin use has been made of what appears to be a fairly standard form: *Institutes*, I, 15, 8 will mean Calvin's *Institutes*, Book One, Chapter 15, Section 8; the edition of the *Institutes* used, unless indicated to the contrary, will be the two-volume, English edition translated by F.L. Battles and edited by J.T. McNeill. *CR*, 7 : 129 means volume 7 in the *Corpus Reformatorum*, page or column 129. *OS*, III, 61 means volume 3, page 61 of the five-volume *Opera selecta* collection edited by Barth and Niesel.
3 An outstanding instance of this is the manner in which Karl Barth has exploited Calvin in his battle with Brunner and others concerning natural theology; see Basil Hall, 'The Calvin Legend,' *John Calvin: A Collection of Distinguished Essays*, ed. Gervase E. Duffield (Grand Rapids, 1966), p. 4. This appears to be the thrust of Shepherd's critique of Gründler's interpretation of Zanchius; see Norman Shepherd, 'Zanchius on Saving Faith,' *The Westminster Theological Journal*, Vol. XXXVI (1973), pp. 31–47.
4 David N. Wiley, 'Calvin's Doctrine of Predestination: His Principal Soteriological and Polemical Doctrine' (Unpublished Ph.D. dissertation, Duke University, 1971), p. 6 n. 1.

Finding one's way through the writings about Calvin is greatly facilitated by the perceptive bibliographical work done by Paul Jacobs and by Wilhelm Niesel.[5] Another factor which aids the researcher is that a certain consistency of position makes it possible to place the interpreters in various schools of thought. Thus Wendel is justified in stating that

After Alexandre Schweizer in 1844 and Ferdinand Christian in 1847 had claimed that predestination was the central doctrine of Calvin's theology and that all the originality of his teaching proceeded from it, historians and dogmaticians went on for three-quarters of a century repeating that affirmation like an article of faith which did not even have to be verified.[6]

Since the time of Schweizer and Christian there have been others who have found predestination to be the central, controlling dogma in Calvin's theology.[7] Thus Schnat el has made the causal comment that 'Calvin's central dogma, as is well known, is that of predestination.'[8] But among recent Calvin scholars there appears to be a growing conviction that predestination is not the key to understanding Calvin's theology.[9] Many would agree with Wendel that 'To recognize that Calvin taught double predestination, and underlined its dogmatic and practical interest, is not to say that this must be taken to be the very centre of his teaching.'[10] Calvin's doctrine of predestination must be understood in relation to his doctrines of the church and the sacraments.[11] Many scholars would now concur with the earlier judgment of Hermann Bauke that there is no basic principle in the theology of Calvin from which everything else can be derived.[12]

5 See Paul Jacobs, *Prädestination und Verantwortlichkeit bei Calvin* (Neukirchen, 1937), pp. 20–40; Wilhelm Niesel, *The Theology of Calvin*, trans. Harold Knight (Philadelphia, 1956), pp. 9–21, 159. I view the volume by Jacobs as perhaps the best single study of Calvin's doctrine of predestination – even though perhaps Calvin is not quite as Christocentric as Jacobs depicts him. A fine one-volume study of Calvin's life and thought is the work of François Wendel: *Calvin: The Origins and Development of His Religious Thought*, trans. Philip Mairet (London, 1963). A few additional works especially helpful are Emile Doumergue, *Jean Calvin, les hommes et les choses de son temps* (7 vols.; Lausanne, 1899–1917); Edward A. Dowey, Jr., *The Knowledge of God in Calvin's Theology* (New York, 1965); Richard Stauffer, *L'Humanité de Calvin* (Neuchâtel, 1964).
6 Wendel, *op. cit.*, p. 263.
7 Otto Ritschl, *Dogmengeschichte des Protestantismus* (Göttingen, 1926), III, pp. 156, 167. Dowey (*op. cit.*, p. 210 n. 286) has cited as egregious instances Gisbert Beyerhaus, *Studien zur Staatsanschauung Calvins; mit besonderer Berücksichtigung seiner Souveränitatsbegriffs* (Berlin, 1910), pp. 48–77 and J.W. Kampschulte, *Johann Calvin; seine Kirche und sein Staat in Genf* (Leipzig, 1869), I, 251–278.
8 *Deutschlands geschichtliche Quellen und Darstellungen in der Neuzeit: Part I: Das Zeit alter der Reformation* (1931), p. 51, cited by Niesel, *op. cit.*, p. 159.
9 See Niesel, *op. cit.*, pp. 159–181.
10 Wendel, *op. cit.*, p. 264; see also Albert-Marie Schmidt, *John Calvin and the Calvinistic Tradition*, trans. Ronald Wallace (New York, 1963), p. 89. There are, however, a number of scholars who view Calvin's doctrine of predestination as the 'crown' or 'capstone' of his soteriology; see Wiley, *op. cit.*, p. 172 n. 1.
11 John Calvin, *Concerning the Eternal Predestination of God*, ed. J.K.S. Reid (London, 1961), pp. 9, 29–30.
12 *Die Probleme der Theologie Calvins* (Leipzig, 1922), pp. 11 ff., 31.

In attempting to appraise the role of predestination in Calvin's theology, it is best to study the major writings of Calvin and to note where and in what context Calvin discussed the topic.[13]

An analysis of Calvin's writings indicates that 'his earliest writings do not contain any systematic statement of the problem, and although, later on ... he accorded a growing importance to it, he did so under the sway of ecclesiological and pastoral preoccupations rather than in order to make it a main foundation of his theology.'[14] Wiley, on the contrary, has argued that the basic orientation of Calvin's doctrine of predestination was soteriological, rather than ecclesiological.[15]

In the first edition of the *Institutes* (1536) there was no special section devoted to predestination. The doctrine appeared clearly only in one passage which dealt with the church.[16] As Jacobs has noted, the word *electio* was used only fifteen times and the word *reprobatio* three times in this section dealing with the church.[17] But even in this short passage concerning the church Calvin touched upon all of those elements that were later to be considered part of his doctrine of predestination.

Here Calvin mentions, one after another and each in a brief sentence, the union of the faithful in Christ, the community of the elect, the consequences of election — namely the calling, justification and glorification — then the perseverance of the elect and their separation from among the reprobate. He points out the close relation between vocation and justification on the one hand and election on the other ...[18]

The only aspect of predestination that did not appear clearly in this passage was the concept of reprobation as the result of a special decree of God.[19]

13 Helpful discussions which focus upon the development of the doctrine of predestination in the theology of Calvin may be found in the following: Wendel, *op. cit.*, pp. 264–270; Peter Barth, 'Die Erwählungslehre in Calvins Institutio von 1536,' in *Theologische Aufsätze, Karl Barth zum 50. Geburtstag* (München, 1936); Peter Barth, 'Die biblischen Grundlagen der Prädestinationslehre bei Calvin,' *Evangelische Theologie* (1938); Jacobs, *op. cit.*, pp. 22 ff.; Heinz Otten, *Calvins theologische Anschauung von der Prädestination* (München, 1938), pp. 19 ff., 99 ff.; Max Scheibe, *Calvins Prädestinationslehre* (Halle, 1897), pp. 9–85; Niesel, *op. cit.*, pp. 159 ff.; Brian Gerrish, *Reformers in Profile* (Philadelphia, 1967), pp. 157 ff.; Wiley, *op. cit.*, pp. 9–172.

14 Wendel, *op. cit.*, p. 264.

15 Wiley, *op. cit.*, p. 291 and *passim*. Wiley goes beyond Dantine ('Die Prädestinationslehre,' p. 36) and others (Doumergue, Lecerf, Moltmann) who affirmed that for Calvin the doctrine of predestination was the 'crown' or 'capstone' of his soteriology. For Wiley the doctrine of predestination was 'a foundation stone as necessary for the whole soteriological structure to stand as gratuitous justification itself' (p. 172).

16 John Calvin, *Opera Selecta*, ed. Peter Barth and Wilhelm Niesel (Munich, 1926–1936), I, pp. 86 ff. (Hereinafter referred to as OS); Wendel, *op. cit.*, p. 265. Wiley (*op. cit.*, pp. 14–26) has argued, contrary to much scholarly opinion, that Calvin did deal with predestination before his treatment of the Creed in the 1536 edition of the *Institutes*. I do not find his arguments concerning this question to be convincing.

17 Jacobs, *op. cit.*, p. 22.

18 Wendel, *op. cit.*, p. 265.

19 *Ibid.*, p. 266.

The Genevan *Catechism* which Calvin wrote in French in 1537 represented a decisive change in his approach to predestination. For the first time the doctrine received special treatment.[20] Yet even in this instance it did not come first: it followed the Law but came before the section dealing with redemption. In this passage Calvin declared the fact of election as an explanation for the varied responses which greet the preaching of the Word, he mentioned the condemnation of the reprobate, and, for the first time, he proclaimed that both the elect and the reprobate would magnify 'the glory of God.'[21] It should be noted that in the *Catechism* 'The practical and ecclesiological point of view is evident and clear ... And this, in spite of the theoretical developments, is what dominates the exposition of predestination to the end.'[22] In the second and final *Catechism* of 1542 there is no longer separate treatment of election. Niesel has suggested that this change reveals an intention on the part of Calvin to indicate that 'the doctrine of election has no intrinsic significance for theology in the sense that other doctrines might stem from it.'[23]

In the 1539 edition of the *Institutes* a chapter was devoted to predestination and providence. In treating providence and predestination together Calvin followed the dogmatic tradition of Augustine whose influence upon his work was pervasive.[24] But the doctrines were not emphasized as critical theological issues which formed the foundation for all theology. Their location in the 1539 edition is a clue to the significance which Calvin gave them: they formed a bridge between his discussion of soteriology and ecclesiology. Calvin's interpretation of predestination was still determined basically by pastoral considerations, rather than by a desire to philosophize.[25] The discussion of predestination was located in the same place in later editions of the *Institutes* up to and including the edition of 1554.[26] Two controversial works produced by Calvin during that period, the *De aeterna Dei Praedestinatione*[27] of 1552, directed against Pighius, and the address of 1551 concerning the 'Congrégation sur l'élection éternelle,'[28] written in the context of the Bolsec affair, produced additional arguments for the reality of predestination and amplified the biblical texts employed in these arguments. But no new significance was ascribed to the doctrine in these works.

Calvin once again revised the textual position of predestination in his 1559 edition of the *Institutes*. In this edition Calvin placed his discussion of providence at the end of the doctrine of God the Creator.[29] Predestination he placed within

---

20 Calvin, *OS*, I, pp. 390 ff. For a discussion of the theological implications undergirding the location of the doctrine of predestination in a theological system, see Karl Barth, *op. cit.*, II/2, pp. 81–88.
21 Calvin, *OS*, I, p. 391.
22 Wendel, *op. cit.*, pp. 266–267.
23 Niesel, *op. cit.*, p. 166.
24 Jacobs, *op. cit.*, p. 69; Otten, *op. cit.*, p. 101.
25 Calvin, *CR*, 30 : 861.
26 Wendel, *op. cit.*, p. 267.
27 Calvin, *CR*, 36 : 85–140.
28 *Ibid.*, 36 : 249–366.
29 Calvin, *Institutes*, I, 16–18.

the discussion of soteriology after his treatment of sanctification and justification.[30] There is no problem in understanding why Calvin placed providence under the doctrine of God, for Calvin has told us: he wanted to counter the view of those who argued that God's work was exhausted in Creation. On the contrary, God actively preserves his creation. 'Moreover, to make God a momentary Creator, who once for all finished his work, would be cold and barren, and we must differ from profane men especially in that we see the presence of divine power shining as much in the continuing state of the universe as in its inception.'[31]

But it is more difficult to understand the structural, organizational relationship between predestination and providence in the 1559 edition of the *Institutes*. This arrangement may have been dictated for Calvin by the consideration that predestination and providence were both the result of one divine, eternal decision which took place outside of time. Or it may be that he was influenced by Thomas Aquinas.[32] Another possibility would be the influence of Augustine, whose impact upon Calvin was great.[33] The most convincing case however has been made by Jacobs and others who have argued that the final location of predestination in the *Institutes* is a logically appropriate location which reflects the Christological orientation of Calvin.[34] Wendel has expressed it well:

> ... he [Calvin] connected predestination with the Christ and his work, in order to show more clearly that it is in Christ that election takes place. Just as the doctrine of providence, placed at the conclusion of the doctrine of God, might be said to complete the latter as the key-stone finishes an arch, so also does the doctrine of predestination complete and illuminate the whole of the account of the Redemption. The link between predestination and providence subsists, then, in the last edition of the *Institutes*, in their two parallel functions.[35]

Some scholars gave argued that Calvin made a wrong decision in placing predestination at the end of book three of the *Institutes*.[36] But, as Armstrong has noted, this argument ignores the statement by Calvin in his epistle to the reader that he was only satisfied with the order of topics in his last edition of the *Institutes*.[37]

30 *Ibid.*, III, 21–24. Helpful discussions of this point may be found in Otto Weber, *Grundlagen der Dogmatik*, (Neukirchen, 1955/62), II, p. 472 and Jürgen Moltmann, *Prädestination und Perseveranz: Geschichte und Bedeutung der reformierten Lehre 'de perseverantia sanctorum'* (Neukirchen, 1961), p. 37.
31 *Institutes*, I, 16, 1.
32 John W. Beardslee III, ed., *Reformed Dogmatics: J. Wollebius, G. Voetius, F. Turretin* (New York, 1965), pp. 16–18; but note Wendel's objection: *op. cit.*, pp. 267–268.
33 Luchesius Smits, *Saint Augustin dans l'oeuvre de Calvin* (Assen, 1957), *passim*.
34 Beardslee, *op. cit.*, pp. 17–18; Jacobs, *op. cit.*, pp. 41 ff., 64, 66, 71, 92, 147; Niesel, *op. cit.*, pp. 159 ff.; Gerrish, *op. cit.*, pp. 157 ff.; Dowey, *op. cit.*, pp. 186–188. In the 1559 edition of the *Institutes* the only new dimension to Calvin's discussion of predestination was the presentation of Christ as the author of election; see Wiley, *op. cit.*, p. 164.
35 Wendel, *op. cit.*, p. 268.
36 Ritschl, *op. cit.*, III, pp. 156–163; A.M. Hunter, *op. cit.*, pp. 88 ff.; MacKinnon, *op. cit.*, pp. 247–251.
37 Armstrong, *op. cit.*, p. 162.

There is every indication that Calvin had considered very carefully the location of topics in the *Institutes*, and, in all probability, he would have objected to placing predestination under the doctrine of God as some of the Protestant scholastics were to do.[38]

At first glance the textual position of predestination in the *Institutes* may appear trivial and insignificant, but it has given us important insight into Calvin's interpretation of predestination and the significance which he ascribed to it. Indeed, his Christological and soteriological interpretations of predestination will be crucial in our attempt to understand the teaching of his follower, Theodore Beza.

There is some disagreement among scholars as to whether Calvin's own understanding of the doctrine of predestination changed in the course of his writings. Otten has asserted that there was a shift from an initial soteriological, religiously oriented interpretation to a later more theoretical and speculative interpretation that was based upon his doctrine of God.[39] Quistorp agrees with Otten's view.[40] Dantine accepts Otten's interpretation but with some qualifications.[41] Wiley takes sharp issue with Otten's position and argues that there were no major breaks in Calvin's doctrine of predestination.[42]

The great caution which Calvin exhibited in deciding where he should place the discussion of predestination in the *Institute* also characterized his exposition of the doctrine. He believed that all of our knowledge of God has been accommodated to the limitations of our human nature.[43] The essence of God is incomprehensible to man, and one who seeks to discover it will simply amuse himself with insipid speculations.[44] Thus for Calvin there is a certain 'learned ignorance' which marks our knowledge of God.[45] But this is not to deny a knowledge of God.

---

38 Ritschl, *op. cit.*, III, p. 163.
39 Otten, *op. cit.*, pp. 130—135.
40 Heinrich Quistorp, 'Sichtbare und unsichtbare Kirche bei Calvin,' *Evangelische Theologie*, IX (1949—50), 95.
41 Dantine, 'Die Prädestinationslehre,' pp. 34, 157. This interpretation of Calvin allows Dantine to view Beza's doctrine of predestination, which Dantine understands to be theological and speculative, as a logical continuation of the later Calvin (*ibid.*, p. 156). Dantine's view has been forcefully criticized by Wiley (*op. cit.*, pp. 169—170) although at other points Wiley is in agreement with Dantine (*ibid.*, p. 9 n. 1).
42 Wiley acknowledges that there was some development in Calvin's doctrine of predestination — for example, a broadening of the definition to include rejection as well as election — but nothing basic (*ibid.*, p. 170). He also acknowledges that there was greater theological precision and more polemical emphasis in Calvin's doctrine after 1537, but 'the increased precision did not distort the earlier doctrine of predestination, making the final formulations both less soteriologically oriented and more immediately derived out of the doctrine of God' (*ibid.*, p. 9).
43 *Institutes*, I, 2, 2; I, 10, 2; see Edward A. Dowey, Jr., *The Knowledge of God in Calvin's Theology* (2nd printing; New York, 1965), pp. 3—17.
44 Calvin, *OS*, III, 35.
45 *Institutes*, III, 21, 2; III, 23, 8. Calvin's use of the term 'docta ignorantia' is another instance of his heavy dependence upon Augustine and of his increasing tendency to buttress his discussions of predestination with expressions and passages taken from Augustine; see Smits, *op. cit.*, I, pp. 45 ff., 61 f., 104 f., 109.

Rather, Calvin warned against an impious curiosity concerning God. That which it is necessary for man to know about God may be known through the revelation of God, the word of God.[46]

Calvin's strictures against speculation are nowhere more evident than in his treatment of predestination. At the very beginning of his discussion of predestination Calvin made the following statement concerning those who were filled with human curiosity:

> Let them remember that when they inquire into predestination they are penetrating the sacred precincts of divine wisdom. If anyone with carefree assurance breaks into this place, he will not succeed in satisfying his curiosity and he will enter a labyrinth from which he can find no exit. For it is not right for man unrestrainedly to search out things that the Lord has willed to be hid in himself, and to unfold from eternity itself the sublimest wisdom, which he would have us revere but not understand that through this also he should fill us with wonder.[47]

That which God desires man to know concerning predestination may be found in Scripture.[48] The very question of predestination should not be formulated apart from the statements of Scripture. To do so would involve us in so much speculation that we would be overwhelmed with a sense of our own genius and would be incapable of grasping the purposes of God. We would also be overwhelmed with a sense of terror as we would realize that, in fact, all of us deserve damnation.[49]

But Calvin's warnings concerning speculation should not be interpreted to mean that one should avoid the topic of predestination. On the contrary, Calvin urged that predestination should be preached and taught because it is part of the revelation of God. The doctrine should not be avoided, but it must be presented in a biblical fashion.[50] Consequently, Calvin stated the general rule 'that we should not investigate what the Lord has left hidden in secret, that we should not neglect what he has brought into the open, so that we may not be convicted of excessive curiosity on the one hand, or of excessive ingratitude on the other.'[51]

And yet, Jacobs has demonstrated that in his own preaching Calvin seldom dealt with the topic of reprobation. It would appear that the large place that the

46 *Institutes*, III, 21, 1–2. Nor should this be interpreted to mean that Calvin denied any value to philosophy. For helpful studies concerning this question, see the following works by Charles B. Partee, Jr.: 'Calvin and Classical Philosophy: A Study in the Doctrine of Providence' (unpublished Th.D. dissertation, Princeton Theological Seminary, 1971); 'Calvin and Experience,' *Scottish Journal of Theology*, XXVI (1973), 169–181.
47 *Institutes*, III, 21, 1.
48 *Institutes*, III, 21, 2. A comparison between Calvin and Bucer at this point has been made by Wendel, *op. cit.*, p. 271 n. 118. For a discussion of the critical literature concerning the influence of Bucer's doctrine of predestination upon Calvin see Wiley, *op. cit.*, pp. 314–324.
49 *Institutes*, III, 24, 4; *CR*, 48 : 314; 54 : 57–58.
50 *Institutes*, III, 21, 3–4; *CR*, 49 : 181; 51 : 282; 54 : 57.
51 *Institutes*, III, 21, 4.

doctrine played in the polemical works of Calvin was dictated by the attacks of his foes rather than by his own evaluation of the significance of the doctrine.[52]

In the theology of Calvin there is no question concerning the fact of predestination. The first chapter in the *Institutes* which deals with predestination is entitled 'Eternal election, by which God has predestined some to salvation, others to destruction.'[53] In most of his uses, Calvin means by predestination a particular form of election: the election of individuals to salvation.[54] This individual, soteriological election is quite distinct in the thought of Calvin and should not be confused with other more general, non-soteriological forms of election, e.g., the national election of Israel, the election to office, etc.[55]

Virtually everything that Calvin taught concerning predestination may be found in two definitions:

We call predestination God's eternal decree, by which he determined with himself what he willed to become of each man. For all are not created in equal condition; rather, eternal life is foreordained for some, eternal damnation for others. Therefore, as any man has been created to one of the other of these ends, we speak of him as predestinated to life or to death.[56]

As Scripture, then, clearly shows, we say that God once established by his eternal and unchangeable plan those whom he long before determined once for all to receive into salvation, and those whom, on the other hand, he would devote to destruction. We assert that, with respect to the elect, this plan was founded upon his freely given mercy, without regard to human worth; but by his just and irreprehensible but incomprehensible judgment he has barred the door of life to those whom he has given over to damnation. Now among the elect we regard the call as a testimony of election. Then we hold justification another sign of its manifestation until they come into the glory in which the fulfillment of that election lies. But as the Lord seals his elect by call and by justification, so, by shutting off the reprobate from knowledge of his name or from the sanctification of his Spirit, he, as it were, reveals by these marks what sort of judgment awaits them.[57]

From the above statements by Calvin it becomes clear that he held to double predestination, i.e., some to election and others to reprobation. Both election and reprobation are the works of a sovereign God and are based in his immutable decrees apart from the works of man. During the present time on earth election is

52   Jacobs, *op. cit.*, pp. 142–152.
53   *Institutes*, III, 21.
54   *Institutes*, III, 21, 5–7; *CR*, 36 : 313, 50 : 46–47; 59 : 29. But note that in his *Defence of the Secret Providence of God* (1558) Calvin used the term predestination in the sense of providence (*CR*, 37 : 287). Jacobs (*op. cit.*, p. 67) has noted the difficulty of determining the relationship between providence and predestination in Calvin's thought. For an extended discussion of this question, rich in bibliographical footnotes, see Wiley, *op. cit.*, pp. 175–222.
55   *Institutes*, III, 21, 6–7; *CR*, 75 : 310–311.
56   *Institutes*, III, 21, 5.
57   *Ibid.*, III, 21, 7.

testified to by a positive response to the Gospel and by the fact of justification. The ultimate manifestation of election will be glorification.

Thus for Calvin it was misleading to speak of 'the elective decrees.' On the contrary, there was only one decree of predestination, but there were two aspects to that decree. Karl Barth has captured this point well: 'In the writings of Calvin, predestination means quite unequivocally double predestination: double in the sense that election and rejection are now two species within the one genus designated by the term predestination.'[58]

In his commentary on Ephesians, Calvin indicates that there are four causes in election. The efficient cause is the good pleasure of the will of God. The material cause is Jesus Christ. The formal cause is the preaching of the gospel. The final cause is the praise of the glory of his grace.[59] A schema of fourfold causation is also found in his comments upon Romans 3 : 24—25 in which Calvin argued that for Paul the efficient cause was the mercy of God, the material cause was the blood of Christ, the formal or instrumental cause was faith conceived by the Word, and the final cause was the glory of the divine justice and goodness.[60]

Yet one must hasten to add that Calvin's use of this fourfold schema of causation does not make him a scholastic.[61] His goal was not to solve the philosophical problems of determinism; nor was he concerned about producing a philosophical theology.[62] On the contrary, the direction of twentieth century scholarship has been to stress the Christological orientation of Calvin's doctrine of predestination.[63] This view is supported by the textual position of the predestination doctrine in the *Institutes*, which has been discussed above.

According to Calvin, Christ is the center of election. It is Christ who is the author and foundation of election.[64] Christ is, himself, elect, and is, therefore, an example to the believer of election.[65] The believer is part of the body of Christ, and his election, as part of that body, is grounded in the election of Christ.[66] It is Christ who is the guarantee and the promise of the believer's election and salvation.[67] The election of Christ is a mirror in which the believer views his own election and gains assurance of salvation.

58 Barth, *op. cit.*, II/2, p. 17.
59 *CR*, 79 : 148—150.
60 *CR*, 77 : 61, as cited by Wiley, *op. cit.*, pp. 71—72.
61 A brief summary of the arguments pertaining to the influence of scholasticism upon the writing of the *Institutes* has been presented by Wendel, *op. cit.*, pp. 126—130. A more recent statement is that of Kilian McDonnell, *John Calvin, the Church, and the Eucharist* (Princeton, 1967), especially pp. 7—25. Unfortunately, the analysis of McDonnell is faulted by building too much upon the assumption that Calvin studied in Paris under the nominalist John Major, a theory that is yet to be proven.
62 Dowey, *op. cit.*, pp. 218—219.
63 See Wendel, *op. cit.*, p. 274; Niesel, *op. cit.*, pp. 162—163; Jacobs, *op. cit.*, pp. 72—93; Thomas F. Torrance, *Kingdom and Church* (Edinburgh, 1956), *passim*; Gerrish, *op. cit.*, pp. 157 ff.; Beardslee, *op. cit.*, pp. 17—18; Dowey, *op. cit.*, pp. 186—188.
64 *Institutes*, III, 22, 7; *OS*, I, 63.
65 *OS*, IV, 380.
66 *OS*, I, 86 ff.; IV, 377, 380—381, 387; *CR*, 36 : 99 f. On the believer's relationship to the lordship of Christ see Alfred Gohler, *Calvins Lehre von der Heiligung* (Munich, 1934), pp. 111—113.
67 *CR*, 36 : 318.

Those whom God has adopted as his sons are said to have been chosen not in themselves but in his Christ (Eph. 1 : 4); for unless he could love them in him, he could not honor them with the inheritance of his Kingdom if they had not previously become partakers of him. But if we have been chosen in him, we shall not find assurance of our election in ourselves; and not even in God the Father, if we conceive him as severed from his Son. Christ, then, is the mirror wherein we must, and without self-deception may, contemplate our own election. For since it is into his body the Father has destined those to be engrafted whom he has willed from eternity to be his own, that he may hold as sons all whom he acknowledges to be among his members, we have a sufficient clear and firm testimony that we have been inscribed in the book of life if we are in communion with Christ.[68]

Thus, for Calvin, election is sealed in Christ who, as second member of the Trinity, participated in the decree of election and 'is also the artisan of this election in his capacity as Mediator.'[69] 'There was a twofold role of Christ in predestination: (1) as mediator he was that one who witnessed to the eternal decree and received the elect into his body; but (2) as eternal Son, member of the Trinity, he was a participant in the decision to predestine.'[70] Wendel has summarized the matter nicely: 'That Calvin insists so much upon predestination is precisely for this reason. It is in the fact that election is founded upon Christ that he finds assurance of the certitude of salvation.'[71] In sum, for Calvin the doctrine of predestination is not an abstract, philosophical, metaphysical consideration; on the contrary, it is rooted and grounded in his soteriology and Christology.

Recent scholarship has also stressed the organic relationship between Calvin's concept of predestination and his doctrine of the church.[72] His point of departure in discussing the doctrine of the mystical body is predestination and election rather than the Incarnation.[73] The church has been based upon election in Christ, and it is this basis which has established the lordship of Christ in the church. Consequently, Calvin's doctrine of election is intricately woven into his concept of the church and is, in fact, the foundation of it.[74]

The crucial point of this discussion is to note that Calvin's doctrine of predestination does not stand as an isolated element in his theology; nor is the purpose of the doctrine to stress the *potentia absoluta* of the nominalists.[75] On the contrary,

68 *Institutes*, III, 24, 5.
69 Wendel, *op. cit.*, p. 274.
70 Wiley, *op. cit.*, p. 276. But Wiley does go on to acknowledge that the latter role of Christ was not stressed in Calvin's works (*ibid.*, pp. 277 ff.).
71 Wendel, *op. cit.*, p. 274.
72 Niesel, *op. cit.*, pp. 189–190; McDonnell, *op. cit.*, pp. 169–172.
73 Alexandre Ganoczy, *Calvin théologien de l'église et du ministère* (Paris, 1964), p. 490.
74 Niesel, *op. cit.*, pp. 189–190. It should also be noted, in passing, that a number of scholars have demonstrated the vital connections between Calvin's doctrine of election and his views of our knowledge of God, the nature of faith, the sacraments, and eschatology; see especially A.D.R. Polman, *De Praedestinatieleer van Augustinus, Thomas van Aquino en Calvijn* (Franeker, 1936), pp. 357–377; Heinrich Quistorp, *Calvin's Doctrine of the Last Things* (Richmond, 1955), p. 24; Torrance, *op. cit.*, pp. 105–107; Dowey, *op. cit., passim*.
75 McDonnell, *op. cit.*, pp. 8–9; Wendel, *op. cit.*, p. 129; Dowey, *op. cit.*, pp. 208–211.

Calvin has stated quite clearly that the threefold purpose of the doctrine of predestination is to humble the believer, to enlighten the believer as to the debt which he owes God, and to provide a firm basis for the believer's confidence (*fiducia*) in the salvation of God.[76]

According to Calvin, the goal, or purpose, of election is twofold. The ultimate goal, or, in Calvin's terminology, the final cause is the glory of God. This is a dominate theme in Calvin's commentaries — especially his comments on Ephesians — but it is not a major thrust in the *Institutes*. In the latter Calvin stresses the proximate end: our sanctification. These two purposes do not engender a conflict in Calvin's thought.

> 'That we should be holy.' Here he considers the proximate, not the ultimate, purpose of election. For it is not absurd that the same thing should have two objectives. For instance, the purpose of a building is that it be a house. But this is the proximate purpose: the ultimate purpose is that it be used as a home. We touch upon this in passing because Paul speaks constantly of another purpose, which is the glory of God. There is no contradiction here. Our sanctification is subordinate to the highest end of election, that is, the glory of God.[77]

Calvin's discussions of predestination presuppose that man is in need of God's salvation because man, apart from the grace of God, is a sinner who is alienated from God.[78] Calvin is not concerned to argue for a pessimistic view of man in contrast to an optimistic view. Indeed, Calvin is willing to grant that man has many wonderful natural gifts that have been given to him by God. The problem is that man is no longer what God intended him to be.[79] In his present state man is alienated from God his creator.[80] There are times at which Calvin speaks very loosely and states that the divine image in man has been destroyed. But at other times he is more careful and says that the image is still there, though it is badly marred.[81] But in any case, that which was originally most valued in man is 'altogether corrupted.'[82] Man is now dominated by an evil tendency which Calvin identifies with concupiscence.[83]

The root of man's problem may be traced back to Adam. When the first man fell, the entire human race fell.[84] For Calvin Adam was much more than an individual man; he was the embodiment of the human race. When Adam sinned he acted on our behalf, and, in some fashion, we acted in him. Thus Calvin rejected

---

76 *Institutes*, III, 21, 1.
77 *Commentary on Ephesians 1 : 4; CR*, 79 : 147.
78 For helpful studies of Calvin's doctrine of man and the nature of sin see Thomas F. Torrance, *Calvin's Doctrine of Man* (London, 1949); Wilhelm A. Hauck, *Sünde und Erbsünde nach Calvin* (Heidelberg, 1938); Niesel, *op. cit.*, pp. 80–91; Wendel, *op. cit.*, pp. 185–196.
79 *Institutes*, I, 15, 4.
80 *Institutes*, II, 1, 4.
81 *Institutes*, I, 15, 4.
82 *Institutes*, II, 1, 9.
83 *Institutes*, II, 1, 8.
84 *Institutes*, II, 1; *OS*, III, 228.

any concept of original sin that would teach that man inherits sin.[85] Rather, we sinned through Adam in much the same way as the elect live a perfect life through Christ.[86] Consequently, we are all guilty through the sin of Adam. Calvin is in agreement with Augustine that the primal sin and the 'beginning of all evils' was pride. It was pride that led man to rebel against God and to leave the Word of God.[87]

The effects of that sin may be clearly seen in men today who are 'saturated' with sin.[88] The sinfulness of man is not limited to one part of man, but, rather, it extends to the total being of man.[89] Yet man is not forced to sin as a result of outside pressure.[90] The problem focused upon the will of men: man sins freely because his will is perverse. Man no longer possesses a healthy will.[91] The only cure for this radical ill is for Christ to change the will.[92] Calvin has summarized the matter by quoting Bernard, 'To will is in us all: but to will good is gain; to will evil, loss. Therefore simply to will is of man; to will ill, of a corrupt nature; to will well, of grace.'[93]

In spite of the pervasive nature of sin, man is still capable of achieving good things and of practicing some virtues.[94] But the terrible irony is that gifted men become proud of their gifts. Hence, in the final analysis, their gifts and virtues do not count before God.[95]

Calvin's emphasis upon the importance of the fall has led some scholars to conclude that Calvin held to a supralapsarian interpretation of the decrees.[96] However, it is my opinion that those conclusions are not justified. The debate itself took place after the death of Calvin, and to apply the terms of that debate to him is anachronistic. Although numerous scholars have taken passages from the works of Calvin and have attempted to draw from them either supralapsarian or

85 *Institutes*, II, 1, 7. Though at times Calvin sounded as though he believed in inherited sin; see *Institutes*, I, 15, 8 and II, 1, 8.
86 *Institutes*, II, 1, 6.
87 *Institutes*, II, 1, 4.
88 *CR*, 33 : 728.
89 *Institutes*, II, 1, 8–9.
90 *CR*, 49 : 128–129.
91 *Institutes*, II, 1, 8; II, 3, 5. For a helpful comparison with Bucer, Luther, and Melanchton at this point see Hermann Barnikol, *Die Lehre Calvins vom unfreien Willen und ihr Verhaltnis zur Lehre der ubrigen Reformatoren und Augustins* (Neuwied, 1927).
92 *Institutes*, II, 2, 7; II, 3, 5–6.
93 *Institutes*, II, 3, 4.
94 *Institutes*, II, 2, 13; II, 2, 18; II, 3, 4; *CR*, 36 : 535.
95 *Institutes*, II, 3, 4.
96 This conclusion has been drawn by Dowey (*op. cit.*, pp. 186, 213) and by Kickel (*op. cit.*, p. 148). The terms 'supralapsarianism' and 'infralapsarianism' were employed in the Calvinistic debates of the sixteenth and seventeenth centuries concerning the order of the decrees. The supralapsarians argued that God's decree to elect and to save some men preceeded his decree to permit the fall (*supra lapsum*). The infralapsarians insisted that God's decree to elect and to save some men followed his decree to permit the fall. See Heinrich Heppe, *Die Dogmatik der evangelisch-reformierten Kirche*, revised and edited by Ernst Bizer (Neukirchen, 1958), pp. 118–120 for a discussion of these distinctions. For a recent discussion of the question of the sequence of the decrees in Calvin's thought and the critical literature surrounding this issue, see Wiley, *op. cit.*, pp. 224–238.

infralapsarian conclusions, the simple fact is that Calvin refused to speculate concerning the order or the decrees.[97] Hall is probably correct in his statement that Calvin would have regarded discussion of the order of the decrees 'as being impertinently precise in setting out God's purposes.'[98] Indeed, as I shall argue, it was Calvin's reluctance to speculate concerning such matters that gave his theology a different hue from that of Beza.

The radical nature of man's sin has alienated man from God. On the one hand, God is horrified by the sin of man and cannot look upon that sin. At the same time man now hates God, for he fears God and anxiously awaits the punishment for his sin. Thus a breach has formed between God and man – a breach that necessitates the work of a mediator. It is precisely this necessity for an intermediary that, in Calvin's mind, distinguishes Christianity from the other religions.[99]

An essential characteristic of the mediator must be his ability to be obedient where men have been disobedient to God. The requirement of obedience can be met only by one who is both God and man – Jesus Christ. God, himself, must come to rescue his people from their sin. 'Our Lord came forth as true man and took the person and the name of Adam in order to take Adam's place in obeying the Father, to present our flesh as the price of satisfaction to God's righteous judgment, and, in the same flesh, to pay the penalty that we had deserved.[100] God the father has, then, accepted as satisfaction for sin the perfect obedience of Christ. The obstacle of sin had prevented God's love from reaching man, but now that obstacle has been removed. The work of Christ is the instrument, or the means by which God brings to pass his elective purposes. Redemption is part of predestination, and the unfolding history of salvation must be viewed as the completion of election.[101] At the same time it must be remembered that Christ, as one of the three persons of the Trinity, took part in election. His role was much more than a mechanical, instrumental one.[102]

There was no question in the mind of Calvin concerning the benefits that the believer received from the work of Christ: the forgiveness of sins (justification) and sanctification (regeneration).[103] However, a crucial question raised by Calvin

97 The following scholars acknowledge that Calvin did not address himself to this problem: Klooster, *op. cit.*, p. 20; Scheibe, *op. cit.*, p. 89; Wiley, *op. cit.*, p. 225.
98 Hall, *op. cit.*, p. 27.
99 For a discussion of the role of Christ as mediator in Calvin's theology, see Wiley, *op. cit.*, pp. 269–276.
100 *Institutes*, II, 12, 3. A guide to the literature on Calvin's Christology may be found in Wendel, *op. cit.*, p. 215 n. 95.
101 Jacobs, *op. cit.*, pp. 178–179.
102 Wendel, *op. cit.*, p. 231. A number of scholars have noted the Trinitarian aspect of predestination in Calvin's formulation; see Hauck, *Die Erwählten*, pp. 48–49; Jacobs, *op. cit.*, p. 74; McDonnell, *op. cit.*, pp. 170, 177; Wiley, *op. cit.*, pp. 276–286. Dantine has been criticized by Wiley (*op. cit.*, p. 282 n. 2, p. 286 n. 1) for minimizing the role played by Christ in Calvin's understanding of predestination.
103 *OS*, I, 69; III, 11, 1. Concise summaries of Calvin's views concerning these doctrines, accompanied by helpful bibliographical references may be found in the following: Niesel, *op. cit.*, pp. 120–139; Wendel, *op. cit.*, pp. 233–263.

was of precisely how one becomes a partaker of the grace of Christ.[104] In a sense one may argue that for Calvin it was simply a matter of exercising faith, for Calvin himself stated that one's position in Christ came about by faith.[105] Yet Calvin also spoke of faith as being similar to an empty vessel with no value for salvation.[106]

This seeming paradox in Calvin's theology is easily resolved by making two distinctions. First, there are two aspects, or types, of faith. One aspect of faith consists of assenting to the existence of God and to the truth of the Gospels concerning Christ. This is not saving faith, for even the devils believe and tremble.[107] At its worst, this is the type of faith whereby the scholastics have made God an 'object' of faith concerning which one may speculate.[108] Distinct from this type of faith, Calvin defined true faith as 'a firm and certain knowledge of God's benevolence toward us, founded upon the truth of the freely given promise in Christ, both revealed to our minds and sealed upon our hearts through the Holy Spirit.'[109]

Another distinction was Calvin's insistence that the value of true or saving faith is derived not from the faith itself, but from the object of faith: Jesus Christ.[110] The faith which unites the believer to Christ has no value nor dignity of itself, apart from Christ; it is only instrumental.[111]

In Calvin's theology the crucial point was the need for one to become united with Christ. Wendel is certainly correct when he states that for Calvin 'Communion with Christ, the *insitio in Christum*, is the indispensable condition for receiving the grace that Redemption has gained for us.'[112] There was no question in the mind of Calvin concerning the centrality of the union with Christ. In his commentary on John 17 : 26 he stated that until a man was united with Christ, he was not included in the love of God.[113]

Union with Christ becomes possible when the Holy Spirit baptizes one into the body of Christ.[114] The believer is bound to Christ through a faith that has been instilled in him through the activity of the Holy Spirit.[115] Christ unites the believer to himself by the Holy Spirit. 'By the grace and power of the same Spirit

---

104 This is the topic of Book III of the *Institutes*.
105 *Institutes*, III, 1, 1.
106 *Institutes*, III, 11, 7.
107 *CR*, 29 : 56; *OS*, I, 68.
108 Dowey, *op. cit.*, p. 153.
109 *Institutes*, III, 11, 7. For a brief discussion of Calvin's changing concept of faith see Wendel, *op. cit.*, pp. 240–241; see also Dowey, *op. cit.*, pp. 184–185.
110 Wendel, *op. cit.*, p. 238; Niesel, *op. cit.*, pp. 123–126; *Institutes*, III, 2, 1; III, 2, 32; *OS*, IV, 415; Dowey, *op. cit.*, p. 187.
111 Wendel, *op. cit.*, p. 241.
112 Wendel, *op. cit.*, p. 235. See also Ronald S. Wallace, *The Doctrine of the Christian Life* (Grand Rapids, 1959), pp. 17–27; Niesel, *op. cit.*, pp. 120–124; Armstrong, *op. cit.*, p. 214.
113 *CR*, 75 : 391.
114 *Institutes*, III, 1, 4. For an extremely helpful study on the function of the Holy Spirit in Calvin's theology see Werner Krusche, *Das Wirken des Heiligen Geistes nach Calvin*, (Göttingen, 1957); and H. Jackson Forstman, *Word and Spirit in Calvin: Calvin's Doctrine of Biblical Authority* (Stanford, 1962).
115 *Institutes*, III, 1, 4; III, 2, 30.

we are made his members, to keep us under himself and in turn to possess him.'[116] Thus Calvin was fond of speaking of the Holy Spirit as the 'bond' whereby Christ binds the believer to himself.[117]

Once again we find Calvin's thought returning to the concept of election: the Holy Spirit, acting sovereignly, elicits from man the faith which is required for one to enter into a soteric mystical union with Christ.[118] Through the faith instilled by the Holy Spirit the believer becomes incorporated into the body of Christ and eventually becomes one with Christ.[119]

The grace that God grants to the believer through the Holy Spirit is irresistible and assures the believer that he will be brought successfully through the struggles of this life.[120] As soon as one has been incorporated into the body of Christ, one has the assurance that in the end he will achieve victory in the fight. The Spirit of God is consistent with himself and will nourish and confirm in the believer the love of obedience that he instilled in the believer from the beginning.[121] 'If we ascribe any reality to predestination, it must be admitted that the decree of election must be able to triumph not only over our initial resistances, but our permanent weaknesses and our liberality to fall back into sin and disobedience.'[122] Dowey had expressed Calvin's logic lucidly:

Faith will never be blotted out in the elect, no matter what doubts attack, for it is God's work rather than man's, and man is thus held by God, not by his own efforts. But . . . the final determination by God is not meant to release man from a present effort. The certainty of final outcome is not seen as nullifying the seriousness of the soul's struggle.[123]

And yet Calvin never taught the permanence of election in general, but rather, the permanence of the election of individuals to the body of Christ. There had been a general election of the people of Israel, but they had lost the benefit of that election. The benefits of election in Christ will never be lost. It was for the purpose of maintaining that distinction that Calvin distinguished several different types of election — especially in the last edition of the *Institutes*.[124]

Calvin acknowledges that there are some individuals who seemed to possess the true faith, but nevertheless, fell away. His explanation is that their faith was apparent, but nor real. 'Such persons never cleaved to Christ with the heartfelt trust in which certainty of election has, I say, been established for us.'[125] Calvin

116 *Ibid.*, III, 1, 3.
117 *CR*, 74 : 953; *Institutes*, III, 1, 1; Wendel, *op. cit.*, p. 239.
118 The relationship between faith and the mystical union with Christ has been explored by Dowey, *op. cit.*, pp. 197–204.
119 *Institutes*, III, 11, 10; III, 2, 24.
120 *Institutes*, II, 3, 10; IV, 1, 3. A comparison with the theology of Bucer on this point has been presented by Wendel, *op. cit.*, p. 278.
121 *Institutes*, II, 3, 11.
122 Wendel, *op. cit.*, p. 278.
123 Dowey, *op. cit.*, p. 197.
124 Wendel, *op. cit.*, pp. 279–280.
125 *Institutes*, III, 24, 7.

then goes on to declare that such instances should not induce us 'to abandon a quiet reliance upon the Lord's promise, where he declares that all by whom he is received in true faith have been given to him by the Father, no one of whom . . . will perish.'[126]

Is there, then, any way in the theology of Calvin whereby one can know whether one is the object of special election and does, in fact, exercise true faith? To this question Calvin gave two responses. First, one may be assured of election by the fact of his faith in Christ and by the sense of union with him. A warm, wholehearted response to the preaching of the Gospel is a sign of election.[127] 'Now among the elect we regard the call as a testimony of election. Then we hold justification another sign of its manifestation, until they come into the glory in which the fulfillment of that election lies.'[128]

But, at the same time, there is in the work of Calvin another vein of argumentation in response to the question of assurance. This second response stresses that proof of election may be found in the presence of works which follow true faith. This has led some scholars to see in Calvin 'the germs of the future puritanism.'[129] But it appears to me that Wendel is entirely correct in pointing out that the *syllogismus practicus* is no evidence of contradiction in Calvin's theology if one interprets it within the general context of his theology. Thus, works are a sign of election, but they are inferior signs because of the sinfulness of all men.[130]

Calvin's understanding of the relationship between good works and assurance is clearly seen in his comments upon I John. Although works may provide a type of support and confidence to men, it is a secondary support that is valueless without the primary support.[131] Again, 'although a good conscience cannot be separated from faith, none should conclude from this that we must look to our works for our assurance to be firm.'[132] A summary of Calvin's view is to be found in his comments upon I John 2 : 23:

> But we are not to conclude from this that faith rests on works. For although everyone has a witness to his faith from his works, it does not follow that it is founded on them, but they are a subsequent proof added as a sign. The godliness and holiness of life distinguish true faith from a fictitious and dead knowledge of God.[133]

126 *Ibid.*
127 *CR*, 51 : 260.
128 *Institutes*, III, 21, 7.
129 Wendel, *op. cit.*, p. 276. Discussions of this second argument, the so-called *syllogismus practicus*, may be found in Niesel, *op. cit.*, pp. 169–180; Klooster, *op. cit.*, pp. 34–35; Wendel, *op. cit.*, pp. 275–277; Barth, *op. cit.*, II/2, pp. 333–340; Wilhelm Niesel, 'Syllogismus practicus?', *Aus Theologie und Geschichte der reformierte Kirche. Festgabe für E.F.K. Muller* (Neukirchen, 1933), pp. 158–179; G.C. Berkouwer, *Divine Election*, trans. Hugo Bekker (Grand Rapids, Michigan, 1960), pp. 288–290.
130 Wendel, *op. cit.*, p. 276.
131 Calvin's comments upon I John 4 reveal this; see John Calvin, *Calvin's New Testament Commentaries*, ed. David and Thomas Torrance, trans. T.H.L. Parker (Grand Rapids, 1959–1968), V, p. 295.
132 *Ibid.*, V, p. 278 (comments upon I John 3 : 19).
133 *Ibid.*, V, p. 281 (comments upon I John 2 : 23). The above references in I John have

For Calvin the doctrine of predestination was a great encouragement to believers during adversity, but it was not the basis for Christian assurance.[134] The only solid foundation for the certainty of salvation was Christ.[135] Those seeking certainty must turn their gaze to Christ.[136]

It was quite clear to Calvin that there were some men who were not of the elect, but he was extremely cautious in commenting upon the question of the extent of the atonement — for whom did Christ die? When Calvin compósed his refutation of the Decrees of the Council of Trent in 1547 he wrote that he did not wish to comment upon the decree which asserted that Christ had died for all men.[137] In this area, as in others, it would appear that Calvin was concerned lest he press the work of God into too precise a mould and become presumptious concerning his knowledge of God.[138] Some scholars are convinced that Calvin believed in a limited atonement, but it appears to me that Calvin made numerous reference to a universal atonement.[139]

Calvin's reluctance to embrace a doctrine of limited atonement did not prevent him from espousing the doctrine of divine reprobation.[140] For Calvin the doctrine of reprobation was necessary to explain the phenomenon of unbelief, and it served as a 'logical counterpart' of election.[141]

Election itself could not stand except as set over against reprobation. God is said to set apart those whom he adopts into salvation; it will be highly absurd to say that others acquire by chance or obtain by their own effort what election alone confers on a few. Therefore, those whom God passesover, he condemns; and this he does for no other reason that that he wills to exclude them from the inheritance which he predestines for his own children.[142]

It is at this point that Calvin deviated from Augustine. In the Augustinian system it was only the elect who received a special decision from God. The reprobate were simply abandoned by God and allowed to experience the full consequences of their sins.[143] But for Calvin reprobation comes about as a result of the counsel of God.[144]

bᵥen called to my attention by Gaylund Olson in a seminar paper that he wrote on Calvin's doctrine of assurance.

---

134 *CR*, 42 : 595; 45 : 132.
135 *CR*, 36 : 321; 37 : 757.
136 *CR*, 36 : 319; 81 : 59—60. For a discussion of Christ as the source of certainty in Calvin's theology see Wiley, *op. cit.*, pp. 264—268.
137 *CR*, 35 : 371 ff.
138 Duffield, *op. cit.*, p. 27.
139 A number of these references have been compiled by Armstrong, *op. cit.*, pp. 137—138.
140 Illuminating analyses of Calvin's understanding of reprobation are found in Jacobs, *op. cit.*, pp. 141—157; Klooster, *op. cit.*, pp. 36—59; Wendel, *op. cit.*, pp. 280—284; Niesel, *op. cit.*, pp. 166—167; Dowey, *op. cit.*, pp. 210—220.
141 Wendel, *op. cit.*, p. 280.
142 *Institutes*, III, 23, 1.
143 Wendel, *op. cit.*, p. 280.
144 *Institutes*, III, 23, 7.

At the same time, Calvin is very wary about justifying the reprobationary activity of God to man. One can say no more than that God has chosen some for reprobation.[145] Any further assertion would touch upon the 'inscrutable judgments of God.'[146] Rather than scrutinize and investigate the decree of reprobation, Calvin advises the believer to remember that there is such depth to the judgments of God that 'all men's minds would be swallowed up if they tried to penetrate it.'[147]

Shortly after having proclaimed the incomprehensibility of the will of God, Calvin asserts that the condemnation of the reprobate is just and is their own fault.[148] But, in the final analysis, the ultimate cause of reprobation is the sovereign will of God.[149]

Calvin's reservations concerning our ability to pierce the causes of reprobation extends also to our inability to identify the reprobate and to distinguish them from the elect. It is true that there are some signs that usually mark the reprobate — such things as a lack of positive response to the preaching of the Gospel and a lack of sanctification — but those marks are not infallible.[150] At times the reprobate exhibits traits very similar to those of the elect.[151] Therefore one must conclude that only God knows the reprobate, and the Gospel must be preached to all.[152]

Scholars have not been unanimous on the importance of reprobation in the theology of Calvin. Much writing has been devoted to the question of whether the doctrine of reprobation was an integral part of Calvin's theology or was simply an insignificant appendage, the result of either metaphysical speculation or of inconsistent biblical exegesis.[153]

There is certainly a body of evidence to support the position that reporbation was not an integral part of Calvin's theology and that the doctrine did not support nor harmonize other doctrines to which Calvin subscribed. In the first place, there was very little treatment of reprobation, or 'negative predestination,' in those works of Calvin that were nonpolemic; that is, his sermons and exegetical works.[154] Calvin, himself, had stated that reprobation was not an appropriate subject for preaching.[155] One finds such more attention devoted to the doctrine in

145 *Institutes*, III, 23, 5.
146 *Institutes*, III, 21, 1; *CR*, 9 : 263.
147 *Institutes*, III, 23, 4.
148 *Ibid.*, III, 23, 8.
149 *Ibid.*, III, 22, 11; III, 23, 1. Cf. his comments on Romans 9 : 11 (*CR*, 77 : 177–179).
150 *Institutes*, III, 21, 7; III, 23, 12.
151 *Ibid.*, III, 2, 11; III, 24, 7.
152 *CR*, 73 : 216; *Institutes*, III, 24, 13–14.
153 A formidable body of secondary literature surrounds this question. A few of the more significant discussions of the question may be found in Dowey, *op. cit.*, pp. 211–220; Jacobs, *op. cit.*, pp. 119–157; Heinrich Quistorp, *Calvin's Doctrine of the Last Things* (Richmond, 1955), pp. 144 ff.; Cornelius van Til, *The Defense of the Faith* (Philadelphia, 1955), pp. 413 ff; Torrance, *op. cit.*, p. 107; Paul van Buren, *Christ in our Place* (Grand Rapids, 1957), pp. 102–103; James Daane, *A Theology of Grace* (Grand Rapids, 1954), *passim*; Klooster, *op. cit.*, pp. 47–54; Wiley, *op. cit.*, pp. 239–253.
154 Jacobs, *op. cit.*, pp. 148–152.
155 *Ibid.*, p. 152.

his systematic works, but, as Jacobs has forcefully argued, that was because Calvin's opponents attacked double predestination. In defending the doctrine, Calvin felt that he was defending the freedom and the sovereignty of God.[156] This has led Dowey to conclude that 'Reprobation is an isolated doctrine for Calvin, literally in its place in the *Institutes*, in its comparative rarity in Calvin's commentaries and sermons, as well as in its theological scope.'[157]

The importance of reprobation in Calvin's theology has also been denied on epistemological grounds by Dowey. His argument is that only believers know the doctrine of reprobation, and they must treat their neighbors as being potentially elect.[158] 'The doctrine . . . enters into neither the relation to God nor the relation to one's fellow man, neither the worship nor the ethics, of the only one for whom it is a doctrine: the believer.'[159] Dowey adds that 'There are in Calvin's theology no ethical, ecclesiastical, or soteriological corollaries to the doctrine of reprobation. It brings about no harmonizing modifications in other doctrines.'[160]

Finally, there are logical problems involved in asserting that reprobation is parallel to the doctrine of election. These problems may be traced to what Dowey has termed 'systematic peculiarities' within the doctrine of reprobation itself.[161]

How have these charges been answered by those who maintain that the doctrine of reprobation is an integral part of Calvin's theology? One response has been to cite passages from the works of Calvin that would indicate that *he* believed the doctrine of reprobation to be 'equally ultimate' with the doctrine of individual election.[162] These passages seem to me to constitute persuasive evidence. This pushes one on to the question of how accurately Calvin evaluated the function of the doctrine of reprobation in his own theology, a question which will be considered at a later point.

Another response has been to demonstrate that Calvin did, in fact, connect the doctrine of reprobation with other doctrines such as the unconditioned character of God's actions, the sovereignty of God, the freedom of God, and God as the ultimate cause of all things.[163] Once again, Calvin's perception of his own system may be questioned.

The fact that Calvin did not devote as much space to the topic of reprobation as he did to that of election does not, in and of itself, demonstrate that Calvin subordinated reprobation to the other doctrines in his own thinking. In the first

---

156 *Ibid.*, p. 148. The basic thrust of Jacobs' entire discussion from p. 119 to p. 157 is the subordinate nature of the doctrine of reprobation.
157 Dowey, *op. cit.*, p. 217.
158 *Ibid.*, pp. 213–215.
159 *Ibid.*, p. 213.
160 *Ibid.*, p. 213.
161 Dowey has spelled out some of these problems on pp. 215–219.
162 An example of this approach may be found in Klooster, *op. cit.*, pp. 48–51.
163 Wilhelm Albert Hauck, *Die Erwählten. Prädestination und Heilsgewissheit bei Calvin* (Gütersloh, 1950), ṛ 0. Wiley (*op. cit.*, p. 240) has argued that Calvin believed in the parity of election and reprobation for two reasons: first, because of the way in which their parity undergirded his soteriology, and second, because he thought that this was the teaching of Scripture.

place, many of Calvin's expositions of election contain discussions of reprobation.[164] Furthermore, the preaching of reprobation would have little positive, pastoral value for Calvin, whereas the proclamation of election would, to Calvin's mind, increase the assurance of salvation for the believers.[165]

A more persuasive rejoinder to those who have denied that election and reprobation are 'equally ultimate' in Calvin's theology has been to focus upon the ambiguity of the expression 'equally ultimate.'[166] Precisely what is meant by those who deny that the two doctrines are equally ultimate? Election and reprobation are equally ultimate if one considers that the ultimate source of both is the will of God.[167] Dowey was certainly correct in his observations concerning the nonparallel relationships between election and reprobation in Calvin's theology,[168] but a certain lack of parallelism does not, in itself, demonstrate that the two doctrines are not 'equally ultimate' within Calvin's theological system.[169]

The conclusions one may then draw concerning the relationship between election and reprobation in the work of Calvin seem to me to be as follows: Reprobation was an important doctrine for Calvin because it was part of God's revelation concerning his nature and activity. Furthermore, Calvin did relate reprobation to other doctrines. But Dowey is certainly correct in his observations that Calvin's doctrine of reprobation is in no way the infrastructure of his theology, nor does it harmonize difficulties presented by other doctrines. In short, Calvin overestimated the role played by the doctrine of reprobation in his theology. Dowey has stated the matter succinctly.

Calvin's doctrine of the decrees, especially the decree of reprobation, cannot by a process of extrapolation be lifted out of its context and set above the doctrines of creation and redemption without being transmuted into a rationalistic metaphysic which would then change the nature of his entire theology. This process is just what Beza and subsequent Calvinist orthodoxy brought about, an extreme but well safeguarded formulation becoming the dominant theme among the epigoni, as has more than once happened in the history of thought.[170]

CALVIN VERSUS THE CALVINISTS

It would simplify matters greatly if one could apply the term 'Calvinist' to those whose doctrine agreed with Calvin on predestination as well as on other points.

164 Klooster, *op. cit.*, p. 52.
165 There were a number of occasions upon which Calvin, himself, called attention to predestination as one of the bases for the believer's assurance of salvation, e.g., *Institutes*, III, 24, 5; *Predigten über das 2. Buch Samuelis*, ed. Hans Rückert (Neukirchen, 1936–1961), pp. 184–185, 212–213, 351, 352, 483, cited by McDonnell, *op. cit.*, pp. 200–201.
166 This refutation has been employed by Klooster (*op. cit.*, pp. 48–54) and by van Til (*op. cit.*, pp. 413–415).
167 Klooster, *op. cit.*, pp. 48–50.
168 Dowey, *op. cit.*, pp. 215–219.
169 Klooster, *op. cit.*, pp. 51–54.
170 Dowey, *op. cit.*, p. 218.

Unfortunately, this avenue has been closed to us because of the weighty historical problems that have developed concerning the meaning of Calvinism.[171]

Some of these problems have long historical lineage and continue to be debated by renowned scholars, e.g., the debate concerning the status of Puritanism as a Calvinist movement.[172] Schmidt has commented upon the difficulty experienced by those who claim to be the disciples of Calvin: the genius of his theology appears to elude them.[173]

Part of the problem may be psychological in nature. In summarizing historical movements, one tends to focus sharply upon a few individuals in an attempt to provide clarity of narrative, but such clarity is achieved at the expense of the richness of the historical phenomena under study. 'Looking back on the scene, Calvin's figure may appear to tower over others, but perspectives are sometimes deceiving, because history tends to concentrate on a few great names.'[174]

Indeed, there were contexts within which Calvin had less influence and authority than did such Reformed theologians as Beza, Bullinger, Martyr, Musculus, Viret, and Zanchi. Bucer, Bullinger, and Martyr had more of an impact upon Edwardian England than did John Calvin. Polish Calvinism was more oriented toward Zurich than it was to Geneva, and Heidelberg had more influence upon German Calvinism than did Geneva.[175]

Such questions as the impact of Calvin upon his contemporaries and upon seventeenth century Calvinism are being raised and considered in a refreshing manner by young historians today.[176] The basic impact of much of this literature has been to minimize the role played by Calvin in the development of Calvinist thought.

Armstrong has presented a strong case for the independence of the French Calvinists from Calvin.[177] It certainly appears, for example, that Calvin had little hand in drawing up the Confession of 1559.[178]

Laplanche has noted the relative obscurity enjoyed by Calvin even on the part of those who have accepted the appellation of 'Calvinist' in the seventeenth century. If Laplanche is correct, the thought of Calvin possessed no normative quality for those seventeenth century divines. Indeed, his thoughts were taken no more seriously than those of other theologians of the day. Any value that adhered to

---

171 For a helpful discussion of the confusions which pertain to this question see Basil Hall, 'Calvin against the Calvinists,' *John Calvin: A Collection of Distinguished Essays*, ed. Gervase E. Duffield (Grand Rapids, 1966), pp. 19–37.

172 See the article by George M. Marsden, 'Perry Miller's Rehabilitation of the Puritans: A Critique,' *Church History*, XXXIX (1970), 91–105.

173 Albert-Marie Schmidt, *Calvin and the Calvinistic Tradition*, trans. Ronald Wallace (New York, 1960), p. 99.

174 Marshall Knappen, *Tudor Puritanism* (Chicago, 1939), p. 137; quoted in Donnelly, *op. cit.*, p. 18 n. 3.

175 Leonard J. Trinterud, ed., *Elizabethan Puritanism* (New York, 1971), p. 81.

176 Armstrong, *op. cit.*, Donnelly, *op. cit.*, Kingdon, *Geneva*. But this insight is not limited to young scholars; see Otto Ritschl, *Dogmengeschichte des Protestantismus* (Göttingen, 1926), III, pp. 243–282, and Bizer's introduction to Heppe, p. xix.

177 Armstrong, *op. cit.*, pp. 22–31.

178 *Ibid.*, pp. 24–30.

the works of Calvin was based upon the fact that he had attempted to produce a theology of the Word.[179]

Armstrong agrees with Laplanche's position and has argued that a chasm existed between the theology of Calvin and that of the seventeenth century Calvinists who engaged themselves in theological conflict with Amyraut (Moses Amyraldus). It was the contention of Amyraut that his position concerning predestination was the position of Calvin, and it would appear that 'these orthodox theologians were not well read in Calvin and so were unprepared to counter the tremendous mass of relevant Calvin material marshalled by Amyraut.'[180] Indeed, Amyraut invoked the name of Calvin so frequently in defense of his position that du Moulin, one of his opponents, complained that Amyraut had made Calvin *coryphoeum theologorum.* [181]

For Amyraut the distinction between the teaching of Calvin and that of seventeenth century orthodox Calvinists was so clear cut that at times he defended Calvin against the charge of having turned God into a tyrant, but he refused to extend that defense to the orthodox Calvinists.[182] Amyraut focused upon Martyr, Zanchi and, especially, Beza as distorters of Calvin's doctrine of predestination.[183] It would appear that there were occasions on which Amyraut would go out of his way to attack Beza even though the circumstance did not demand it.[184]

The research of Armstrong and Laplanche, if accepted as reliable, would lead one to the conclusion that the impact of Calvin upon the Calvinistic movement has been greatly overrated. It may well be that some of the epigoni, particularly Beza, Martyr, and Zanchi, had a greater influence upon the formulation of Reformed doctrine that did Calvin.

It was quite common in the late sixteenth century for opponents of the Calvinists to set the work of Calvin against the position of contemporary Calvinists. They would then exploit what they viewed as weak spots in the apologetics of their Calvinist foes.[185]

In the field of ecclesiology it was clear that the later Calvinists moved away from Calvin's doctrine at some critical points.[186] A central figure here appears to have been Beza whose doctrinaire presbyterianism is viewed by Basil Hall as a distortion that upset the 'balance of Calvin's theology.'[187] Maruyama has noted the role played by Beza in altering the Reformed understanding of the church. 'For the early Protestant Reformers the classical marks of the Word and the Sacrament were the symbol of the church's unity. This is no longer the case. The

---

179 François Laplanche, *Orthodoxie et Prédication: L'Oeuvre d'Amyraut et la querelle de la grâce universelle* (Paris, 1965), p. 273.
180 Armstrong, *op. cit.*, p. 188.
181 *Ibid.*, p. 158.
182 *Ibid.*, p. 151.
183 *Ibid.*, p. 158.
184 *Ibid.*, pp. 159–160.
185 Maruyama, *op. cit.*, p. 238.
186 Kingdon, *Geneva*, pp. 37–148; Maruyama, *op. cit.*, pp. 303–313.
187 Basil Hall, 'Calvin against the Calvinists,' *John Calvin*, ed. Gervase E. Duffield (Grand Rapids, 1966), pp. 19–37.

mark of orthodoxy has become the symbol of the ecclesiology of Reformed Orthodoxy as well as of the mature Beza.'[188]

We have already noted the rise of Protestant scholasticism and the differences between the theology of that movement and the position of Calvin.[189] Calvin's attitude toward scholasticism and toward Aristotle differed radically from the attitudes of many later Reformed theologians.[190] Peter Martyr is a good example of this different attitude.

> Martyr's general attitude toward the scholastic differs sharply from Calvin's ... Calvin's reference are almost uniformly hostile and derisive ... Martyr cites the opinion of scholastics nearly as often to agree with it as to oppose it. Martyr's friend Zanchi carried this a step further; his references to particular scholastic authors, especially St. Thomas, are almost uniformly friendly. Martyr's reading in medieval theology seems much broader than that of Calvin.[191]

Martyr did not view Aristotle as a deadly foe of Reformed theology. For Martyr Aristotelian philosophy was not even a neutral tool to be used in constructing theological arguments. On the contrary, Martyr viewed Aristotle as an ally for the Reformed cause.[192]

In summary, the problem of 'Calvin versus the Calvinists' is not an easy one to unravel. There was certainly a large gap between the theological position of Calvin and that of other 'Calvinists.' And yet it is difficult to ascertain the exact nature of that gap because of the heterogeneity of those theologians known as 'Reformed.' It is within this confused theological milieu that Theodore Beza forged his theology. Much of the difficulty of understanding Beza's theology may be traced to the factors discussed above.

BEZA AS COMBATANT IN THE PREDESTINATION CONTROVERSIES

Although Amyraut was one of the first to focus upon Beza as a distorter of Calvin's theology, he certainly was not the last. Since that time numerous scholars have cited Beza as a crucial figure in the formation of orthodox, scholastic Calvinism. His imprint, according to these scholars, has been particularly profound in formulating the doctrine of predestination.[193]

---

188   Maruyama, *op. cit.*, p. 302.
189   See above, Introduction.
190   See Armand A. LaVallee, 'Calvin's Criticism of Scholastic Theology,' (Unpublished Ph.D. dissertation, Harvard University, 1967).
191   Donnelly, *op. cit.*, pp. 42—43.
192   *Ibid.*, p. 314.
193   The following studies depict Beza as a transformer of Calvin's theology: Beardslee, *op. cit.*, pp. 19—20; Ernst Bizer, *Frühorthodoxie und Rationalismus* (Zürich, 1963), pp. 5—15; Karl Barth, *Church Dogmatics*, trans. Geoffrey W. Bromiley et al. (Edinburgh, 1957), II/2, pp. 335—340; Johannes Dantine, 'Das christologische Problem im Rahmen der Prädestinationslehre von Theodor Beza,' *Zeitschrift für Kirchengeschichte*, LXXVII (1966), pp. 81—96; Dantine, 'Les Tabelles sur la doctrine de la prédestination par Théodore de Bèze,'

There is certainly good reason to associate Beza with the Calvinistic doctrine of predestination. One of the first theological controversies in which Beza became involved was the Bolsec affair which broke out in 1551 at Geneva. The basic issue was Calvin's doctrine of predestination.[194] There is no question concerning the position of Beza during the controversy: he served as Calvin's right-hand man and defended Calvin's theological stance as his own. Beza wrote a letter to Bullinger, his spiritual father, which contained Beza's interpretation of the Bolsec affair. Beza included a summary of Calvin's doctrine of election which he equated with his own.[195] At about the same time, in a letter sent to Calvin, Beza again testified to his complete agreement with Calvin's formulation of predestination as expressed in Calvin's work *De aeterna praedestinatione*. Beza then proceeded to suggest to Calvin certain changes of strategy in handling the Bolsec affair.[196]

The controversy with Bolsec was also related to problems of jurisdiction between Geneva and Berne. As a consequence Beza, who had become closely identified with the doctrinal authority of Calvin and of Geneva, became *persona non grata* in the Vaud. During the acrimonious debate which followed the banishment of Bolsec from Geneva, Beza wrote a number of theological works that considered the topic of predestination. The most famous of these was his *Tabula Praedestinationis*.[197]

Predestination was also a major issue in the conflict that broke out with Castellio in 1558. Although Castellio had served as a pastor in Geneva, he left the city in 1544 as a result of controversies that had surrounded his translation of the Bible, the canonicity of the *Song of Solomon*, and the doctrine of Christ's descent into hell.[198] From the safety of Basel he later attacked the execution of Servetus in Geneva, and his treatise concerning toleration elicited Beza's response in the form of his work *De haereticis a civili magistratu puniendis*.[199] Thus there was a

---

Revue de Théologie et de Philosophie, XVI (1966), pp. 365–377; Dowey, *op. cit.*, p. 218; Basil Hall, 'Calvin against the Calvinists,' *John Calvin: A Collection of Distinguished Essays*, ed. Gervase E. Duffield (Grand Rapids, 1966), pp. 19–37; Basil Hall, 'The Calvin Legend,' *John Calvin*, ed. Gervase E. Duffield (Grand Rapids, 1966), pp. 1–18; Laplanche. *op. cit.*, p. 25; Pontien Polman, *L'Elément historique dans la controverse religieuse de XVIᵉ siècle* (Gembloux, 1932), p. 127; Walter Kickel, *Vernunft und Offenbarung bei Theodor Beza* (Neukirchen, 1967), *passim.*

---

194 Monter, *op. cit.*, pp. 128–131; Léonard, *op. cit.*, pp. 342–343; Geisendorf, *op. cit.*, pp. 74–75, 204.
195 Beza to Bullinger, January 12, 1552, text in Meylan, *Correspondance*, I, pp. 76–80; see also Geisendorf, *op. cit.*, pp. 74–75, CR, 42 : 243.
196 Beze to Calvin, January 21, 1552, text in Meylan, *Correspondance*, I, pp. 81–84; see also CR, 42 : 254.
197 The historical context has been provided by Geisendorf, *op. cit.*, pp. 74–75.
198 For the definitive biography of Castello see Ferdinand Buisson, *Sébastien Castellio* (Paris, 1892), 2 vols. An outstanding bibliography of works concerning Castellio may be found in Léonard, *op. cit.*, I, pp. 430–432.
199 Geisendorf, *op. cit.*, pp. 64–68.

long tradition of hostility and tension between Beza and Castellio before they clashed over the doctrine of predestination.[200]

In 1558 Beza responded to Castellio's attack upon Calvin's doctrine of predestination by publishing a new work, *Ad sycophantarum quorumdam calumnias, quibusunicum salutis nostrae fundamentum, id est aeternam Dei predestinationem evertere nituntur, responsio Theodori Bezae Vezelii.*[201] When this treatise was reprinted with variations in the *Tractationes theologicae*, the expression 'sycophantarum' was replaced by the name 'Sebastiani Castellionis' in the title of the work, and the name 'Sebastien Castellion' was placed in the body of the work in lieu of 'Sycophanta.'[202] Beza chose to defend Calvin's doctrine of predestination in this work because he equated it with the doctrine of Christ. This was clearly indicated by the heading that Beza placed on the first page of the original work: 'The preface of the slanders against the doctrine of John Calvin (or, rather, of every faithful congregation) of the secret providence of God.'[203]

Predestination was also one of the topics of discussion at the colloquy of Montbéliard in 1586. Beza interacted with Jakob Andreae at the colloquy, but his position had become inflexible, and he simply restated his earlier formulations of the doctrine.[204]

Beza was certainly a major combatant in the predestination controversies of the sixteenth century. He was viewed both as the successor of Calvin and as his spokesman.[205] Furthermore there is good evidence to support the thesis that this was also the manner in which Beza viewed himself. Besides the letters to Bullinger and Calvin in 1552 and Beza's response of 1558 to Castellio, there is also the instance of the *Confessio de la foi chrétienne* which Beza produced as a defense of Calvin.[206]

But an important question remains: was Beza justified in viewing his doctrine of predestination as a faithful replica of Calvin's doctrine? And it is to that question that we shall now direct our attention.

---

200 For a description of the personal antagonism between Beza and Castellio see Geisendorf, *op. cit.*, pp. 232–236.

201 *Ibid.*, p. 68; Gardy, *op. cit.*, pp. 55–58.

202 Gardy, *op. cit.*, p. 55.

203 *Ibid.*

204 *Acta Colloquii Montis Belligartensis* (Tübingen, 1587), pp. 502–560; Réponse aux actes de la conférence de Montbéliard (Geneva, 1587); Léonard, *op. cit.*, II, p. 34; P. Pfister, *Le colloque de Montbéliard* (Geneva, 1873); A. Lods, 'Les Actes du colloque de Montbéliard, 1586. Une polémique entre Théodore de Bèze et Jacques Andreae,' *Bulletin de la Société de l'histoire du protestantisme français* (1897), pp. 192–215.

205 Borgeaud, *op. cit.*, I, pp. 228, 323–324; Polman, *op. cit.*, p. 127.

206 See Geisendorf, *op. cit.*, p. 78; Gardy, *op. cit.*, pp. 60–80; Walter Hollweg, *Neue Untersuchungen zur Geschichte und Lehre des Heidelberger Katechismus* (Neukirchen, 1961), pp. 86–123.

CHAPTER III

THE POSITION OF PREDESTINATION IN BEZA'S THEOLOGY

This chapter will be the first of three dedicated to an exposition of Beza's doctrine of predestination. The basic thrust of this chapter will be to determine the systemic significance of predestination for Beza. Precisely what role did the doctrine play in Beza's theology? Did Beza view predestination as a central dogma, or did he treat it as a secondary issue?

THE SIGNIFICANCE OF THE QUESTION

Predestination became the keystone of Protestant scholasticism.[1] If the doctrine of predestination did not possess crucial importance for Beza, then any attempt to link Beza with the rise of Protestant scholasticism would be foredoomed to failure.

Numerous scholars have labeled Beza as a distorter of Calvin's theology. Indeed, a number of these scholars have focused upon Calvin's doctrine of predestination as one of the areas in which Beza distorted the teaching of Calvin by ascribing to predestination a significance and function far different from that which it played in Calvin's theology.[2] The result, in the words of Basil Hall, was that 'Beza re-opened the door to speculative determinism which Calvin had attempted to close.'[3] Recently this interpretation has been lucidly stated by David Steinmetz.

Perhaps the most important distinction between the theology of Beza and that of Calvin, and the most difficult to understand, is their difference over the

---

1 Johannes Dantine, 'Les Tabelles sur la doctrine de la prédestination par Théodore de Bèze,' *Revue de Théologie et de Philosophie*, XVI (1966), 365.
2 For instance of this interpretation see Brian Armstrong, *Calvinism and the Amyraut Heresy* (Madison, 1969), pp. 37–42, 136–137, 198–199; John W. Beardslee (ed.), *Reformed Dogmatics* (New York, 1965), pp. 19–20; Edward A. Dowey, Jr., *The Knowledge of God in Calvin's Theology* (New York, 1952), p. 218; François Laplanche, *Orthodoxie et Prédication* (Paris, 1965), p. 25; Walter Kickel, *Vernunft und Offenbarung bei Theodor Beza* (Neukirchen, 1967), pp. 99, 106–107, 116, 120, 136–137, 141, 149–150, 167–169; Dantine, *loc. cit.*, 365, 371–372, 374–376; Bèze, *La Confession de foi du Chrétien*, ed. and trans. Michel Réveillaud in *La Revue réformée*, VI (1955), Parts 3–4, Introduction, p. 5 n. 1.
3 Basil Hall, 'Calvin against the Calvinists,' *John Calvin: A Collection of Distinguished Essays*, ed. Gervase E. Duffield (Grand Rapids, 1966), p. 27; see also E. Wolf, 'Erwählungslehre und Prädestinationsproblem,' *Die Predigt von der Gnadenwahl, Theologische Existenz heute*, Neue Folge XXVIII (1951), 93, cited in Dantine, *loc. cit.*, 372–373.

doctrine of predestination. The key to the difference lies not so much in the language they employ as in the larger theological context within which they view the doctrine of predestination.

Predestination is clearly the nerve center of Beza's theology. For many years it was believed to be the center of Calvin's theology as well, partly because Calvin's theology was read by later generations with the spectacles of Beza . . .

. . . One sees in the theology of Beza the worst fears of Melanchthon come to pass. Predestination becomes in the hands of this speculative theologian a form of philosophical determinism scarcely distinguishable from the Stoic doctrine of fate. It is Beza, therefore, and not Calvin, who becomes the father of the hyper-Calvinism of Reformed Orthodoxy.[4]

One reason, perhaps, why some contemporary scholars stress the importance of predestination in Beza's theology has been the strong association of Beza with the doctrine of supralapsarianism. In the opinion of a number of scholars, there is no question concerning the validity of this association.[5] Indeed, at numerous times Beza assumed a theological stance that could only be called supralapsarian.[6] In contrast to Calvin, whose writings contain no statement of the order of the decrees, Beza was very specific concerning the proper order. In a letter to Calvin, dated July 29, 1555, Beza described two approaches to the order of the decrees, an infralapsarian approach and a supralapsarian approach. He opted for the latter order.[7]

There was a very strong methodological link between the supralapsarian position and the tendency to stress the centrality of predestination.[8] Consequently, there is some basis for the claim that predestination was a crucial doctrine for Beza, but the paucity of the evidence and argumentation presented thus far are not completely convincing.

THE LOCATION OF PREDESTINATION IN BEZA'S
MAJOR THEOLOGICAL WORKS

The first major work in which Beza considered the question of predestination at any length was the *Tabula Praedestinationis* (1555).[9] The circumstances surrounding the origins of the *Tabula* are exceedingly vague. To large measure this

4 David C. Steinmetz, *Reformers in the Wings* (Philadelphia, 1971), pp. 168–169.
5 Armstrong, *op. cit.*, pp. 41–42, 136–137, 160; Heinrich Heppe, *Die Dogmatik der evangelisch-reformierten Kirche*, revised and edited by Ernst Bizer (Neukirchen, 1958), pp. 118–120; Steinmetz, *op. cit.*, p. 169; Hall, *loc. cit.*; Kickel, *op. cit.*, pp. 102, 143.
6 Beza, *Quaestiones et Responsiones* (Geneva, 1570), pp. 105, 109–111; *Tractationes theologicae* (Geneva, 1570–1582), I, 173, 179, 344, 362, 418; III, 404, 426.
7 Meylan, *Correspondance*, I, pp. 169–172.
8 Armstrong, *op. cit.*, pp. 136–137.
9 For a definitive treatment of the origins of this work, the various editions and the translations see Frédéric Gardy and Alain Dufour, *Bibliographie des oeuvres théologiques, littéraires,*

vagueness may reflect the fact the Seigneurie of Berne had tried to minimize the controversy associated with the topic of predestination. On November 17, 1554, the Seigneurie issued a decree outlawing sermons on the topic of predestination. This was followed on January 26, 1555, by a prohibition against any discussion in the Vaud on the matters connected with the issue of Bolsec.[10] In light of these factors one would hardly expect Beza to publicize his progress on a new treatise which would focus upon predestination. The *Tabula* represented another phase of the doctrinal conflict between Calvin and his opponents. The polemical purpose of this work was responsible for its form.

In all probability the *Tabula* first took shape in 1555.[11] Reference to it was made by Beza in a letter to Calvin dated July 29, 1555.[12] The *Tabula*, itself, consists basically of a diagram in which all of mankind is divided into two groups: the elect and the reprobate. According to this diagram, the decree of God is the foundation upon which is built a number of other doctrines: God's calling, conversion, grace, faith, justification, sanctification, the glorification of believers and the damnation of sinners, eternal life and eternal death.[13] It may be that the diagram itself was secretly circulated by Beza without the benefit of a text, for Peter Martyr wrote to Beza in March, 1555, and suggested that an explanatory text be appended to the diagram.[14] The earliest extant edition of the diagram and the text is the English translation of 1556. The earliest extant Latin edition is that prepared for the 1570 edition of the *Tractationes theologicae.*[15]

In some respects it is unfortunate that the *Tabula* was the first major work in which Beza dealt with the doctrine of predestination because it has mislead some scholars in their attempt to ascertain the role that the doctrine played in Beza's general theology.[16] They have overlooked the fact that the *Tabula* was composed by Beza in the midst of attacks upon the doctrine of predestination taught by his master, John Calvin. Under these circumstances one would expect Beza to focus upon the doctrine of predestination and to ascribe to it an importance that one might not find if Beza had set out to write a general summary of the Christian faith.

---

historiques et juridiques de Théodore de Bèze (Geneva, 1960), pp. 47—53. The historical context within which the work was produced has been sketched by Paul F. Geisendorf, *Théodore de Bèze* (Geneva, 1949), pp. 74—75. A helpful analytical summary of the *Tabula* is to be found in Joannes Dantine, *loc. cit.*, 365—377. The *Tabula* was reprinted in the *Tractationes theologicae*, I, pp. 170—205. All references to the *Tabula* in this monograph will be taken from that source.

---

10 Henri Vuilleumier, *Histoire de l'Eglise Réformée du Pays de Vaud sous le régime bernois* (4 vols.; Lausanne, 1927—1933), I, pp. 349—350.
11 Gardy, *op. cit.*, p. 47; Dantine, *loc. cit.*, 367.
12 Meylan, *Correspondance*, I, pp. 169—173.
13 A copy of this diagram may be found in Heppe-Bizer, *op. cit.*, p. 119; Gardy, *op. cit.*, p. 49.
14 Meylan, *Correspondance*, I, pp. 153—155. Martyr never came out with such a schema himself, but the *Tabula* had great influence and was copied by Perkins; see Donnelly, *op. cit.*, p. 252 n. 109.
15 Gardy, *op. cit.*, pp. 47—50.
16 Kickel and, to a lesser degree, Dantine have erred at this point.

The fact that Beza referred to this work on predestination as the *Summa totius Christianismi* increased the possibility of misinterpretation.[17] Kickel, for example, understood this to mean that for Beza the doctrine of predestination summarized all of Christian theology.[18] It appears more probable that *Summa totius Christianismi* should be interpreted to mean the sum total of the Christian life or of the redemption promised to the faithful. This interpretation is supported by the fact that in his more comprehensive theological works Beza did not attempt to interpret all other doctrine, such as the Eucharist, in the light of predestination.[19]

The doctrine of predestination is central in the *Tabula*. It provided the foundation upon which was built the entire body of evangelical dogma. The decree of predestination, itself, was based upon and derived from the nature of God.

In the *Tabula* Beza placed predestination within the context of providence.[20] Beza may have done this because of the influence of Calvin upon him, but, in any case, it was certainly a logical consequence of his doctrine of God as developed in the *Tabula*. Indeed, according to the theological framework developed by Beza, all of redemptive history is simply the unfolding of the decree of God. The will of God has become a metaphysical principle with a logic of its own from which all else may be derived. The logical necessity of the will of God is reflected in Beza's frequent use of such expressions as *oportet* and *necesse est*.[21] In contrast to the will of God, all else has assumed the pale dimension of logical symbolism. 'The work of Christ becomes only the execution of the long and resolved decree and is indicated in the description only with an annotation.'[22]

If one knows the attributes of God, one can deduce from them the whole plan of salvation, including the necessity of atonement by the God-man. The drama of redemption stands from first to last under Beza's speculative doctrine of predestination.[23]

The basic diagram that Beza had employed in the *Tabula* was revised and reprinted at a much later date (1582) in conjunction with a series of lectures that he had presented on Romans, Chapter 9. The lectures were edited by his faithful disciple Raphael Egli who then had them published in the *Tractationes* along with a simplified form of Beza's diagram.[24]

17 Gardy, *op. cit.*, p. 47.
18 Kickel, *op. cit.*, p. 99.
19 See Jill Raitt, *The Eucharistic Theology of Theodore Beza* (Chambersburg, Pennsylvania, 1972), *passim*.
20 At this point he may have been following the lead of Calvin who treated predestination and providence together in the 1539 edition of the *Institutes* and did not separate them until his 1559 edition; see Wendel, *op. cit.*, p. 267. Augustine had also considered them together.
21 Ernst Bizer, *Frühorthodoxie und Rationalismus* (Zürich, 1963), p. 10.
22 *Ibid.*, p. 7.
23 Steinmetz, *op. cit.*, p. 169.
24 Beza, *Tractationes*, III, 402—447. The new work was published under the title *De Praedestinationis doctrina et vero usu tractatio absolutissima. Ex Th. Bezae praelectionibus in nonum Epistolae ad Romanos caput a Raphaele Eglino Tigurino Theologiae studioso in schola Genevensi recens excepta* (Genevae, 1582). (Hereinafter cited as *De Praedestinationis doctrina.*) For bibliographical information concerning this work see Gardy, *op. cit.*, p. 187.

Although there are strong similarities between the *Tabula* of 1555 and Beza's *De Praedestinationis doctrina* of 1582, the differences are consistent and significant. By 1582 it appears that the scholastic, rationalistic tendencies within Beza have come more to the fore. The basic terms used in both works — decree, predestination, foreknowledge — are given a more precise, rationalistic definition. By 1582 Beza has dropped such anthropocentric terms as 'love' and 'hate'. There has been an infusion of Thomistic terminology.[25] And, perhaps most significantly, Beza's earlier strictures which reminded one of the mystery involved in predestination are almost entirely absent from this later work. It would appear that now the only mystery consists of determining who is to be included in the ranks of the reprobate.[26]

In spite of the fact that the lectures upon which *De Praedestinationis doctrina* was based were, ostensibly, an exegesis of Romans 9, in fact, the text of Romans 9 has been exploited by Beza as an opportunity to expound his theory of predestination. Thus one discovers that Beza has read into the text of Romans 9 controversies in which he himself was involved; he has sought justification in Romans 9 for his own theories concerning predestination; and he has drawn conclusions from the text far beyond what many exegetes would view as justified. At the same time, one must remember that Romans had provided an opportunity earlier for Luther and Calvin to expound their theories of predestination. The difference is that Beza's comments were far more systematic and scholastic.[27]

The *Praedestinationis doctrina* is similar to the *Tabula* in that both of them were polemical works geared to defend Calvin's doctrine of predestination. In the *Praedestinationis doctrina* predestination is presented as the foundation for all evangelical dogma, and especially for the doctrine of justification. Apart from predestination, the doctrine of justification would be useless.[28] Kickel has commented that Beza would lead us to believe that predestination is the basic theme of the entire epistle of Paul to the Romans.[29]

Predestination was certainly the central doctrine for Beza in both the *Tabula* and the *De Praedestinationis doctrina*, but these were not Beza's only theological works. His involvement in the Castellio controversy led to the publication in 1558 of another work on predestinatiom: *De la prédestination, contre Castellion*.[30] This was an important work on predestination, but in it Beza essentially limited himself to refuting the accusations of Castellio. Hence the structure of Beza's treatise was determined by the order of Castellio's accusations. As a result we cannot determine the significance of Beza's doctrines by examining the order in which he presents them. The substance of *De la prédestination, contre Castellion* and the arguments utilized there by Beza were, however, in harmony with the tenor of the *Tabula*.

25 Raitt (*op. cit.*, p. 71) has noted that Beza's later Eucharistic works were increasingly scholastic in their method.
26 Dantine, *loc. cit.*, 373–374.
27 These points have been discussed at length by Kickel, *op. cit.*, pp. 136–146.
28 Beza, *Tractationes*, III, 412–417.
29 Kickel, *op. cit.*, pp. 136–137.
30 Gardy, *op. cit.*, pp. 55–58; Geisendorf, *op. cit.*, p. 68.

The *Confession de la foi chrétienne*, published in 1559, presents a very difficult form of exposition.[31] In this work predestination does not determine the framework for the theological exposition. Rather, the *Confession* is organized in a traditional trinitarian pattern. In this work providence is dealt with as a subdivision of Part I which is devoted to the topic of the Trinity. Predestination is not considered as an aspect of providence. Indeed, there is no separate treatment of predestination in the entire work. This does not mean that Beza denied the doctrine in this work. Allusions to it are made in Chapter I under the general topic of God, it may be seen in his discussion of Christology, and it emerges in his analysis of soteriology. But in the *Confession* predestination is given the status of a basic concept, rather than a fundamental doctrine upon which all other doctrines must be based.[32] Even in the statement on soteriology predestination, as a general doctrine, is not explored; instead, it is considered in highly personal terms as part of the answer to the question of the assurance of salvation.[33]

It is certainly clear that the ecclesiology of the *Confession* is not subordinated to the doctrine of predestination.[34] On the contrary, in this work Beza's ecclesiology depends less upon predestination that did Calvin's.

In sharp contract to Calvin who maintains the dual aspects of the church, it appears that Beza makes no attempt to relate the visible church to the invisible church. Certainly he would say that the church as the congregation of the faithful is 'chosen' by the grace of God in Christ. In no way, however, does the term come close to Calvin's predestinarian description of the invisible church. As far as ecclesiology is concerned, therefore, he avoids a strongly predestinarian position.[35]

The lack of emphasis upon predestination in the *Confession* has created serious problems for scholars, such as Kickel and Dantine, who have argued for the centrality of predestination in Beza's theology. It is true that the *Confession*, later utilized in a revised form as the *Confessio Hungarica*, was originally written in an attempt to justify to his French father Beza's conversion to Protestantism.[36] But it is unsatisfactory to argue, as has Dantine, that the lack of emphasis upon predestination in this work was caused by Beza's fear of offending his Catholic father.[37]

31 Gardy, *op. cit.*, pp. 60–80; Geisendorf, *op. cit.*, p. 78; Walter Hollweg, *Neue Untersuchungen zur Geschichte und Lehre des Heidelberger Katechismus* (Neukirchen, 1961), pp. 86–123. The work may be found in the *Tractationes*, I, 1–79.
32 Raitt's exposition of the eucharistic doctrine found in the *Confession* (Raitt, *op. cit.*, pp. 10–30) refutes Kickel's argument that for Beza all doctrine, including sacramental theology, was founded upon predestination (Kickel, *op. cit.*, pp. 167–169, 223 ff.).
33 Théodore de Bèze, *La Confession de foi du Chrétien*, ed. and trans. Michel Réveillaud in *La Revue réformée*, VI (1955), Parts 3–4, Introduction, p. 5.
34 For an analysis of the ecclesiology of the *Confession*, see Maruyama, *op. cit.*, pp. 6–22.
35 *Ibid.*, pp. 36–37.
36 Réveillaud, *op. cit.*, pp. 2–3; Hollweg, *op. cit.*, pp. 88–89; E.F. Karl Müller, *Die Bekenntnisschriften der reformierten* (Leipzig, 1903), pp. 376–449.
37 Dantine, 'Les Tabelles,' 374–375. Maruyama (*op. cit.*, p. 242 n. 25) has presented three objections to Dantine's explanation: 'This cannot explain, for example, why the entire

The basic mistake is to assume that the position held by predestination in the *Tabula* is normative for Beza, and then to try and explain deviations from that pattern. On the contrary, there are good reasons for starting with the *Confession* as normative for Beza's theology and then explaining deviations from that structure. The *Confession* was Beza's most comprehensive theological work.[38] As such, it would be the most appropriate place to analyze the importance and the position of the doctrine of predestination in his general theology. The *Confession* was written in a clear, vigorous, unsophisticated style that would allow Beza to communicate the essence of Reformed doctrine to the average Frenchman.[39] In the preface of the French edition of 1559 Beza himself explained why he wrote the *Confession*:

> Brief, puis que nommeement tous chrestiens sont admonestez par la bouche de sainct Pierre de se tenir prests à rendre response à quiconques leur demande raison de leur esperance, il appert que le devoir d'un vray chrestien est d'avoir prest et en main quelque sommaire et resolution des principaux points de la religion, et des principales raisons par lesquelles d'un costé il se puisse confermer en icelle, et d'autre part aussi resister selon sa vocation aux ennemis de verité, et communiquer ses richesses spirituelles à un chacun. Parquoy estant desja de cest avis, et mesmes outre cela estant requis de rendre raison de ma foy par un personnage auquel après Dieu je suis le plus tenu d'obeir, j'ay dressé ces jours passez ce recueil, que j'ay intitulé Confession de foy, auquel j'ay comprins par le meilleur ordre que j'ay peu ce que l'ay apprins en la religion chrestienne, par la lecture du Vieil et Nouveau testament, avec la conference des plus fideles expositeurs.[40]

The deemphasis of predestination in the *Confession* would by itself create serious problems for those who see predestination as the foundation of Beza's theology. But the *Confession* was not the only work by Beza in which predestination did not serve as the organizing principle. The short work *Altera brevis fidei confessio* was not organized according to predestination doctrine.[41] Nor was the *Petit Catéchisme* of 1575.[42]

A somewhat different picture emerges when one studies Beza's more extensive work *Quaestiones et responsiones*. The first part of this work was published in 1570; the second part in 1576.[43] Part One of the *Quaestiones* begins with the

Confession is so polemically anti-Catholic, why it contains Point seven, "a brief comparison of the doctrine of Papacy with that of the Universal Church," and why its Latin edition, designed for the learned public, maintained the same non-predestinarian scheme.'

---

38 Maruyama, *op. cit.*, p. 241.
39 Geisendorf, *op. cit.*, p. 79.
40 Meylan, *Correspondance*, III, p. 260.
41 Gardy, *op. cit.*, pp. 69–72; *Tractationes*, I, 80–84.
42 Gardy, *op. cit.*, pp. 167–169; *Tractationes*, I, 689–694.
43 Gardy, *op. cit.*, pp. 148–157; Geisendorf, *op. cit.*, p. 280. This treatise has been published in the *Tractationes*, I, 669–707; in the second edition, from which I shall cite, I, 654–694. At times citations will be taken directly from Part I as published in Geneva in 1570.

topic of God and then moves on to consider Scripture, the Trinity, satisfaction and Christology, man, sin, faith, the order of salvation, providence and predestination. Part Two considers pneumatology, ecclesiology, prayer and hope.

The *Quaestiones* clearly reflects the organizational principles of Calvin: one begins by considering the question of our knowledge of God and then moves on to our knowledge of man.[44] The dependence upon Calvin is especially pronounced at the beginning of the *Quaestiones* where Beza poses the precise questions with which Calvin began his Catechism of 1542/45 — though Beza has revised their order somewhat.[45] But Beza has departed from Calvin in the emphasis that he has given to predestination in his treatise. Although Beza did not begin his work with questions concerning predestination, the doctrine undergirds his entire discussion. More than one third of part one of the *Quaestiones* is devoted to the specific topics of predestination and providence. In addition to this, such closely related questions as the freedom of man, original sin, etc., have been dealt with earlier in his work.

Predestination was certainly an important doctrine in the *Quaestiones* in terms of the attention given to it. But in no way did it serve as an organizing principle in this work. The extensive attention given to predestination may reflect questions that had been raised by the publication of the *Tabula* in 1555 and the work against Castellio in 1558. In any case, predestination played no role in Part Two, *pars altera quae est de sacramentis*, that was published in 1576.

Beza's treatment of predestination in the *Quaestiones* also differs from Calvin's in that Beza has adopted an 'analytical' approach to the issue. The distinction between an analytical approach and a synthetic approach was spelled out by Polyandre.[46] The analytical approach begins with effects and, on the basis of the effects, attempts to ascend to the causes.[47] The synthetic method begins with cause and descends to effect. Beza usually did not employ the analytical method in his treatment of predestination, but he used it increasingly in later life. The importance of the method may be seen in Beza's lectures on Romans (1582) in which he uses it as an important aid in developing the *syllogismus practicus.*[48]

Another systematic work connected with the thought of Beza from which one may gain some idea of the importance which he ascribed to predestination was the collection of theses done under him at Geneva.[49] Although the theses were composed by the students at Geneva, rather than by Beza and Fayus directly, the two professors supervised the theses so closely that they may be viewed, to some

44 , Calvin, *Institutes*, I, 1, 1.
45 Dantine, *loc. cit.*, 375. Compare Beza, *Tractationes*, I, 654, with Calvin, *OS*, II, 75.
46 Dantine, *loc. cit.*, 375.
47 Beza employed the analytical method in his exposition of Romans 9–11; see Dantine, *loc. cit.*, n. 4.
48 *Tractationes*, III, 402–447.
49 Theodore Beza and Antonio Fayus, *Theses theologicae in Schola Genevensi ab aliquot Sacrarum literarum studiosis sub DD. Theod. Beza & Antonio Fayo SS. Theologiae professoribus propositae & disputatae. In quibus methodica locorum communium S.S. Theologiae epitome continentur* (Genevae, 1586). (Hereinafter cited as Beza, *Theses*.) See Gardy, *op. cit.*, pp. 219–220.

degree, as a product of their own scholarship. Neither of the professors would have accepted theses that were out of accord with their own theological method. Thus the theses composed under the direction of Beza, covering the period 1581–1586, may be viewed as at least a partial index of his own theology.[50] The *Theses* were published, according to Fayus, 'So that it may appear by this pattern of wholesome words both what is taught in our university and in what fashion the same is delivered.'[51] Fayus went on to state that the *Theses* were presented not only in his own name 'But also in the name of that worthy man, M. Theodore Beza, who took the greatest pains with this work . . .'[52]

The *Theses* begin with the topic of God, rather than with the issue of predestination, and the early pattern of the work is very similar to the trinitarian structure found in the *Confession* (1559). The first nine sections of the *Theses* concern themselves with questions pertaining to the doctrine of God. They are followed by another seven sections which consider, respectively, providence, predestination, creation, angels, man, the faculties of the soul of man, and free will. This work differs from the Confession in that a separate, substantial section is devoted to predestination, which is dealt with before creation and is conjoined with providence.

One must also consider Beza's Latin translation of the New Testament with annotations which was published in 1556.[53] In his attempt to provide helpful aids to the reader of the New Testament Beza may perhaps unwittingly have injected his own theological formulations and focus upon predestination. An analysis of Beza's annotations upon Romans 9–11 has led me to the conclusion that Beza did utilize the Biblical text as an opportunity to defend his own interpretation of predestination. There is a noticeable trend toward scholasticism in his exegetical comments.[54] But one must also note that his comments upon Romans 9–11 in 1556 were not nearly as scholastic as were his lectures on Romans 9 which were published in 1582. This observation may be interpreted, broadly speaking, in two ways: by reference to the nature of the work and by consideration of the time that lapsed. His annotations in the *Novum Testamentum*, by virtue of the nature of the work itself, needed to be compressed. This may have led to a reduction in the number and in the length of the comments that he may have chosen to make reflecting his own theological stance. The verse-by-verse structure of the annotations would tend to dilute any tendency toward large-scale metaphysical observations. Another interpretation would be that the greater use of scholastic terms in

50 Henri Heyer, *Catalogue des thèses de théologie soutenues à l'Académie de Genève pendant les XVIᵉ, XVIIᵉ et XVIIIᵉ siècle* (Genève, 1898), pp. 9–20.
51 *Theses*, Preface.
52 *Ibid.*
53 See Geisendorf, *op. cit.*, p. 70, and Henri Clavier, *Théodore de Bèze: Un aperçu de sa vie aventureuse, de ses travaux, de sa personnalité* (Cahors, 1960), p. 41. The full title of Beza's work was *Novum D.N. Jesu Christi Testamentum Latine jam olim a veteri interprete, nunc denuo a Theodoro Beza versum: cum ejusdem annotationibus, in quibus ratio interpretationis redditur* (Hereinafter cited as *Novum Testamentum*).
54 Examples of this rationalistic component in Beza's annotations will be cited below in Chapter VI which will consider the general impact of rationalism upon Beza.

1582 represented a reaction to the theological polemics in which Beza had been involved. His theological conflicts may have pressed him in the direction of greater theological precision – a precision to which scholastic terms lent themselves well.[55] The greater use of scholastic terminology would not, in and of itself, mean that the substance of Beza's theology had become more scholastic. We have commented earlier upon the increase of scholastic terms in the revisions of the diagram found in the *Tabula*.

There are in the *Novum Testamentum* additional testimonies to the importance of predestination for Beza. He ascribed to various texts a relevance for his predestination teaching that many would question. The degree to which he has rationalized Calvin's doctrine may be seen by comparing their comments upon certain key passages of Scripture.[56] An analysis of these texts will show that there is frequently a polemic quality to Beza's comments and an attempt to orient the texts toward the doctrine of predestination that is not to be found in the work of Calvin. But one must be careful not to make too much of these passages, for at other points Beza is in such accord with the comments of Calvin that he uses even the technical terminology employed by Calvin.[57]

Beza's sermons are the last set of materials that will be examined in our quest to determine the importance that predestination held for him. For our purposes his most significant sermons are those upon the first three chapters of Song of Solomon,[58] the book of Ecclesiastes,[59] the history of the passion of Christ,[60] and his sermons concerning the history of the resurrection of Christ.[61]

It should be noted that Beza's sermons differ significantly from the standard sermonic form. They really fit into no set homiletical genre. They are not true sermons because they lack an outline and a unifying theme. The absence of a

---

55 Beza's increased use of scholastic terminology is obvious in his exposition of eucharistic doctrine; see Raitt, *op. cit.*, pp. 42, 60.
56 Some revealing texts for our purposes are John 6 : 37; 13 : 18; Acts 13 : 48; Galatians 1 : 15; I Thessalonians 5 : 24; II Thessalonians 2 : 13; I Peter 2 : 9; II Peter 1 : 10; 3 : 9; I Timothy 2 : 4; II Timothy 1 : 9.
57 A ready instance of the latter tendency may be found in Beza's comments upon Ephesians I. His enumeration of efficient cause, final cause, material cause, and formal cause is very similar to that of Calvin.
58 *Sermons sur les trois premiers chapitres du Cantique des Cantiques, de Salomon, par Theodore de Bèze, ministre de la Parole de Dieu en l'Eglise de Geneve* (Geneve, 1586) (Hereinafter cited as Beza, *Sermons sur des Cantiques*). See Gardy, *op. cit.*, pp. 193–195; Geisendorf, *op. cit.*, p. 336. For a helpful analysis of the ecclesiology found in Beza's sermons on the Song of Solomon, see Maruyama, *op. cit.*, pp. 257–275.
59 *Ecclesiastes* (Genevae, 1588). See Gardy, *op. cit.*, p. 200; Geisendorf, *op. cit.*, pp. 336–337.
60 *Sermons sut l'Histoire de la Passion et Sepulture de nostre Seigneur Jesus-Christ descrite par les quatre Evangélistes, par Theodore de Besze* (Geneva, 1592) (Hereinafter cited as *Sermons sur la Passion*). See Gardy, *op. cit.*, pp. 207–208; Geisendorf, *op. cit.*, pp. 390–391.
61 *Sermons sur l'Histoire de la Résurrection de nostre Seigneur Jésus-Christ* (Geneve, 1593) (Hereinafter cited as *Sermons sur la Résurrection*). There is some question concerning the dating of this set of sermons. Gardy, *op. cit.*, p. 209, has ascribed to these sermons the date 1593. Yet Dückert, in his thesis which was presented at the University of Toulouse, has argued that these sermons were preached between 1593 and 1597 – see Armand Dückert, *Théodore de Bèze: Prédicateur* (Genève, 1891), p. 93.

central idea precludes classifying them as homilies. They are not paraphrases because they do not follow the text that closely. Furthermore, Beza's comments are so extensive that no one sermon ever covers more than four verses of text.[62] In modern parlance Beza's sermons might be better called dissertations or theological discussions.[63] But if one adopts these weightier labels, one must not lose sight of the fact that Beza's sermons were also marked by eloquence − even more eloquence than that exercised by his esteemed teacher Calvin.[64]

Beza's sermons would be a prime source for studying the role ascribed to predestination by Beza in later life, for all of his preserved sermons come from the last part of his life. If it is true, as some have asserted, that predestination became an increasing concern with Beza, then one would be justified in anticipating that these sermons would focus especially upon that topic. Beza's sermons would also provide a valuable key to his thought because of the heavy burden that they placed upon him; he preached several times a week and sometimes twice a day.[65] When one bears in mind his other duties, this would increase the probability that Beza's sermons sprang directly from the man without passing through a long period of intellectual incubation that might, to some degree, obscure from us his authentic response to a variety of topics.

In actual fact the question of predestination seldom emerges in these sermons. One would be hard pressed to identify the author of these sermons as the same man responsible for the *Tabula* and the *De praedestinationis doctrina*. In the course of these sermons Beza dealt with virtually all aspects of Reformed doctrine, but he placed the greatest emphasis upon the doctrine of Christology and the topics of man and God − in that order. Less attention was given to the areas of the Holy Spirit, the Word of God, the church, and the Trinity.[66] He seldom considered the question of predestination.

Various explanations have been offered for the absence of extended treatments of predestination in Beza's sermons: the topic did not come up naturally in the text; it would have had little practical value for Beza's hearers; it is inappropriate to expect complete theological systems to be spun out in sermons.[67] There is certainly some merit in these explanations, but they have all missed the point. If Beza were obsessed by the doctrine of predestination and if he were pursuing it doggedly to the exclusion of other considerations, these eighty-seven sermons would certainly reflect this strong interest.

In addition to this consideration, there is an almost total absence in these sermons of any evidence to support the image of Beza as a scholastic.[68] In his introduction to his *Sermons sur des Cantiques* Beza explained that one of the

---

62 Dückert, *op. cit.*, p. 71.
63 *Ibid.*, pp. 14−15.
64 *Ibid.*, p. 9.
65 *Ibid.*, p. 11.
66 *Ibid.*, pp. 24−44.
67 *Ibid.*, p. 43.
68 In Chapter VI specific citations will be taken from Beza's sermons as well as from other sources, to support our contention that it is erroneous to view Beza as a thoroughgoing Protestant scholastic.

reasons that he had not preached upon this portion of Scripture earlier was his fear of speculation. One may object that it was simply a stock in trade for Protestant theologians to denounce speculation and then to proceed to speculate. But the point is that Beza did not speculate in these sermons.

Nor did Beza present a scholastic orientation toward God in these sermons. The main attributes of God that were presented were omnipotence and infinite goodness. It is also true that God is infinite and incomprehensible, but this should not be interpreted to mean that God is a tyrant. For Beza, God is essentially a father whose goodness has been demonstrated to us in many ways, but especially in his creation of the church and in the death of Christ for our sins.[69]

Neither does the image of Christ presented in the sermons conform to a scholastic stereotype. Beza has not presented Christ as an impersonal, logical symbol whose main value is to support one aspect of an impersonal schema of predestination. On the contrary, the primary picture of Christ given by Beza in his *Sermons sur la Passion* and his *Sermons sur la Résurrection* is that of being the suffering savior.[70]

Hence it appears that a basic tension underlies the treatment of predestination in the structure of Beza's works. On the one hand, in some works Beza gave predestination a structural centrality which one does not find in Calvin. But these works are basically the polemical works in which Beza was defending Calvinism rather than presenting a complete theological system. This tendency was first seen in the *Tabula* (1555). It was also pronounced in the *De Praedestinationis doctrina* of 1582. The publication in 1558 of Beza's work, *De la prédestination, contre Castellion*, followed Calvin's pattern of refuting the basic accusations of opponents. Hence it is of no value in determining the structural centrality of predestination in Beza's thought.

But, on the other hand, when Beza attempted to present a total theological system, he did not use predestination as the organizing principle nor as the foundation of his theology. The clearest instance of this second approach is the *Confession* (1559), written for a general audience, that reverted to a more traditional structure and avoided an undue emphasis upon predestination. The *Quaestiones* (1570–76) were in the catechetical tradition established by Calvin and reflected Calvin's organizational principles. There was an unusual emphasis upon predestination in Part One of this work, but very little mention of it in Part Two. In no sense was predestination the organizing principle of this work. The *Theses* (1586) did not begin with the doctrine of predestination, nor did that doctrine serve as an organizing principle. But, at the same time, the position of predestination before creation in the *Theses* was a testimony to the growing emphasis upon supralapsarianism at Geneva and the rationalism which unusually accompanied

---

69 For a collection of texts that have been drawn together to support these generalizations see Dückert, *op. cit.*, pp. 36–38. The present writer's analysis of Beza's sermons has led him to agree with these conclusions by Dückert.

70 Dückert, *op. cit.*, pp. 27–28. It is my conclusion that Dantine has gone much too far in his emphasis upon the impersonal role played by Christ in Beza's theology; see Johannes Dantine, 'Das christologische Problem im Rahmen der Prädestinationslehre von Theodor de Beze,' *Zeitschrift für Kirchengeschichte*, LXXVII (1966), pp. 81–96.

that position.[71] The lack of emphasis upon predestination was in keeping with Calvin's pattern and may say much about Beza's view of the pastor and his function. But we would certainly expect more of a focus upon predestination in the sermons if it was, in reality, the central, organizing doctrine for Beza.

Therefore we conclude that the location of predestination in Beza's major theological works does not support the claim that the doctrine was a central organizing principle in his theology.

THE SIGNIFICANCE OF PREDESTINATION IN BEZA'S GENERAL THEOLOGY

Calvin had taken the position that predestination should be taught and preached because it was part of God's revelation, but the teaching and preaching should be biblical in nature.[72] Beza agreed with this verbal formula and devoted Chapter I of the *Tabula* to an argument stressing the need to teach predestination. Beza reasoned that all revealed truth must be preached even though some may misunderstand it. It is certainly true that some hearers might use the doctrine of predestination as an excuse for a lax, immoral life, but that did not stop the Apostles and the church fathers from proclaiming the doctrine. Furthermore, if the doctrine is not preached, then some who might benefit from it could be caught in the snare of the Devil. 'In the same way that we must preach the fear of God in order to truly serve God, so must we preach predestination so that he who has ears to hear may hear and rejoice in God and the grace of God towards him rather than in himself.'[73]

In teaching and preaching predestination, one should not ignore or sidestep the issue of reprobation, for even the doctrine of reprobation has a positive impact upon the elect. One benefit which the elect receives from the doctrine of reprobation is a greater fear and awe of God which will encourage the elect to confirm in themselves the testimony of Election in Christ. Furthermore, the elect will be impressed with the fact that all are subject to the same curse of sin, and this will help them to embrace the goodness of God. A third benefit is that the elect will be more alert to receive the special gift of faith and cause it to increase if he knows that it is not within the power of every man to repent when he will. Finally, when the elect is being persecuted he will be reminded by the doctrine of reprobation that God is in charge of all and that nothing happens according to change.[74]

But this should not be interpreted to mean that Beza believed in no restrictions upon the preaching and the teaching of predestination. On the contrary, Calvin had taken a strong stand against the speculative use of reason in the attempt to

---

71 Rationalism, when used within this context, does not imply a rejection of revelation. Rather, it connotes an emphasis upon the ability of man to use reason and logic in such a fashion as to arrive at a doctrinal position in accord with that given by revelation. This use of reason may technically be referred to as instrumental rather than as majesterial.
72 Calvin, *Institutes*, III, 21, 3—4.
73 *Tractationes*, I, 171.
74 *Ibid.*, I, 203—204.

fathom the mysteries of predestination, and Beza echoed those sentiments. In teaching predestination one must be careful not to replace the 'pure and simple truth' of God with vain and curious speculation.[75] Beza stipulated that there were two limitations placed upon the articulation of the doctrine of predestination. 'The one is that we speak no farther here than God's Word does limit us. The other is that we set forth the same teaching as that of Scripture in a spirit of edification.'[76]

Earlier in this chapter we had analyzed the structure of Beza's major theological works in our attempt to ascertain the significance of predestination for his general theology. At this juncture we shall look more closely at the precise statements of Beza concerning the importance of predestination. Is it true, as Kickel has asserted, that for Beza the doctrine of predestination has determined the theological role of the doctrines of justification, the Trinity, the two natures, and the sacraments?[77]

In response to this question one discovers a certain ambivalence within Beza's thought. On the one hand, there are statements within Beza's works which indicate that the divine decree was the basis and the cause of all of redemptive history — the creation, the fall, and the pattern whereby redemption was accomplished.[78] Beza can even refer to predestination as 'the principle ground and foundation of our salvation.'[79] The impact that this had upon other doctrine — such as the work of Christ and the role of works — is clearly seen in the following statement by Beza:

Therefore, when the Scripture confirms the children of God in full and perfect hope, it is not content to call attention to the testimony of the second causes, that is to say, the fruits of faith, nor to the second causes themselves — faith, and calling by the Gospel. Nor does it remain at the level of Christ himself, who, as our head, has, nevertheless, elected and adopted us. But it [Scripture] ascends higher — even to that eternal purpose which God has determined only in himself.[80]

For Beza predestination has become more basic than even justification by faith. The degree to which Beza has deviated from the Reformers' stress upon *sola fide* may be seen in his statement that to understand the question of faith one has to return 'to the very headsprings, that is, to providence and predestination.'[81] The

---

75 *Ibid.*, I, 197.
76 *Ibid.*, I, 171. There is a basic ambiguity in Beza's strictures against the use of reason; this ambiguity has been discussed below in Chapter IV.
77 Kickel, *op. cit.*, p. 169.
78 *Tractationes*, I, 173, 177–179, 349; III, 404. This impression is reinforced by Beza's letter to Calvin, dated July 29, 1555, in which Beza argued for a supralapsarian position in which all events would be subordinated to the Godly purpose of predestination; see Meylan, *Correspondance*, I, pp. 169–173.
79 *Tractationes*, I, 199.
80 *Ibid.*, I, 175.
81 *Quaestiones et responsiones* (Geneva, 1570), p. 92.

doctrine of justification by faith is useless without predestination.[82] Salvation requires perseverance in faith, but how will one know about perseverance apart from election? [83] Perseverance is the result of true faith, and faith comes from the mercy of God only upon those who have been ordained to eternal life.[84] Consequently, Beza has argued that in Romans 9–11 Paul *had* to rise from sanctification to faith, and from faith to God's conclusion of predestination.[85]

If the statements above by Beza were all that we knew about his doctrine of predestination, then we would be forced to conclude that for him it was the central doctrine and the organizing principle for his theology. This impression would be reinforced by the visual impact of the diagram in Beza's *Tabula*. However, at this point the observations of Karl Barth are relevant:

> In any case there can be no historical justification for taking the concept 'central dogma' to mean that the doctrine of predestination was for the older Reformed theologians a kind of speculative key — a basic tenet from which they could deduce all other dogmas. Not even the famous schema of T. Beza . . . was intended in such a sense. Its aim was rather (rightly or wrongly) to show the systematic interconnection of all other dogmas with that of predestination in the then popular graphic fashion. There was no question of making the latter doctrine a derivative principle for all the rest.[86]

Our previous study of the location of predestination in Beza's major theological works has demonstrated that it was not given a structural centrality by him in those works. Furthermore, there is evidence within Beza's theology that he did not intend that the doctrine of predestination should be employed as a key to harmonize and explain all theological issues. For example, Beza cautioned that one should not try to explain all phenomena of belief and of unbelief simply in terms of predestination by citing the 'eternal decree of God.' Rather, one must explain belief and unbelief in terms of the middle causes — faith, sin, etc.[87]

Jill Raitt's analysis of Beza's eucharistic theology has already been cited above a number of times. Her conclusions do not support the contention that predestination was the foundation and the organizing principle of all of Beza's theology.

Nor did Beza attempt to define salvation history in terms of a predestinarian schema.[88] On the contrary, Beza was willing to follow Calvin's lead and employ an incarnational model.[89]

Another facet of Beza's theology that has been subjected to careful scrutiny in

82 *Tractationes*, III, 412–413.
83 *Ibid.*, I, 199.
84 *Quaestiones*, p. 121.
85 *Tractationes*, III, 417.
86 Barth, *op. cit.*, II/2, pp. 77–78.
87 The only exception to this is certain categories of blasphemers; see *Tractationes*, I, 197.
88 Maruyama, *op. cit.*, pp. 354–355.
89 For recent studies of this point in Calvin's theology see J.M. Tonkin, *The Church and the Secular Order in Reformation Thought* (New York and London, 1971), pp. 93–130, and Benjamin C. Milner, Jr., *Calvin's Doctrine of the Church* (Leiden, 1970), pp. 46–98.

recent years is his ecclesiology. The authoritative work concerning this question is that by Maruyama.[90] His research indicates that Beza's ecclesiology was not determined by the doctrine of predestination. For example, the *Confession* (1559) contained an ecclesiology that was strongly Christological.[91] Beza avoided a strongly predestinarian position.[92] The same may be said of the Colloquy of Poissy (1561) where Beza's approach to ecclesiology was Christological rather than heavily predestinarian.[93] The *Tabula* (1555), as Maruyama has pointed out, 'took no notion of the church in its predestinarian scheme.'[94] Nor was predestination related to the church in Part One of the *Quaestiones* (1570).[95] In fact, there were some ways in which Beza's treatment of the church was less influenced by predestination than was Calvin's. For example, when Calvin spoke of the church as the 'mystical body of Christ' he would then connect it with predestination. This was not done by Beza.[96] However, Maruyama notes that in Beza's later works, especially the *De Praedestinationis doctrina*, his sermons on Song of Songs and the Passion of Christ, and his commentary on Job, Beza attempted to relate the doctrine of predestination to his ecclesiology.[97] Maruyama has interpreted Beza's later interest in relating predestination and ecclesiology to his desire to bridge the dualism between doctrine and practice that marked his earlier theology.[98] And yet even Beza's mature ecclesiology continued to be marked by a Christocentric emphasis.[99]

We conclude that predestination was not a central, organizing doctrine in Beza's theology. Beza did not give predestination the type of emphasis that one finds in the work of such divines as Zanchi and Perkins. The doctrine was of great value to Beza in his polemics for Calvinism — so great that he himself overestimated the centrality of the doctrine in his own theology. His mistake, at that point, was a repetition of Calvin's overemphasis upon the role that the doctrine played in his theology. There were other ways in which Beza's treatment of predestination was similar to Calvin's. Both argued that election to salvation should be preached under certain circumstances because the doctrine was capable of providing a type of assurance for the believer. Reprobation should be avoided in sermons and was dealt with by both men primarily in their polemical, systematic works.

Yet there were some ways in which Beza's treatment of predestination differed from Calvin's. The basic difference was that Beza was much more of a systematizer than was Calvin — clearly seen in the *Tabula* and in a number of other works by Beza. This appears to be an important step toward the rigid systems that

---

90 Maruyama, *op. cit.*.
91 *Ibid.*, p. 9.
92 *Ibid.*, p. 37.
93 *Ibid.*, pp. 80—81.
94 *Ibid.*, p. 244.
95 *Ibid.*, pp. 244—245.
96 *Ibid.*, pp. 351—352.
97 *Ibid.*, pp. 244—245. The same was true of Augustine; *ibid.*, p. 245 n. 31.
98 *Ibid.*, p. 250.
99 *Ibid.*, p. 246.

marked the work of the Protestant scholastics. He also had a greater degree of confidence in the ability of man's reason to penetrate the mysteries of God than did Calvin, but one must be careful not to draw too large a gulf between Calvin and Beza on this point. He made far greater use of scholastic terminology in his treatment of predestination than did Calvin.[100] He also attributed greater significance to the *syllogismus practicus* than had Calvin. The differences were subtle but significant.[101]

100 For the development of these last two points see Chapter VI below.
101 See Chapter V below.

CHAPTER IV

BEZA'S DOCTRINE OF PREDESTINATION

The basic thrust of Chapter III was to demonstrate the importance that the doctrine of predestination held for Beza and to show the manner in which he built other doctrine upon it. The purpose of this chapter will be to present Beza's interpretation of the positive side of predestination: election. The extent of election and the doctrine of reprobation will be considered in Chapter V.

THE DEFINITION OF PREDESTINATION

The topic of predestination crops up frequently in Beza's writings, and at times there are problems in harmonizing some of his occasional references to the question. But there are also several summary statements in Beza's works that draw together most of the significant dimensions of his doctrine of predestination. The following statement, taken from the beginning of the *Tabula*, captures the important aspects of his formulation of the doctrine.[1] The bulk of his work on predestination may be viewed as an elaboration of the themes found below.

God, whose judgments no man can comprehend, whose ways can not be discovered, and whose will should close the mouths of all men, has, in keeping with the fixed and unchangeable purpose of his will, ... determined within himself from before the beginning of all things to create everything at the appropriate time for his glory. This is specifically the case with men whom he created according to two types that are contrary to each other. The one type, which it pleased him to choose by his secret will and purpose, he makes partakers of his glory through his mercy. These we call, in keeping with the Word of God, the vessels of honor, the elect, the children of promise, those predestined to salvation. The other type it pleased him to ordain to damnation so that he might be glorified in them by showing forth his wrath and power. This second type we call the vessels of dishonor and wrath, the reprobate, those cast off from all good works.

This election, or predestination to eternal life, ... is the original source of the salvation of the children of God. Nor is it grounded, as some have said, upon

---

1 Another summary statement by Beza may be found in his *Quaestiones,* pp. 132–133.

God's foreknowledge of their faith or good works. Rather, it is based upon God's good will which is the source of election, of faith, and of good works.

Therefore, when the Scripture confirms the children of God in full and perfect hope, it is not content to call attention to the testimony of the second causes, that is to say, the fruits of faith, nor to the second causes themselves — faith, and calling by the Gospel. Nor does it remain at the level of Christ himself, who, as our head, has, nevertheless, elected and adopted us. But it [Scripture] ascends higher — even to that eternal purpose which God has determined only in himself.

Likewise, when mention is made of the damnation of the reprobate, it is usually stressed that the fault of the reprobate is to be found in themselves. In spite of this, sometimes it is necessary for Scripture to declare the great power of God, his patience, and the riches of his glory towards the vessels of mercy by which is the first cause of the damnation of the reprobate. The only cause of this decree known to man is the just will of God. We must all obey his will reverently as it comes from him who is just and incomprehensible.

It is necessary that we note a difference between the decree of reprobation and reprobation itself. It is the will of God that the secret of his decree should be kept hidden from us. At the same time, God's word expresses very clearly the causes of reprobation and damnation: corruption, lack of faith, and iniquity. These causes are both necessary and voluntary in the vessels made to dishonor.

In similar fashion, when we describe the causes of salvation of the elect, we must draw a distinction between the decree of election itself, which God has determined in himself, and the execution of election which has been appointed in Christ. The decree goes before all things that follow upon it.[2]

Even a cursory attempt to locate a definition of predestination by Beza immediately forces one to note the close ties between predestination and providence in his thought.[3] At times Beza came very close to equating predestination with providence. 'Predestination, speaking generally, is the same thing that we have called God's determination or ordinance, however with specific reference to the end or work of the ordinance itself.'[4] Fortunately, Beza did provide a precise definition of providence in the *Quaestiones*:

In summary, what you have said about providence is this:
nothing in the entire world comes to pass rashly and casually without God's will or knowledge. But everything happens in the manner in which God ordained them from eternity. He disposed the intermediate causes in such a powerful and

2 Beza, *Tractationes*, I, 171—177.
3 Dantine, 'Les Tabelles sur la doctrine de la prédestination par Théodore de Bèze,' *Revue de Théologie et de Philosophie*, XVI (1966), 371.
4 Beza, *Quaestiones*, p. 116; see also *Theses*, p. 16.

effective fashion that they are necessarily brought to the appointed end to which he had ordained them. And yet he [God] is not the author or permissive agent whereby evil is brought into being, for he always deals justly with the instruments whereby he executes his work.[5]

For Beza providence was much more than just God's foreknowledge; it was the cause of all things and that which provided direction and goals for all phenomena.[6] But Beza refused to equate providence with a mechanical fatalism, for the living God was the author of providence.[7]

Although at times Beza came very close to equating predestination with providence, in his more guarded comments he defined predestination as that aspect of providence which pertained to the salvation and damnation of men. 'I say it (predestination) is God's eternal and unchangeable ordinance, which came before all of the causes of salvation and damnation, and by which God has determined to glorify himself — in some men by saving them through his simple grace in Christ and in other men by damning them through his rightful justice in Adam and in themselves.'[8]

But not all men have been chosen to salvation, and Beza rejected the theory of universal election as 'indefinite.'[9] Rather, there are two types of predestination: a predestination to salvation, which Beza usually termed 'election,' and a predestination to damnation and reprobation.[10] In no way may one gain access to the circle of the elect by virtue of good works that one has done.[11] Beza certainly believed that God desired good works of men, but these works could never serve as the basis for salvation.[12] When the question of good works arose in the *Petit Catéchisme*, after he denied their efficacy for salvation, Beza went on to state that the purpose of good works was 'to set forth God's honor, to win or to strengthen one's neighbors, and to make us know and feel within ourselves that we are the children of God.'[13] Salvation is not the result of good works; rather, it is based upon the mercy of God which has been activated by the hidden, mysterious will of God.[14] It is expected that the lives of the elect should be marked by good works, but in no sense was their election based upon God's foreknowledge of those works.[15] 'The doctrine of foreseen faith and foreseen works is contrary to the doctrine that preaches and teaches the grace of God.'[16]

5 Beza, *Quaestiones*, p. 107; see also p. 92.
6 Beza, *Theses*, p. 16; *Quaestiones*, p. 92; *Tractationes*, III, 402; *Sermons sur la Passion*, p. 494. Beza's use of 'cause' will be discussed below.
7 *Theses*, p. 16; Beza, *Commentaires sur Job* (Geneva, 1589), pp. 4–5.
8 *Quaestiones*, p. 116; see also *Theses*, pp. 16–17.
9 *Ibid.*, pp. 122–123.
10 *Tractationes*, I, 174, 203–204; *Quaestiones*, pp. 117–118.
11 *Quaestiones*, pp. 83–84; *Novum Testamentum*. comments upon Ephesians 2.
12 *Tractationes*, I, 188.
13 Beza, *Petit Catéchisme* (Geneva, 1575), pp. 291–293. This work was usually published as an appendix to Calvin's catechism; see Gardy, *op. cit.*, p. 168.
14 Armand Dückert, *Théodore de Bèze: Prédicateur* (Genève, 1891), pp. 37–38; Théodore de Bèze, *Chrestiennes Méditations*, trans. and ed. by Mario Richter (Geneva, 1964), pp. 54, 91–92; *Sermons sur la Passion*, p. 15.
15 *Tractationes*, III, 415; *Novum Testamentum*, Ephesians 1 : 5; *Theses*, pp. 12, 16, 18.
16 *Novum Testamentum*, II Timothy 1 : 9.

One would anticipate that this doctrine would strike many of Beza's contemporaries as harsh and unreasonable, and that was precisely what did happen. As a consequence, the major theological works of Beza are studded with his answers to the objections lodged by others against his understanding of predestination.

Beza denied that his doctrine would lead to a dissolute life of sin by the elect. He argued that it was only the elect who would give themselves to good works and repentance.[17] A proper understanding of the purpose of God is a prerequisite to being able to honor, love, and fear him.[18]

Nor has God become partial by acting according to the decree of predestination. Beza contended that God would be partial only if he treated two similar men differently because of some factor *outside* of himself.[19] To call God unrighteous because of reprobation would involve one in a contradiction, for 'the will of God is the only rule of righteousness.'[20] On the contrary, Beza argued that it was only a proper understanding of predestination that would allow one to realize that the glory of God was uniquely demonstrated in election. It was in election that God declared himself to be most just and most merciful.

> . . . Most just, I say, in that he has punished with extreme rigor and severity the sins of his elect in the person of his son. Nor did he receive them into the fellowship of his glory until he had completely justified and sanctified them in his son. And he is most merciful in that he freely decided to elect them, according to his purpose, and he chose them freely in his son by calling, justifying, and glorifying them by means of the very faith that he had given them through grace and mercy.[21]

The damned cannot complain because God has chosen mercy for some. They should marvel at his goodness.[22]

Furthermore, Beza maintained that God did not hate the reprobate, for then he would hate his own creation. Rather, God hates sin.[23] Beza protested that he never said that the reprobate were appointed to damnation. Rather, he said they were appointed to *just* damnation. No one is damned except God ordain him to damnation, but, at the same time, no one is damned except those who 'are found to have in themselves just causes of damnation.'[24] The reprobate are condemned because of their corruption, unbelief, and sin.[25] 'For between the ordinance and its execution, sin intervened, and what is more appropriate than that God should

---

17 *Tractationes*, I, 199; *Quaestiones*, pp. 130–131.
18 *Tractationes*, I, 201.
19 *Quaestiones*, pp. 127–129.
20 *Ibid.*, p. 127.
21 *Tractationes*, I, 196.
22 *Sermons sur la Passion*, p. 551.
23 *Quaestiones*, p. 127.
24 *Ibid.*, p. 120.
25 *Novum Testamentum*, Romans 9 : 18; *Tractationes*, I, 190.

punish sin?[26] The justice of God is reflected in the fact that the reprobate are accused and condemned by their own conscience.[27]

In some ways the rejection of the reprobate might seem harsh, but, Beza argued, what are the options? The rejection of predestination would limit one to essentially three options. First, that God created man with no goal for that creation. This option was rejected by Beza on the ground that it contradicted the principle that an acting person acts with a goal in mind. May one say less of God? The second option would be that God had an uncertain goal in mind for man. The third option would be that God made his decision concerning the salvation of man dependent upon the will of man. In that case, as Augustine had expressed it, the power would be in the clay rather than in the potter. Furthermore, it would lead to the consequence that faith originated in man rather than with God. This would clearly be a violation of that which we know through revelation and must, therefore, be rejected.[28]

If the foes of Beza persisted in attacking his doctrine as illogical and as unbiblical, then Beza would wheel out his last defense: it is impossible for man's naked reason to penetrate the mysterious decree of God. It is foolish men who go about trying to harmonize the infinite wisdom and justice of God with the crooked standard of their own weak and slender capacity. Rather, men should close their mouths 'and learn that the secrets of God are to be highly reverenced, rather than to be searched into deeply and curiously.'[29] There is a secret will of God which the reason of man cannot fathom.[30] In a very real sense it is impossible for us to describe God except as he has revealed himself to us.[31] Beza went so far as to assert that 'God is infinite and incomprehensible in all of his works, even the smallest.'[32]

Because of God's incomprehensibility, Beza denounced speculation as a vain exercise with potentially dangerous consequences.[33] In teaching predestination, one must be careful not to replace the 'pure and simple truth' of God with vain and curious speculation.[34] The only source of clear answers to the questions connected with predestination is the Word of God.[35] One should speak no further concerning predestination 'than God's Word does limit us.'[36]

---

26 *Quaestiones*, p. 131.
27 *Tractationes*, I, 196, 205. A more detailed analysis of the relationship between the will, reprobation and culpability will be provided in Chapter V.
28 *Quaestiones*, ɔp. 124–125.
29 *Commentaires sur Job*, pp. 4–5.
30 *Quaestiones*, p. 130; see also Bizer, *Frühorthodoxie und Rationalismus* (Zürich, 1963), pp. 11–12; *Tractationes*, I, 197.
31 Beza, *Ecclesiastes* (Genevae, 1588), p. 44; *Theses*, p. 2.
32 Beza, *Sermons sur des Cantiques*, Third sermon, as cited by Dückert, *op. cit.*, p. 36.
33 *Tractationes*, I, 203–204; Dückert, *op. cit.*, p. 13. Beza's comments concerning the inscrutability of election and the incomprehensibility of God are very similar to the observations made by Calvin (*Institutes*, III, 21, 1–2; III, 23, 8). But in practice Beza granted to reason and logic a role far greater than that allowed by Calvin.
34 *Tractationes*, I, 197.
35 *Ibid.*, I, 200.
36 *Ibid.*, I, 171.

At first blush it might appear ironic that Beza, who spoke so strongly against speculation, should be labeled retrospectively by many twentieth century scholars as a Protestant speculative theologian.[37] But, upon reflection, this very fact should serve as a key to unlock much of his thought. One of the techniques utilized by intellectual historians is to take those elements in the thought of a man which appear to be contradictory to an outsider and show why, in the mind of the individual under study, they were not contradictory or illogical. If one is capable of engaging in that type of intellectual inquiry, then there is a good chance that the researcher will be able to penetrate the logic and thought patterns of his subject and discover there whatever may be fresh, vital, or original.

This is precisely what happens when one takes as his cue in Beza the strictures against reason and speculation and contrasts them to what many would regard as the abundance of speculation and logical/rational analysis within Beza's own works. This avenue of inquiry draws one to Beza's sharp distinction between God's decree of election and the execution of that decree. Although it is true that Thomas Aquinas had drawn a distinction between providence and the execution of providence, it was Beza who modified Thomas' distinction in order to meet certain problems raised by Augustine and by Calvin. The result — Beza's distinction between the decree of election and the execution of that decree — became Beza's most significant original contribution to the question of predestination. It provided the foundation upon which Beza developed his doctrine of predestination.[38]

Beza drew a distinction between the decree and its execution a number of times in his works.[39] One of his clearest statements is to be found toward the beginning of the *Tabula*.

Likewise, when mention is made of the damnation of the reprobate, it is usually stressed that the fault of the reprobate is to be found in themselves. In spite of this, sometimes it is necessary for Scripture to declare the great power of God, his patience, and the riches of his glory towards the vessels of mercy by leading us to the high secret: the secret decree of God which is the first cause of the damnation of the reprobate. The only cause of this decree known to man is the just will of God. We must all obey his will reverently as it comes from him who is just and incomprehensible.

It is necessary that we note a difference between the decree of reprobation and reprobation itself. It is the will of God that the secret of his decree should be kept hidden from us. At the same time, God's word expresses very clearly the causes of reprobation and damnation: corruption, lack of faith, and iniquity. These causes are both necessary and voluntary in the vessels made to dishonor.

37 David C. Steinmetz, *Reformers in the Wings* (Philadelphia, 1971), pp. 168–169; Basil Hall, 'Calvin against the Calvinists,' *John Calvin: A Collection of Distinguished Essays*, ed. Gervase E. Duffield (Grand Rapids, 1966), p. 27.
38 Dantine, *loc. cit.*, 372.
39 *Tractationes*, I, 176–177, 452; *Quaestiones*, p. 126.

In similar fashion, when we describe the causes of salvation of the elect, we must draw a distinction between the decree of election itself, which God has determined in himself, and the execution of election which has been appointed in Christ. The decree goes before all things that follow upon it.[40]

Beza's discussion of this distinction in the *Quaestiones* contains some additional emphases.

... The execution of the ordinance of election ... depends upon faith that takes hold of Christ, and the execution of the ordinance of reprobation ... depends upon sin and the fruits of it ... The only cause that we know of this ordinance whereby some men are chosen to be saved by grace and others are allowed to be damned through their own sins is that the Lord, who is incomparably merciful and righteous, will be glorified in this way. He who will not be content with this but seeks some higher and more righteous thing than the will of God, deserves to be reproved by the Apostle as a babbler.[41]

A recognition of the importance of Beza's distinction between the elective decree and the execution of the decree provides the key to understand Beza's apparently contradictory attitude toward the use of reason. Reason will show us nothing concerning the decree of election itself. One must be content with the Biblical statements that God chose his elect before the foundations of the world according to the good pleasure of his will. But it is a different matter when one comes to the *execution* of the divine decree. The execution of the decree involves the use of secondary means by God, and there is nothing in Scripture that would prevent the employment of reason by pious men to determine the mode whereby God executes his decree. It is quite legitimate for one to study logically and analytically the secondary means employed by God in the execution of his elective decree, and this is the nature of most, if not all, of the 'speculative' theologizing done by Beza. In short, Beza allowed to reason an instrumental function in understanding the execution of the decree, but he refused to grant it a magisterial function in judging the justice of either the decree or its execution.

Beza's application of these principles may be seen in the *Tabula*, the basic structure of which was built upon the distinction between the decree and its execution. The stages by which God executes his decree are named in the diagram which accompanied the text of this work. The secondary means employed by God are synonymous with these stages of execution, and the bulk of the *Tabula* is devoted to explicating the various stages and secondary means.

With so much of the predestination doctrine now thrown open to rational analysis it is no wonder that one finds in Beza fewer and fewer references to paradox and to the limits of reason. Indeed, reason, for Beza, became a marvelous tool for dispelling the mystery that had formerly shrouded the execution of predestination. Beza's growing confidence in this selective use of reason was one of the

40 *Tractationes*, I, 176—177.
41 *Quaestiones*, pp. 126—127.

basic distinctions between his theological method and that of Calvin.[42] Eventually, for Beza, there was only one aspect of the execution of the decree veiled to reason: the distinguishing marks of the reprobate. One could never be certain who were the members of that group.[43] Otherwise, the revelation of God was extremely clear and logical.

It is obviously a small step from the position of Beza to that of the later Protestant scholastics, such as du Moulin, in whose works there are practically no acknowledgements of the difficulty of probing the divine mind.[44] The scholastics also shared with Beza a passion for logical consistency that is missing from the works of Calvin.[45]

Beza's distinctions are paramount in attempting to grasp his doctrine of predestination, and they will dominate the remainder of this chapter. We turn next to an analysis of the elective decree itself and what it meant for Beza, reserving until later an exposition of the execution of that decree.

THE DIVINE DECREE OF ELECTION

The ingenious distinction that Beza drew between the decree of election and the execution of the degree provided him with important methodological advantages. On the one hand he could continue to proclaim the mysterious element in predestination, while, at the same time, engaging in a highly sophisticated analysis of the doctrine on the level of its execution. This allowed him to defend rationally his understanding of predestination against his doctrinal foes. But if, on the other hand, it appeared that Beza's foes had pierced his logical defenses, then Beza could cover the breach with the rubric 'the reason is hidden in the mystery of God.' An additional benefit was that Beza could cite verses of Scripture to undergird whichever of the two postures he had assumed at a given moment.[46] It became exceedingly difficult for Beza's theological opponents, who suspected that he had departed from the teaching of Scripture, to locate precisely the points at which that departure took place. Furthermore, Beza's interpretation of predestination was sufficiently sophisticated to obscure the crucial differences between his position and that which had been held by Calvin. Indeed, there is no evidence that Beza ever viewed himself as anything other than a faithful disciple of Calvin.

42 Dantine, loc. cit., 366–367, 375–376.
43 *Tractationes*, I, 192, 197, 203–204; III, 439; *Novum Testamentum*, Romans 11 : 2; *Theses*, p. 19. At this point Beza was in agreement with Calvin; see Calvin, *Institutes*, III, 23, 14.
44 Brian Armstrong, *Calvin and the Amyraut Heresy* (Madison, 1969), p. 194.
45 *Ibid.*, pp. 137, 183–185; Edward A. Dowey, Jr., *The Knowledge of God in Calvin's Theology* (New York, 1965), p. 241.
46 The above statement should not be interpreted to mean that Beza was simply a polemicist who became so ego involved with a theological position that he was willing to sacrifice intellectual integrity in order to win a dispute. On the contrary, I am impressed by Beza's integrity and convinced that Beza's basic intention was to be true to Scripture and to the teachings of his master, Calvin. It is another question whether or not Beza was able to maintain a position that was, in fact, synonymous with that of Calvin and the teaching of Scripture.

Beza's important distinction in reference to predestination resembles the distinction later drawn by Kant dividing all of reality into two realms: the noumenal and the phenomenal. In Kant's work there was a certain dualism which made it impossible to give a simple answer to such questions as freedom or necessity. Much depended upon the viewpoint from which the question was being posed.

A similar elusive quality is detected in Beza's theology when one inquires about the cause of predestination. It might appear that Beza could answer simply — and at times he did. But when one looks at the entire body of his writings and takes into consideration his distinction between the decree and its execution, no simple answer may be given to the question.

Even those passages in Beza's works which appear to give a clear, schematic answer to this question lead, upon closer analysis, to complications. For example, in his comments upon Ephesians 2 and the causes of salvation presented by the Apostle Paul, with whom Beza viewed himself as being in agreement, Beza observed that Paul 'beats this into our heads that the efficient cause of this benefit is the free mercy of God; Christ himself is the material cause; faith is the instrument which is also the free gift of God; and the end is God's glory.'[47] And yet earlier in the same work Beza had noted that the efficient cause was God, who chose us from everlasting according to the good pleasure of his will; the material cause was Jesus Christ, who made us acceptable to God; the formal cause was the preaching of the Gospel; and the chief final cause (of which there were two lesser final causes) was the glory of God the father.[48] In this case faith was not cited as an instrumental cause.

A somewhat altered schema was presented in the *Theses*. There the efficient cause was the mercy and love of God; the material cause was Christ crucified and risen for us; the formal cause was the imputation of Christ's righteousness; the instrumental cause was twofold: Christ who justifies us and the faith which embraces the promises of God; the final cause was also twofold: the self-glorification of God and also his desire that men should lay hold of the life that he had reserved for them in heaven.[49]

In addition to the above schematic representations, one find numerous occasional observations in Beza's works concerning the cause(s) of predestination. The picture has been further muddied by Beza's employment of different terms for the secondary causes of predestination.[50] There is, therefore, good reason for the differences among scholars concerning the basic cause of predestination in Beza's theology.

The most significant of these controversial questions has been whether, in Beza's theology, predestination was the result of the love and grace of God. Or did Beza build his doctrine upon the nature of God in such a fashion that some aspect of God's nature — perhaps the purpose of self-glorification — dictated the predestination event?

---

47 *Novum Testamentum,* Ephesians 2.
48 *Ibid.*, Ephesians I.
49 *Theses*, pp. 43–44.

The latter position has been most aptly presented by Ernst Bizer and Walter Kickel. For Bizer the ultimate ground of predestination, in Beza's theology, was the will of God. Everything else was derived from this. 'Thus election is proof of his compassion, and reprobation is proof of his justice.'[51] According to this analysis, predestination has simply become part of the self-actualization of God.

The interpretation offered by Bizer has been elaborated and developed in the scholarly monograph by Kickel. 'What catches one's eye immediately in a consideration of Beza's doctrine of predestination is the severity with which all events from creation to the judgment are subordinated to a godly design of self-glorification.'[52] For Beza God's will was the highest cause (causa summa) of predestination, and Beza interpreted the entire predestination event from the perspective of the godly purpose.[53] The force of Kickel's interpretation may be seen where he summarizes some of Beza's observations and then comments upon them.

... God's final and highest purpose is self-glorification ... Thus God is glorified in that his existence is manifested. His being consists in this since he is the highest justice and highest mercy. Therefore he manifests his existence when he reveals his justice and mercy. God creates the world in order to manifest his justice and mercy ...

There are two dimensions to the glorification of God which correspond to the division of men through election and condemnation. One group of men manifest the goodness and mercy of God. The other group make known his power and righteousness ... Thus the difference between election and condemnation is reduced to a difference in God's own nature. He [God] is sustained by necessity and can be understood through the recognition of suppositions, all of which are logically necessary.[54]

There is certainly a basis in Beza's works for Kickel's interpretation of his theology. Beza stated very clearly that in the final analysis salvation is based solely upon 'that eternal purpose which God has determined only in himself.'[55] Nothing is higher than this will of God.[56] Furthermore, some of Beza's allusions would lead one to believe that in some way election is based upon the nature of God. 'Inasmuch as God is justice itself, it is necessary that he should save the just and condemn the unjust.'[57] The topic of the glory of God crops up with great regularity in

50 Dantine has noted the following terms as found in Beza's Tractationes: causae (I, 177, 313, 677); causae secundae (I, 313); causae intermediae (I, 681); causae mediae (III, 402–404, 411); instrumenta (I, 317, 683); instrumenta media (I, 372). Beza never used the typical term employed by Calvin: causae inferiores. See Dantine, loc. cit., 370 n. 1.
51 Bizer, op. cit., p. 8; see also p. 60.
52 Walter Kickel, Vernunft und Offenbarung bei Theodor Beze (Neukirchen, 1967), p. 120.
53 Ibid., p. 140.
54 Ibid., p. 102.
55 Tractationes, I, 175.
56 Ibid., III, 417.
57 Ibid., I, 194.

Beza's works.[58] And at times it appears to have been linked with the concept of God manifesting his nature. Thus we read that 'it pleased him to ordain [the reprobate] to damnation in order that he might show forth his wrath and power and to be glorified also in them.'[59]

Despite all these considerations, Beza appears in Kickel's interpretation to have been unduly pressed into the role of a reformed philosopher, rather than a theologian. Perhaps one should have anticipated this interpretation from Kickel because the main purpose of his entire monograph was to show the formative impact of reason and of philosophy upon Beza's theology. Given this purpose it would be easy for Kickel to overemphasize the role of a rational, philosophical principle in Beza's predestination doctrine.

Another limitation of Kickel's monograph is that virtually the only sources that he employed in his discussion of Beza's doctrine of predestination were the systematic works of Beza. Armstrong has expressed the point well: 'Kickel's conclusions regarding Beza's scholasticism are probably overdrawn, since he seems to have considered only those writings of Beza which pertain to systematic theology, an approach which would be apt to lead one to conclude that Beza was overly concerned with systematization.'[60]

Furthermore, Kickel has failed to make a distinction between those systematic works, such as the *Tabula*, in which Beza was writing as a defender of Calvinism, and other works in which Beza was commenting upon Scripture or attempting to summarize it for the edification of believers. One would expect the former works to focus to an unusual degree upon the doctrine of predestination because of the important place given to it in the polemics of the era.

Kickel is certainly justified in his basic contention that Beza distorted Calvin's doctrine of predestination by overemphasizing the rational dimension of that doctrine at the expense of the religious, personal, and existential dimensions of his thought.[61] It is also true that Beza's rationalization of Calvin's theology — to the degree that it took place — was based upon an Aristotelian philosophical system.[62]

58 For representative instances see *Tractationes*, I, 173, 190, 196; *Quaestiones*, pp. 109–111, 116–118, 126–127, 132–133; *Novum Testamentum*, Ephesians 1 : 17, 2 : 4 f.; II Timothy 1 : 9 *Theses*, pp. 16–18, 20, 165; *Ecclesiastes*, p. 25; *Sermons sur la Passion*, p. 1046; Meylan, *Correspondance*, I, pp. 169–172.
59 *Tractationes*, I, 173; see also in the same work I, 190, 196. For an especially strong statement of this position, probably written under Beza's supervision, see *Theses*, p. 17: 'We call predestination that eternal decree ... whereby he has unalterably decided from all eternity to manifest himself by his effects. That is, to demonstrate that he is most merciful and most just by saving some in his great mercy and by damning others on his most just severity.'
60 Armstrong, *op. cit.*, p. 39. However, one should not interpret these critical comments concerning Kickel as an attempt to discredit his work. On the contrary, Kickel's work on Beza's theology is the only modern, comprehensive treatment that has been presented to us, and it is dominated by a fruitful question: what were the respective roles played by reason and revelation in the formulation of Beza's theology? But the task now before us is to test Kickel's conclusions by means of more detailed analysis of the different facets of Beza's theology. It is in that spirit that these criticisms have been offered.
61 Kickel, *op. cit.*, p. 159.
62 *Ibid.*, pp. 167–169.

But Kickel has erred in oversimplifying Beza's theology and in making too much of a formal principle – the principle that the cause of predestination is hidden in the mysterious will of God. To be sure, in some of Beza's works, as Kickel asserted, 'all events from creation to the judgment are subordinated to the godly design of self-glorification.'[63] But this was not true of all of Beza's works. Our earlier analysis of the structure of Beza's works demonstrated that in no sense was Beza so obsessed with predestination that he allowed this obsession to ride roughshod over all other considerations.

A proper understanding of Beza must take into consideration two basic tensions within the man that were then reflected in his works. The first tension was between his earlier humanistic orientation, with its emphasis upon the principle of returning *ad fontes* and its aversion to systematization. The second tension involved, on the one hand, the strong pull of Aristotelian philosophy and Beza's rationalistic drive to provide logical solutions for theological problems, and, on the other hand, his determination to be true to the biblical revelation.

The collision between reason and revelation is exemplified in Beza's view of the cause and ground of predestination. On the basis of Kickel's interpretation, one would expect Beza to be consistent and to maintain at all times that the cause and ground of predestination was the hidden will of God. But at times, under the pressure of biblical formulations, Beza spoke of other causes.

In Beza's annotations to Ephesians 1 and 2 he cited as causes of salvation and predestination the mercy of God, Christ himself, faith, the glory of God, and the will of God.[64] These were not isolated instances. At other times Beza referred to the goodness, love, and mercy of God as the causes of man's salvation and predestination.[65]

But the inhibiting impact of Scripture upon Beza's tendency toward philosophical rationalization is seen most clearly in the *Tabula* itself. The main thrust of Chapter VII of that work was the need to be biblical in the proclamation of predestination and to avoid any formulation that would violate the pattern whereby predestination was taught in Scripture. Thus the teacher/preacher of predestination is warned to avoid 'any strange manner of speech not approved by God's Word' and he is instructed to use 'such words and phrases which the Scriptures approve.'[66]

Beza cited the example of the Apostle Paul writing in Romans to show how predestination should be developed as a doctrine. One is expressly forbidden to explain salvation and damnation simply as a result of the hidden decree of God. One must point to faith as the basis of salvation and sin as the cause of damnation, as Paul did in Romans. One is not to 'leap from one extremity to another as from the eternal purpose to salvation or, much worse, from salvation to the eternal purpose; nor should one jump from God's eternal counsel to damnation nor backwards from damnation to his purpose.'[67] The practice of Paul was to

63 *Ibid.*, p. 120.
64 *Novum Testamentum*, Ephesians 1–2.
65 *Sermons sur la Passion*, p. 15; *Chrestiennes Méditations*, pp. 54, 91–92.
66 *Tractationes*, I, 197.
67 *Ibid.*

move from the law and the fact of sin to the forgiveness of sin and, step by step, gradually up to the highest cause of the mystery. But if one began with the mystery, then there would be the danger of causing blindness in the eyes of one who had not been trained to behold the brightness of God's majesty. The only exception to this procedure would be for open blasphemers who must be pricked by the clear judgment of God, or mature believers who have been made able to bear the majesty of God.[68]

Thus, for Beza, the divine decree of election was based upon the hidden will of God. But, at the same time, Beza's captivity to the authority of Scripture kept him from assuming a purely rationalistic approach to the question of causation. He himself used biblical language in proclaiming the doctrine for popular understanding and insisted that others do likewide. He did not utilize the idea of predestination, grounded in the hidden will of God, as a simple device whereby one would explain all instances of belief and of unbelief. It was necessary for the teacher and the preacher to thread their way meticulously through the secondary means whereby God effected his will in his creation. Indeed, there is a basic dualism in Beza's theology which led him to answer the same question in different ways dependent upon who was raising the question and the perspective from which it was to be answered.

THE EXECUTION OF THE DIVINE DECREE

For Beza the execution of the divine decree referred to the historical process whereby God employed secondary means to bring to pass that which had been decreed through the mystery of his will. Beza attempted to demonstrate the centrality of predestination within redemptive history, and to expound the logical, rational connections between that doctrine and other cardinal Christian doctrines. It should be noted that he began with the 'highest cause' as his starting point, but he did not intend that this perspective should be proclaimed by preachers or by teachers of the common folk. One could almost label it as a logical exercise in which Christian source material provided the basic data which was then manipulated according to certain logical patterns. It was in this type of enterprise that Beza emerged most clearly as one driven by strong rational interests.

In order for the elective decree to be executed there must first be the creation of objects upon which God could bestow his grace. Thus for Beza the creation of man was a necessary event in order that the elective decree might be fulfilled.[69] Furthermore, the very qualities of man were determined by the decree. Man had to be created good because God, who was good, could not create evil.[70] But another reason for the goodness of created man was that God desired, through the elective decree, to manifest his mercy toward man. If man had been created evil, then he might have argued against the creator that man was not culpable for his

---

68 *Ibid.*
69 *Tractationes*, I, 177; III, 404.
70 *Quaestiones*, pp. 93–98; *Tractationes*, III, 404; *Theses*, p. 21.

sin because evil could produce only evil. That would have prevented God from demonstrating his mercy. Therefore man was created good.[71]

But the goodness of man could not be immutable; there had to be the possibility for man to sin. Otherwise, the elective purpose would be frustrated. Therefore two of created man's qualities were reason and will. This combination of qualities would make it possible for man to understand and to choose sin.[72] Thus the first man was created with freedom. Not with an absolute freedom, for that belongs only to God, but with 'understanding and will by which he was made capable of knowledge and understanding.'[73] Man was created free in that he was 'the lord of his own actions, that is, endued with free will,' but his real liberty consisted in possessing an understanding and a will that were completely subject to the commandment of God.[74] This original freedom and integrity would have been communicated to man's posterity had it not been for the fall.[75]

The majority of scholars state that Beza held to a supralapsarian interpretation of the fall.[76] They are certainly correct. Even if there were a total absence of any other support for this generalization, Beza's letter to Calvin, dated July 29, 1555, would be conclusive.[77] But there are, in fact, a number of other clear-cut supralapsarian references in Beza's works. Thus the fall was necessary to insure the elective work of God.[78] When Adam chose to sin, he chose the option that 'was set down in the everlasting ordinance of God.'[79] Man had to fall from his original state in order that 'a way might be opened both to the mercy and the justice of God.'[80] All of this was done according to the ordinance of God, for 'we cannot think that anything happens contrary to God's will unless we deny blasphemously that he is omnipotent and almighty.'[81] Beza summarized the matter nicely in the following words:

> . . . We conclude, therefore, that the fall of Adam came forth as the result of his own will, but not without the will of God. It pleased God, by a marvelous and incomprehensible means, that sin, which he does not allow, should not happen without his will. And this is done, as we have already said, in order that he might show the riches of his glory towards the vessels of mercy and, at the same time, show his wrath and power upon those vessels that he had created to set forth his glory by their shame and confusion. For the final end of God's counsel is neither the salvation of the elect nor the damnation of the reprobate. Rather, it consists of the setting forth of his glory both in saving the one by his

71 *Tractationes*, I, 2; I, 349.
72 *Ibid.*, III, 404; *Theses*, p. 29.
73 *Theses*, p. 29.
74 *Ibid.; Quaestiones*, p. 47.
75 *Theses*, p. 21.
76 This understanding of Beza has been presented by Armstrong, Bizer, Hall, Kickel, Steinmetz, *et al.*
77 Meylan, *Correspondance*, I, pp. 169–172.
78 *Tractationes*, I, 178–179.
79 *Quaestiones*, pp. 104–105.
80 *Theses*, p. 17.
81 *Tractationes*, I, 179.

mercy and in condemning the other by his just judgment . . . Let us confess that the corruption of man, God's principle work of creation, did not happen by chance nor without the will of him who, according to his incomprehensible wisdom, makes and governs all things to his glory.[82]

Beza presented his understanding of the logical necessity of the fall very clearly in the *Quaestiones*. The death of Christ was needed to show the glory of God. Redemption was based upon the need to be freed from sin and death. Therefore sin and death played a positive role in Beza's theology, and he could remark that 'It was good that sin and death should enter into the world.'[83] One should not lament Adam's fall, rather it should be the cause of great rejoicing.[84] Beza could even speak of Adam's fall as 'the best and the most profitable thing that could be done for us,' because it was the prerequisite for man gaining through the work of Christ benefits far greater than those originally enjoyed by Adam.[85]

Adam's decision to sin was both necessary, and, at the same time, the result of his own will. It was spontaneous, but contingent.[86] Here we find that Beza has drawn upon the medieval distinction between *coactio* and *necessitas* which served as an important element also in the thought of Luther and Calvin. According to this distinction, man sinned necessarily and in accord with the divine decision, but he was not forced to sin. Man's decision for sin was free and spontaneous.[87] For Beza necessity was not synonymous with compulsion.

Then remember . . . that there is a difference between compulsion and necessity. For many things that are of necessity are also done willingly An example that I would not expect you to deny is Christ's death. But nothing can be the result of both compulsion and willingness.[88]

Beza's attempt to harmonise Adam's will and God's will as they pertained to the fall was made immensely more complicated by Beza's insistence that God was the author of all things, that nothing comes about without his will, but that God was not the author of sin.[89] One possible solution – that at times God permitted what he did not desire – was rejected by Beza as a violation of the omnipotence of God. One cannot separate a permissive will of God from his will and sure knowledge. 'For seeing he has appointed the end, it is necessary also that he should appoint the causes which lead us to the same end.'[90] The result of Beza's methodology here was a series of antinomial statements: God does not will sin, but it does not happen without his will; the fall was necessary and was determined

---

82 *Ibid.*
83 *Quaestiones*, pp. 109–111.
84 *Sermons sur des Cantiques*, p. 348.
85 *Quaestiones*, pp. 110–111; see also *Theses*, p. 34.
86 *Tractationes*, I, 178–179; *Quaestiones*, pp. 44–48, 93–98, 104–105.
87 Dantine, *loc. cit.*, 368, n. 4; *Theses*, pp. 17–18.
88 *Quaestiones*, p. 46.
89 *Ibid.*, pp. 93–98.
90 *Tractationes*, I, 179.

before the foundations of the world, but Adam was free. In spite of prodigious efforts, Beza was never able to resolve these antinomies.[91] The closest that he came was to redefine terms in such a way that God did will evil, but only in the sense that it must serve his will. He did not will evil in the special sense of approving of it.[92]

To Beza there was no ambiguity concerning the immediate consequence of the fall upon mankind: they were disastrous. Man plunged into darkness and died spiritually.[93] The corruption extended to both his body and soul. The very substance of the body has been corrupted, and this is reflected in its mortality. With the soul it is different. The substance of the soul has not been corrupted; the corruption has extended only to the qualities of the soul — will and reason.[94]

The reason of man has been so dimmed that at times Beza referred to the state as one of blindness.[95] But at other times Beza acknowledged that man still had some understanding after the fall, but the reason did not discern things as it ought.[96] Men thought that they were reasoning clearly, yet they did not realize that death and damnation hung over their heads.[97] Furthermore, one of the original tasks of reason had been to provide guidance to the will, but in its fallen state the reason assaulted the will and drove it to sin.[98] Fallen man still has some sparks of knowledge of God, but they are insufficient for salvation and simply render man inexcusable before God.[99]

Corruption has extended not only to the reason but also to the will. Fallen man has not been stripped of his ability to will, but now his will chooses vice rather than virtue.[100] Man can will, but apart from grace he cannot will the good.[101] Thus Beza could state that 'such a liberty remains as can will nothing except that which is evil.'[102]

Beza could state that 'such a liberty remains as can will nothing except that which is evil.'[102]

As a consequence of the corruption of reason and will the unregenerate man always does wrong.[103] Even the philosophical virtues are sins in the sense that they depart somewhat from the law of the lord.[104] In the final analysis man 'delights only in evil.'[105]

Yet Beza softened this judgment somewhat by acknowledging that man still

---

91 *Ibid.*. The precise relationship between free will, sin, and responsibility will be considered in Chapter V with special reference to the reprobate.
92 *Tractationes*, I, 374—376.
93 *Quaestiones*, pp. 38—42; *Theses*, pp. 18, 34.
94 *Quaestiones*, pp. 38—40. There appears to be some conflict between this statement and the assertion in the *Theses* (p. 34) that in the fall both the body and the soul died.
95 *Tractationes*, I, 183.
96 *Theses*, p. 18; *Quaestiones*, pp. 47—48, 74—75.
97 *Tractationes*, I, 183.
98 *Quaestiones*, pp. 42—43.
99 *Theses*, p. 2; *Quaestiones*, pp. 41—42.
100 *Quaestiones*, p. 41—42; *Theses*, p. 31.
101 *Quaestiones*, pp. 47—48.
102 *Theses*, p. 29.
103 *Quaestiones*, p. 44.
104 *Ibid.*, pp. 43—44.
105 *Ibid.*, pp. 105—106.

possessed some freedom.[106] Man may be dead in his ability to do supernatural things, but he is still free to do some natural things.[107] This is especially true on the plane of interpersonal relations where God has granted man special grace. Otherwise, all of society would disintegrate.[108]

But the general picture is dismal indeed. The sins of Adam deprived his posterity of all the gifts that God had intended for them. His posterity resemble him in that they hate God.[109] In a very real sense Adam was the author of damnation.[110] His original sin has been spread by nature and is confirmed by imitation. The proof of this may be seen in the universality of death.[111] Even the infant is a sinner in need of the grace of God. Good parents are not enough.[112]

In spite of this dismal picture, Beza also spoke of the fall as the occasion for great rejoicing.[113] The event was necessary and good, for it opened the door whereby mankind would benefit from the blessings of Christ. The relationship of the redeemed creature to God is far greater than a relationship would have been that was based upon creation. Ergo, the fall was a good thing.[114]

But it is crucial to note that when Beza spoke of the positive consequences of the fall and of the benefits that accrued from the work of Christ, he did not mean to imply that these benefits would be enjoyed by all men.[115] On the contrary, it was only the elect who would receive these benefits. On the level of the execution of the elective decree, the fall has provided the first occasion whereby God will distinguish the elect from the reprobate. All men, by virtue of their sin' deserve damnation. But mankind has been divided by the hidden decree of God whereby some have been chosen to salvation, and others have been selected for damnation. This hidden decree provides the basis for God's response to fallen man. To the elect, God responds with love because they have been chosen for salvation in Christ. They do not receive the damnation that they deserve. But God responds to the reprobate with the hatred that their sin deserves. The reprobate are judged and condemned on the basis of their own works; the elect are judged on the basis of Christ's works for them. And so mankind has been divided into two parts, and Beza attempted to demonstrate with the diagram which accompanied the *Tabula* the two separate lines which designated the execution of the divine plan. The end of the elect was glorification in Christ. The reprobate were condemned to damnation in hell.[116]

106 *Theses*, p. 18.
107 *Ibid.*, p. 29.
108 *Quaestiones*, pp. 41–42.
109 *Theses*, pp. 32–33.
110 *Tractationes*, I, 190.
111 *Quaestiones*, p. 50.
112 *Sermons sur les Cantiques*, pp. 94–95.
113 *Ibid.*, p. 348.
114 *Quaestiones*, 109–111; *Theses*, p. 34.
115 The matter of limited atonement will be discussed in Chapter V.
116 For a photographic reproduction of Beza's diagram see Gardy, *op. cit.*, p. 49. The remainder of this chapter will focus upon a brief summary of the line of execution for the elect. The process whereby the reprobate work out their destiny of damnation will be sketched in Chapter V.

In the execution of the divine decree the efficient cause which brings about the glorification of the elect is the love, grace and mercy of God.[117] This love was manifested in the life, death, and resurrection of Christ which was the material cause of salvation.[118] The death of Christ should be viewed as one of the extraordinary signs by which God communicated his goodness to man.[119] It was the mode by which God made man acceptable to himself.[120] The son was ordained by God for the purpose of our reconciliation to God.[121] It is the sacrifice of Christ, by the mercy of God, that 'is imputed unto us for the forgiveness of sins.'[122]

The basic role of Christ, as seen in Beza's systematic works, was that of mediator.[123] It was necessary that man should have a mediator before the love of God could be poured out upon him. For man was a sinner, and the justice of God demanded that sin be dealt with. 'In order that this [reconciliation] might be done without impeaching his justice, he appointed a mediator who would perform all of the things that were required.'[124] The mediator bore the person of all men, and it was his office 'to pay all of their debts and to suffer punishment for all of them.'[125]

And so it was that Beza summarized the chief work of the mediator as that of justification and of sanctification.[126] A careful statement of this position is to be found in the *Theses*.

The material cause [of our salvation] is Christ crucified and risen for us. Three things are to be noted here. The first is the punishment by which he has fully satisfied our sins. The next consists of his obedience and fulfillment of the entire law for us. The third was the perfect healing and covering up of our filthy natures in the flesh by Christ who took it upon himself so that it does not come into the sight of God.[127]

But the work of Christ did not end with his resurrection. Even now he intercedes with the father on behalf of the elect and makes their prayers acceptable

---

117 *Novum Testamentum*, Ephesians 2; *Sermons sur la Passion*, p. 15; *Chrestiennes Méditations*, pp. 54, 91–92; *Theses*, p. 43. Dantine has argued that the appropriate term to be employed in this context is efficacious vocation; see Dantine, *loc. cit.*, 368, n. 5.
118 *Novum Testamentum*, Ephesians 1–2; *Theses*, p. 43.
119 Dückert, *op. cit.*, p. 38.
120 *Novum Testamentum*, Ephesians 1.
121 *Ibid.*, John 13 : 18.
122 *Ibid.*, Ephesians 1 : 7.
123 *Theses*, p. 38. In his sermons Beza stressed Christ as saviour. But this image was not antithetical to that presented in the systematic works, for the threefold task of the saviour was to intercede, to mediate, and to redeem; see Dückert, *op. cit.*, pp. 27–28.
124 *Theses*, p. 38; see also *Quaestiones*, pp. 10–11; *Tractationes*, I, 180.
125 *Theses*, p. 38.
126 *Tractationes*, I, 180–182.
127 *Theses*, p. 44; see also pp. 42–43.

to God the father.[128] Ultimately history will culminate in the return of Christ who will judge the wicked world and set forth the salvation of the elect.[129]

The knowledge of God that one may have through nature is insufficient. In order to be saved 'it is necessary for us to know God not only as God, but also as our father in Christ.'[130] To believe in God is much more than to grant assent to intellectual propositions concerning the nature of God and faith. It is to yield ourselves to God and to agree with him concerning the nature of salvation in Christ as it pertains to us particularly — rather than in general.[131]

Yet the question remains: How may the elect exercise the faith necessary to make their own this work of Christ? There are many ways in which one may be called: through nature, conscience, or the law.[132] But effectual calling comes only through the preaching of the Gospel.[133] There is a sense in which all men are called through the preaching of the Gospel, but the Gospel is foolishness in the eyes of all except the elect.[134] Effectual calling is experienced only by the elect, and it consists of God granting his Holy Spirit to the elect in such manner that they are capable of responding positively to the preaching of the Gospel.[135]

True faith, which Beza carefully distinguished from intellectual assent,[136] is a gift from God.[137] As such, God has chosen to grant it only to his elect who have been ordained to eternal life.[138] Consequently, one may say that in Beza's theology one exercises faith because he has been ordained to life, rather than as a prerequisite to being ordained to life.[139] The Holy Spirit, as the effector of faith, does not restore free will in order that man may choose Christ and respond positively to the preaching of the Gospel.

On the contrary, [the Holy Spirit] changes their hard hearts of stone into soft hearts of flesh, draws them, teaches them, enlightens them, opens their senses,

128 *Ibid.*, p. 107.
129 *Ibid.*, p. 109.
130 *Tractationes*, I, 191.
131 *Novum Testamentum*, Romans 10 : 11. One detects little scholasticism in this statement.
132 *Quaestiones*, p. 123.
133 *Tractationes*, I, 175; *Novum Testamentum*, I Corinthians 1 : 22–24; *Theses*, p. 40.
134 *Quaestiones*, p. 123; *Novum Testamentum*, I Corinthians 1 : 22–24. But at other times Beza referred to some as having received no calling; see *Tractationes*, III, 415–416.
135 *Tractationes*, I, 185–186; *Novum Testamentum*, I Peter 2 : 9; *Quaestiones*, pp. 130–131; *Theses*, pp. 48, 113.
136 *Tractationes*, I, 186.
137 *Quaestiones*, pp. 37, 91–92, 126; *Tractationes*, I, 177, 186, 188; *Theses*, pp. 40, 113; *Novum Testamentum*, John 6 : 37.
138 *Quaestiones*, pp. 61–62, 121; *Petit Catéchisme*, pp. 281–282; *Novum Testamentum*, John 6 : 37.
139 *Quaestiones*, pp. 124–215; *Novum Testamentum*, Acts 13 : 38; Ephesians 1 :5. Beza might object to this formulation on the basis that it is a violation of the distinction between the hidden decree and the execution of the decree which he sought to maintain in his theologizing. But it should be noted that at times Beza himself violated this dichotomy — his references in the *Quaestiones* (pp. 61–62) concerning the point at which one of the elect becomes united with Christ.

their hearts, their ears, and their understanding in order to do two things: first, to inform them of their own misery; second, to plant in them the gift of grace whereby they may exercise the conviction that is joined to the preaching of the Gospel.[140]

It appears that there may have been a shift in Beza's theology concerning the relationship between faith and conversion.[141] In the first edition of the *Tractationes* faith, as shown in Beza's diagram, appeared to be a consequence of conversion. But in the second edition he placed faith at the side of conversion in such a manner as to indicate that they appeared simultaneously.[142]

The saving faith which Beza described should not be equated with intellectual assent. It is a 'true knowledge' which drives one's person toward a personal commitment to Christ.[143] When a question was raised in the *Petit Catéchisme* concerning the nature of true faith, Beza responded that it was 'A certain persuasion and assurance that every true Christian man ought to have that God the father loves him for the sake of his son Jesus Christ.'[144] The same query elicited a more complex response in the *Quaestiones*.

> The faith, or belief, by which the children of light differ from the children of darkness is not just that insight ... by which a man acknowledges the truth of the writings of the Apostles and Prophets. But, in addition to that, there is a stedfast assent of the mind by which each man applies the promise of everlasting life in Christ to himself as if he were already in full possession of it.[145]

The work of the Spirit does not end with the implanting of faith within the elect which regenerates the elect and causes them to bring forth the fruit of repentance.[146] But the Spirit continues to work in the elect by increasing the faith of the elect and by enabling the elect to persevere in the faith throughout their earthly sojourn until, eventually, they are glorified with Christ.[147] 'Faith in Christ Jesus is a sure sign of our election and therefore of our glorification which is to come.'[148]

> The same Spirit increases faith in us who are now under the grace of effectual regeneration rather than under the authority of the law and the flesh. He also

---

140 *Tractationes*, I, 185.
141 On the other hand, it may simply reflect a change in his thinking concerning the best way to present the doctrine.
142 Dantine, *loc. cit.*, 368 n. 6.
143 *Novum Testamentum*, Romans 10 : 11; *Tractationes*, I, 186; *Theses*, pp. 39–40.
144 *Petit Catéchisme*, pp. 281–282.
145 *Quaestiones*, p. 37.
146 *Ibid.*, pp. 130–131.
147 *Theses*, pp. 41–42, 44, 48, 113; *Tractationes*, I, 187–188, 192, 199; *Quaestiones*, pp. 130–131, 134, 135–136.
148 *Novum Testamentum*, John 6 : 37.

teaches, comforts, raises, and confirms us in all of our conflicts against Satan until we obtain the crown which is a free gift reserved for those who strive in the proper manner and overcome.[149]

True, effectual saving faith is such a clear mark that the elective decree is being executed within one that Beza could speak of eternal life as 'following necessarily' from that faith.[150] Faith leads to justification, and Beza even wrote that faith 'caused' both justification and sanctification.[151] This faith is sealed for one as he partakes of the two sacraments: baptism and the Eucharist.[152] The elect who die in infancy will be immediately taken up by God.[153]

It is quite clear that in Beza's theology virtually all of the traditional cardinal Christian doctrines could be viewed from the perspective of the execution of the divine elective decree. Beza was convinced that if one began with revelation and then applied reason to the material given by revelation, the Christian faith did make sense and was capable of withstanding rational analysis. Redemptive history makes sense when seen as the outworking of God's elective decree.

149 *Theses*, pp. 42–43.
150 *Novum Testamentum*, John 6 : 37.
151 *Tractationes*, I, 200; see also III, 405.
152 *Ibid.*, I, 187.
153 *Ibid.*, I, 189–190.

CHAPTER V

THE ASSURANCE AND THE EXTENT OF ELECTION

This is the third of three chapters in which we have presented Beza's doctrine of predestination. This chapter will focus upon three intellectual problems with which Beza had to cope in formulating his doctrine of predestination. One problem was whether and how the elect are identifiable. A second problem was that of limited atonement, or the question of for whom Christ had died. The third problem was how the reprobate proceed to their decreed end.

THE MARKS OF ELECTION

In Beza's theology one could have assurance of one's election to salvation.[1] One could be as certain of salvation as if one 'had heard from God's own mouth his eternal decree and purpose.'[2] Nor was there any presumption in wanting assurance, for the thief on the cross showed the possibility of that assurance.[3] But assurance may be given to one only in reference to one's own salvation for 'true faith can assuredly be discerned only by the Lord and by those in whom it is.'[4] In none of these points of doctrine did Beza deviate from the teaching of Calvin.[5]

In other respects, however, it is possible to trace within Beza's doctrine of assurance subtle, yet significant, movement from Calvin's doctrine. For Calvin, assurance was based upon faith and the person of Christ; for Beza the primary factors were works and perseverance.[6] It could be argued that the difference between Calvin and Beza was, in reference to this point, simply a matter of emphasis. After all, Calvin made use of the *syllogismus practicus*,[7] and Beza had contended that 'We receive assurance of election from Christ himself rather than

---

1 *Tractationes*, I, 203–204.
2 *Ibid.*, I, 200.
3 *Sermons sur la Passion*, pp. 871–872.
4 *Theses*, p. 114. An exception to this would be a minister who, while visiting the sick, would comfort them with a reminder of their election in Christ. But even then he must remember that his is not the final word; see *Tractationes*, I, 197.
5 See above, Chapter II.
6 An expansion of this point may be found in Walter Kickel, *Vernunft und Offenbarung bei Theodor Beza* (Neukirchen, 1967), pp. 150–153. The Christo-centricity of Calvin has been discussed above, Chapter II.
7 See above, Chapter II.

from the secondary causes of salvation.'[8] But what might appear at this point to be a minor difference of emphasis between Calvin and Beza is in fact symptomatic of a crucial difference in their theological orientation. The lessened Christocentrism in Beza's treatment of the question is a correlate of his more rationalistic theological methodology.[9]

It is certainly true that Beza asserted Christ to be the basis for the believer's assurance, but he did not emphasize that source of assurance. In the same passage he also stipulated that the Scripture, when speaking of salvation, at times does not stop with Christ but 'ascends higher, even to the eternal purpose which God has determined only in himself.'[10] But Beza also cautioned that the believer should not seek assurance by going directly to the higher cause of predestination for he would not be able 'to bear the shining light of God's majesty.'[11]

Nor should one look to material prosperity as a mark of election. Though some of the elect may prosper in a material sense, at times God sends adversity in order to teach men things which they could not learn otherwise.[12]

For Beza the rock of assurance was not to be found in the person and work of Christ, as it had been for Calvin. Nor did he intend to base assurance upon an apprehension of the divine elective decree. In his search for a means whereby the believer could gain assurance Beza eventually seized upon an application of the *syllogismus practicus*.[13]

Beza's concept of assurance was based unequivocally upon the effects of slavation. 'The certainty of election is not be gained from that eternal decree known only to God, nor does it come from a general calling; rather, it comes from the gifts inherent within us and from the effects appropriate for the elect.'[14]

The logic that undergirded Beza's argument was simple enough. One should begin the quest for assurance at the 'lowest order.' That is, the fact that one responded to the Gospel positively and exercised faith is a mark of the redeemed.[15] True, saving faith – in contrast to faith for a season – is known by justification and by sanctification. The testimony that one has been justified and sanctified is twofold: good works and the witness of the Holy Spirit.[16]

The Christian has been rescued from the bondage of sin, and one discovers in Beza's works a bald, almost brutal, demand for good works.[17] For example, in the *Petit Catéchisme* Beza's response to the question of how one may know whether

8 *Tractationes*, I, 175. Beza also stated that 'Faith in Christ Jesus is a sure witness of our election;' see *Novum Testamentum*, John 6 : 37.
9 For a study of the Christological problems within Beza's theology see Johannes Dantine, 'Das christologische Problem in Rahmen der Prädestinationslehre von Theodor Beza,' *Zeitschrift für Kirchengeschichte*, LXXVII (1966), 81–96.
10 *Tractationes*, I, 175.
11 *Ibid.*, I, 200–201; see also III, 434–435.
12 Beza, *Ecclesiastes* (Genevae, 1588), p. 36.
13 The clearest statement of Beza's doctrine of assurance is to be found in the *Tractationes*, I, 200–201.
14 *Theses*, p. 18.
15 The same point may be found in Calvin; see *Institutes*, III, 21, 7; *CR*, 51 : 260.
16 *Tractationes*, I, 200–201; see also III, 434–435.
17 *Ibid.*, I, 186, 188.

or not he has faith was simply: 'By good works.'[18] When Beza spoke of good works he meant following the commandments of God.[19] These commandments, in summary form, stressed the need to love God and to love one's neighbor.[20]

Another evidence of justification and sanctification for Beza was the witness of the Spirit. On a number of occasions he declared that 'the children of God are those who are governed by his Spirit.'[21] The witness of the Spirit may be seen in a strong desire to please God and to bring forth fruits pleasing to him. It is the Holy Spirit who gives the believer a sense of adoption and sonship whereby he can cry 'Abba, Father.'[22] Even when the believer falls into sin, it is the Holy Spirit who prevents him from 'giving liberty willingly to our vile concupiscences.'[23]

For Beza the witness of the Spirit did not imply that one would lead a sinless life. One would, in fact, fall into sin. But when the believer falls into sin the Spirit witnesses to his sonship by generating within him a revulsion and a reaction against that sin. The groaning which sin generates within the believer is motivated by a love of God rather than by a fear of his punishment.[24] The believer should not allow his reaction to sin to cast him into despair; rather, he should rejoice in this testimony to his adoption. The conflict itself is a sign of his adoption.[25] 'For except the spirit of adoption (which is also the spirit of holiness, righteousness, faith, and life) were present in us, there would be no striving in us, but sin would reign at its pleasure.'[26]

> . . . . What is the source of this bewailing of my sins, this hatred of myself, this confidence to call upon you, this desire to amend? What is the source from which I still have the ability to call you my God? Certainly it comes from your grace.[27]

The normal Christian life is one of conflict. So it was that Beza could place within the mouth of every believer the words taken from the Apostle Paul: 'I do the evil that I would not, and I would not do the good that I would do. Woe is me, who shall deliver me from this body of death?' But the believer will gain his victory in the next world and will then declare 'I do the good that I would do; and I do no evil, nor do I desire to do any.'[28]

The effects of good works and the witness of the Spirit testify to the existence of justification and sanctification. The latter two, in turn, are manifestations of

18 *Petit Catéchisme*, p. 285; see also *Ibid.*, pp. 290–293; *Tractationes*, I, 186, 195; *Quaestiones*, pp. 83–84.
19 *Petit Catéchisme*, p. 285.
20 *Theses*, p. 113.
21 *Novum Testamentum*, Romans 8 : 14; for similar observations see *Theses*, pp. 19, 42–43; *Sermons sur la Passion*, pp. 871–872.
22 *Tractationes*, I, 200; see also *Quaestiones*, pp. 133–134.
23 *Tractationes*, I, 200.
24 *Ibid.*, I, 201.
25 *Quaestiones*, pp. 134–135.
26 *Ibid.*, p. 89.
27 *Chrestiennes Méditations*, p. 57; see also *Tractationes*, I, 201.
28 *Quaestiones*, pp. 136–137. The statement by Paul is from Romans, Chapter 7.

true faith. 'Wherefore, if we can gather by these effects that we have faith, it follows that we are called and drawn effectually.'[29] The gift of perseverance has been given to all those who have been effectually called and drawn. 'It follows, I say, that the hope of our perseverance is certain and so, consequently, our salvation.'[30] At another point Beza assured his readers that 'Whosoever is elected craves perseverance and obtains it.'[31]

The problem in Beza's doctrine of assurance emerges very clearly in reference to those who are not certain whether or not they are of the elect. Beza had acknowledged that there are times at which the experience of sanctification is very weak, and one can hardly be certain whether or not the Holy Spirit is witnessing to him.[32] How, then, may one distinguish real faith? Beza acknowledged that at times either the testimony of santification or the witness of the Spirit may be weak. In that case, one should lean even harder on whichever one of these two anchors of assurance has remained fast. In the event that both anchors are weak, then one should realize that participation in Christ does not demand a perfect faith but only a true faith. The crucial factor is the presence of true faith rather than a certain quantity of faith. But Beza did noy answer the basic question of how one may distinguish a weak but real faith from no faith. Rather he went on to remind the believers that difficult experiences such as this also plagued the saints and great figures of biblical times. One should follow their example by confessing whatever sin may be present in one's life, repenting, and rectifying the errors. As a consequence, one will be restored to full fellowship with God. True believers may go through temporary barren periods in their spiritual lives, but that barrenness should not be interpreted as death. The absence of leaves from a tree during winter is not a testimony to the absence of life. A final suggestion that Beza made for believers troubled by lack of assurance was that they should follow the example of David who, when he had no sense of security concerning his salvation, meditated upon the godly fruit that he had seen earlier in his life. The soul who is questioning his faith should ponder the past and remember that in the past he had experienced certain effects of faith and instances of God's benevolence toward him. One thing of which he may be certain is that the divine decree does not change, because God is immutable. For Beza the 'true and certain remedy' for the question of assurance is to be found in the immutability of God. Evidence from the past that one was in the circle of the elect is proof conclusive that one still belongs to the elect.[33]

It is striking that in the above argument Beza did not follow the pattern of Calvin and turn to Christ as the ultimate resolution for the question of assurance.[34] Beza's doctrine of assurance was based far more upon works and the

29 *Tractationes*, I, 201.
30 *Ibid.*
31 *Quaestiones*, pp. 135–136. For other references which stress the necessity of perseverance see *Tractationes*, I, 192, 199; *Theses*, pp. 18, 44, 113.
32 *Quaestiones*, pp. 134–136.
33 *Tractationes*, I, 16–17. For a summary of Beza's arguments concerning these points see Kickel, *op. cit.*, pp. 118–120.
34 Calvin had argued that the only solid foundation for the certainty of salvation was Christ, and that those seeking certainty must turn their gaze to him; see *CR*, 36 : 319, 321; 37 : 757; 81 : 59–60.

doctrine of predestination than was the case in Calvin's thought In spite of Beza's admonitions that the believer should look to the middle causes for his assurance, the coercive, systematic force of his doctrine of predestination had become so great that he was forced back to it as the ground of assurance.[35]

And yet one should not conclude from the above that Beza approached the question of assurance in the manner of a Protestant scholastic. Although at times Beza used scholastic terminology and approached the question much more systematically than had Calvin, his work continued to be dominated by biblical categories. Even the connection that Beza drew between assurance and the immutability of God contained strong biblical overtones.[36] There is no evidence that in the passage under discussion Beza was attempting to ground the doctrine of assurance upon a philosophical argument of God's immutability. It is certainly going too far to argue, as has Barth, that 'Beza, Gomarus, the men of Dort and Wolleb' developed the *syllogismus practicus* into an independent system.[37] Beza did move beyond Calvin in the importance that he attached to the *syllogismus practicus*, but his goal was not to develop it into a system whereby one could distinguish the elect from the reprobate. It is clear, for example, in the *Confession* (1559) that Beza's concern is pastoral: his discussion of assurance is intended to help the faithful who may be suffering from doubt.[38]

Calvin had viewed the doctrine of predestination as a great encouragement to believers during a time of adversity, but he argued that the true basis for Christian assurance was Christ.[39] Beza moved beyond Calvin on the question of assurance by virtue of his tendency to systematize, his emphasis upon the *syllogismus practicus*, and his lessened Christocentrism. And yet the difference between the two treatments was quantitative, not qualitative.

In two of his later works (*Sermons sur l'Histoire de la Passion et Sepulture de nostre Seigneur Jesus Christ* and *Sermons sur l'Histoire de la Résurrection de nostre Seigneur Jesus Christ*) Beza showed a growing concern about the relationship between conscience and assurance. However, he never developed this question systematically as did William Perkins.[40]

LIMITED ATONEMENT

As to the extent of the atonement, one finds in the works of Calvin the cautious restraint that generally marked his theological method. He was concerned that he not become presumptuous in clarifying the work of God beyond the limits laid down by revelation, for he believed that all of our knowledge of God was of an accommodated variety. Thus when he wrote his refutation of the Decrees of the

35 , *Tractationes*, III, 434.
36 *Tractationes*, I, 17; cf. Philippians 1 : 6, Romans 8 : 28–39.
37 Barth, *op. cit.*, II/2, pp. 335–336.
38 Théodore de Bèze, *La Confession de foi du Chrétien*, ed. and trans. Michel Réveillaud in *La Revue réformée*, VI (1955), Parts 3–4, Introduction, p. 5. This point has been noted by Maruyama (*op. cit.*, pp. 253–257).
39 *CR*, 42 : 595; 45 : 132.
40 This point has been noted by Maruyama (*op. cit.*, pp. 256–257).

Council of Trent in 1547 he decided not to comment upon the decree which stipulated that Christ had died for all men.[41] Some scholars are convinced that Calvin believed in a limited atonement. Others dispute that interpretation. Whichever view is correct, the more important fact is undisputed, namely, the restraint with which Calvin approached the issue.

Twentieth century scholarship is agreed that no such reservation marked the work of Beza. He was forthright in his proclamation of a limited, or particular atonement.[42] He argued for a 'specific' atonement in which Christ died for the sins of only some men — the elect.[43] One index of the degree to which Beza deviated from Calvin in this regard may be seen in their respective treatments of those passages of Scripture that many interpret as teaching a universal atonement. Calvin stayed with what was at least the apparent universal emphasis of the passages, whereas Beza became involved in a controverted, polemical exegesis the main thrust of which was to argue for a limited atonement.[44]

For one not familiar with the logic of theological systems even the assertion of limited atonement may appear to be an oddity. After all, why should any Christian teach that Christ did not die for all men? But in Beza's doctrine of limited atonement, there was a consistency that was derived from his interpretation of predestination. The logical force of Beza's argument, and the argument of subsequent Reformed scholastics, has been captured by Armstrong.

... For even this doctrine [limited atonement], as developed by orthodox Calvinism, is a consequence of the starting point in the divine decrees. If one approaches theology in this way, accepting the idea that the order of decrees has a strict logical sequence, a universal atonement becomes untenable. For the decree of election for both infra- and supralapsarian theologians was thought to be the basis for the decree of sending Christ. That is, Christ is sent to redeem the elect. In this schematization any idea of a universal atonement becomes an affront to the God who does all things decently and in order.[45]

Once again we find that Beza has been pushed beyond the limits of Calvin's theology by the compelling logical force latent within his doctrine of predestination. It was Beza's formulation of limited atonement that became normative for seventeenth century Reformed scholasticism.[46]

41 CR, 35 : 371 ff.
42 For affirmations of this position in twentieth century literature see Brian Armstrong, *Calvinism and the Amyraut Heresy*, (Madison, 1969), pp. 41–42, 137–138; Basil Hall, 'Calvin against the Calvinists,' *John Calvin: A Collection of Distinguished Essays*, ed. Gervase E. Duffield (Grand Rapids, 1966), p. 27; David C. Steinmetz, *Reformers in the Wings* (Philadelphia, 1971), p. 166.
43 *Quaestiones*, pp. 120–121; see also *Tractationes*, I, 171, 183.
44 Especially clear instances of this may be found in their comments upon I Timothy 2 : 4 and II Peter 3 : 9; see Beza, *Novum Testamentum* and Calvin's *Commentaries.*
45 Armstrong, *op. cit.*, pp. 137–138.
46 Steinmetz, *op. cit.*, p. 166.

112

THE DECREE OF REPROBATION

For Beza, as for Calvin, there was no question about the fact of reprobation.[47] Beza's theology marks out two parallel lines in predestination. There was a predestination to salvation, which he usually referred to as election, and there was a predestination to damnation and to reprobation.[48]

> ...I say it [predestination] is God's eternal and unchangeable ordinance, which came before all of the causes of salvation and damnation, and by which God has determined to glorify himself — in some men by saving them through his simple grace in Christ and in other men by damning them through his rightful justice in Adam and in themselves.[49]

Beza also agreed with Calvin concerning the need to teach reprobation as one aspect of the wisdom of God.[50] For Beza the teaching of reprobation performed a pastoral function: it served as a spur to godliness for the elect and strengthened them during adversity by reminding them that the sovereignty of God embraced all phenomena — even the fact of damnation.[51]

When Beza was commenting upon Romans 9 he had indicated that in reference to election there were three types of men: those who are outside the church and have experienced no calling; those whose calling was only outward (such as Israel); and the elect, whose calling was both outward and inward.[52] Yet Beza was in firm agreement with Calvin that one could never be certain who belonged to the ranks of the reprobate.[53]

In spite of this agreement, Beza's bent toward logic and rationalism may be seen in his attempt to place the reprobate, very systematically, into neat categories. One consists of reprobate infants who have been chosen for reprobation and die before they reach maturity. A second category are those who have never heard the Gospel. They have walked in their own ways without having been called to the Gospel. Nature has provided them with a testimony to divinity, but that testimony has served only to condemn them and to render them inexcusable. Their punishment is just, for they are corrupt. Another category are those who have exercised only the 'general faith' by which the devils believe and tremble. The fifth category is the most miserable of all. They were so moved by a taste of the heavenly gift that they appeared to receive the word and seemed to take root in the church. They may even have shown the way of salvation to others. But they

---

47 For a summary of Calvin's doctrine see above, Chapter II.
48 *Tractationes*, I, 174, 203–204; *Quaestiones*, pp. 117–118; *Theses*, p. 17.
49 *Quaestiones*, p. 116.
50 *Tractationes*, I, 171: see Calvin, *Institutes*. III, 21, 3–4; *CR*, 49 : 181; 51 : 282; 54 : 57.
51 *Tractationes*, I, 204.
52 *Ibid.*, III, 415–416. In another work the reprobate were divided into two groups: those who had been called and those that had not been; see *Theses*, pp. 18–19.
53 *Institutes*, III, 23, 14; *Novum Testamentum*, Romans 11 : 2; *Tractationes*, I, 192, 197, 203–204; III, 439.

did not have the spirit of adoption, for they did not remain with the elect to the end. They returned to their vomit and were cast into the fire.[54]

There was no ambiguity in Beza's mind concerning the fate of the reprobate. Upon death their souls will fall into endless pain. After their bodies and souls have been rejoined, 'they will enter into everlasting fire which is prepared for the devil and his angels.'[55]

In considering the cause of this reprobation, we reach another of those crucial junctures at which Beza departed from the spirit and the texture of Calvin's theological method. Calvin had, upon occasion, attempted to justify the reprobatory activity of God by arguing that the condemnation of the reprobate was their own fault and was just.[56] But in spite of these lapses, Calvin's basic assertion was that, in the final analysis, the ultimate cause of predestination was a decision by the sovereign God which is beyond our comprehension.[57] If one attempts to go beyond the fact that God has chosen some for reprobation, then one is touching upon the inscrutable judgments of God and runs the risk of having his mind swallowed up by the depth of God's judgments.[58]

Beza went far beyond Calvin in examining the causes of reprobation. Beza's solution was much more complex in its argument and reflected the greater importance ascribed to reason and logic in Beza's theology. The arguments by which Beza attempted to justify reprobation also occupied a larger and more central role in his theology than in Calvin's.[59]

Beza began his explanation of the causes of reprobation by drawing the same distinction between the decree itself and the execution of it that he had drawn in reference to election which had as its end salvation. 'It is necessary that we note a difference between the decree of reprobation and reprobation itself.'[60] This is another indication of the importance that reprobation held for Beza and the degree to which he viewed it as parallel to the doctrine of election for salvation − a parallelism that one does not find in Calvin.

It is impossible for the mind of man to plumb the reasons for 'that eternal purpose which God has determined only in himself.'[61] The decree of God is secret, and 'the only cause of this decree known to man is the just will of God.'[62] In the final analysis, 'the only cause that we know of this ordinance . . . is that the Lord,

---

54 *Tractationes*, I, 190−193.
55 *Ibid.*, I, 196; the fact that Beza believed in degrees of punishment may be seen in *Quaestiones*, p. 85.
56 *Institutes*, III, 23, 8.
57 *CR*, 77 : 177−179; *Institutes*, III, 22, 11; III, 23, 1.
58 *Institutes*, III, 21, 1; III, 23, 4−5.
59 Beza attempted to justify his emphasis upon reprobation on the grounds that the predestination of the reprobate is mentioned in Scripture as often as the predestination of the elect; see *Quaestiones*, p. 119. Beza's emphasis upon reprobation was probably partially a result of the fact that the doctrine was under heavy attack. As the spokesman for Calvinism and the defender of Calvin's theology, one would expect Beza to devote much attention to this question.
60 *Tractationes*, I, 176; see also I, 452; *Quaestiones*, pp. 126−127.
61 *Tractationes*, I, 175.
62 *Ibid.*, I, 176; see also III, 416, *Quaestiones*, p. 130.

who is incomparably merciful and righteous, will be glorified in this way.'[63] The elect glorify God by showing forth his mercy and goodness; the reprobate also glorify God by demonstrating his wrath and power.[64] Beza summarized his position concisely in the *Tractationes*.

> . . . And this is done [the entrance of sin], . . . in order that he might show the riches of his glory toward the vessels of mercy and, at the same time, show his wrath and power upon those vessels that he had created to set forth his glory by their shame and confusion. For the final end of God's counsel is neither the salvation of the elect nor the damnation of the reprobate. Rather, it consists of the setting forth of his glory both in saving the one by his mercy and in condemning the other by his just judgment.[65]

But Beza was insistent that the reprobate were never appointed to damnation. Their appointment was to a *just* damnation. No one is damned except God ordain him to damnation, but, at the same time, no one is damned except those who 'are found to have in themselves just causes of damnation.'[66] The just causes of damnation are sin, corruption, and unbelief.[67] God does not hate the reprobate, for then he would hate his own creation. The cause of his hatred is sin.[68]

And yet, in a sense, one may speak of Adam as the first author of the hatred and of the damnation that one associates with the reprobate. It was his fall which began the process of sin that has polluted the human race.[69] The corruption of original sin, which one finds in all men, would be sufficient to condemn them to hell.[70] This judgment even includes infants. So it was that Beza could assert 'those who remain in Adam's pollution and death are justly hated and condemned by God, with no exception being made for those who die before they sin as Adam did.'[71]

Objection was made to Beza's doctrine on the grounds that some men must perish because they are ordained to damnation. Beza agreed that there was a sense in which this was true, and yet the damnation was caused by the fact that they were sinners. 'For between the ordinance and its execution there stepped in sin . . . what is more rightful than that God should punish sin?'[72]

Great logical importance attached to the distinction that Beza drew between the

---

63 *Quaestiones*, pp. 126–127. For other significant references in Beza's works that stress the glory of God within this context see *Quaestiones*, pp. 109–111, 116–118, 132–133; *Novum Testamentum*, Ephesians 1 : 17; 2 : 4 f.; II Timothy 1 : 9; *Theses*, pp. 16–18, 20, 165; *Ecclesiastes*, p. 25; *Sermons sur la Passion*, p. 1046.
64 *Tractationes*, I, 173, 190; III, 403; *Quaestiones*, pp. 75–76; *Theses*, p. 17.
65 *Tractationes*, I, 179.
66 *Quaestiones*, p. 120.
67 *Novum Testamentum*, Romans 9 : 18; see also *Tractationes*, I, 176, 179; *Quaestiones*, pp. 126, 131.
68 *Quaestiones*, p. 127.
69 *Tractationes*, I, 190.
70 *Quaestiones*, pp. 123–124.
71 *Tractationes*, I, 195.
72 *Quaestiones*, p. 131; see also p. 126.

decree of reprobation and the execution of that decree through secondary means which employed the will of man. It allowed him to maintain, simultaneously, that God was the sovereign lord of all, that nothing happened apart from the will of God, that the fall had been ordained by God, and yet that God was not the author of sin or of evil.[73] Beza usually insisted that the secondary causes of reprobation should be stressed. But at times he clearly juxtaposed the two levels of causation. One of the sharpest juxtapositions may be found in the *Tractationes*.

Likewise, when mention is made of the damnation of the reprobate, it is usually stressed that the fault of the reprobate is to be found in themselves. In spite of this, sometimes it is necessary for Scripture to declare the great power of God, his patience, and the riches of his glory towards the vessels of mercy by leading us to the high secret: the secret decree of God which is the first cause of the damnation of the reprobate. The only cause of this decree known to man is the just will of God. We must all obey his will reverently as it comes from him who is just and incomprehensible.

It is necessary that we note a difference between the decree of reprobation and the reprobation itself. It is the will of God that the secret of his decree should be kept hidden from us. At the same time, God's word expresses very clearly the causes of reprobation and damnation: corruption, lack of faith, and iniquity. These causes are both necessary and voluntary in the vessels made to dishonor.

In similar fashion, when we describe the causes of salvation of the elect, we must draw a distinction between the decree of election itself, which God has determined in himself, and the execution of election which has been appointed in Christ. The decree goes before all things that follow upon it.[74]

The parallelism that Beza drew between election and reprobation did break down at points. Thus in reprobation the secondary cause, human sin, arose from man himself; but in election even the secondary causes may be traced back to the first cause.[75] The ordinance of reprobation was not the cause of unbelief in the same manner in which the ordinance of election was the cause of faith.[76]

The decree of reprobation has been executed by God primarily through the medium of allowing man to do that which he wills. The first wayward will was

73 There was general agreement between Beza and Calvin concerning such issues as God not being the author of sin and of man being responsible for his own sin. But one does not find in Calvin the sharp distinction between God acting and the instruments through which he acts which is an important ingredient in Beza's theology. This may have reflected the greater emphasis in Beza's work upon reprobation and, consequently, the need to separate God from the instruments whereby sin takes place and the decree of reprobation is executed. See Johannes Dantine, 'Les Tabelles sur la doctrine de la prédestination par Théodore de Bèze,' *Revue de Théologie et de Philosophie*, XVI (196), 371–372.
74 *Tractationes*, I, 176–177.
75 *Ibid.*, p. 176.
76 *Quaestiones*, pp. 125–126.

exercised by Adam, and we have all followed in his train. So it is that 'through God's forsaking of man's will, sin has crept into mankind and remains there, producing bad fruit in as many as God decides to leave in their own lust in order that they may be the cause of their own damnation.'[77]

The sin of Adam has infected all men in such a manner that they are driven by their will to sin. Man consistently choses vice rather than virtue.[78] Man 'delights only in evil.'[79] Without grace, the will of man does not will the good.[80]

In the case of the elect, their wills were altered (enlightened) by the Holy Spirit in such a fashion that they chose to respond positively to the Gospel.[81] This was the method by which God imparted to the elect his gift of faith.[82] But the reprobate have not been effectually drawn by the Holy Spirit and have not received the gift of faith.[83] As a consequence, they go their own way into sin and corruption and eventually receive the damnation that they have earned.

In summary, reprobation does not take place because God does something to the reprobate that forces them to sin. On the contrary, God simply leaves them to their own devices and does not give them the faith received by the elect. The reprobate then choose to sin and, eventually, receive the just deserts of their sin.

Of the many objections raised to Beza's doctrine of reprobation, one of the most frequent was that his view of the corruption of the will was so extreme that it effectively denied free will. Beza was vigorous in his refutation of this charge. In the first place, he argued, man does have freedom of choice in many natural and moral matters.[84] But, more to the point, he insisted upon a careful definition of freedom. True freedom does not demand a real choice between good and evil. For if it did then God, who cannot choose evil, would not be free.[85] The reprobate have true freedom in the sense that they are not compelled to act by forces outside of themselves.[86] Although man sins by necessity, he does not sin by compulsion; one should be careful not to confuse the two.[87]

The reprobate are responsible for their sin because they sin of their own will.[88] In doing evil, no man can claim that God is using him as a hammer or a hatchet.

77 *Ibid.*; see also *Tractationes*, p. 179.
78 *Quaestiones*, pp. 41–44; *Theses*, pp. 29, 31.
79 *Quaestiones*, pp. 105–106.
80 *Ibid.*, pp. 47–48.
81 *Tractationes*, I, 185–186; *Novum Testamentum*, I Peter 2 : 9; *Quaestiones*, pp. 130–131; *Theses*, pp. 48, 113.
82 *Tractationes*, I, 177, 186, 188; *Quaestiones*, pp. 37, 91–92, 126; *Novum Testamentum*, John 6 : 37; *Theses*, pp. 40, 113.
83 *Quaestiones*, pp. 61–62, 121; *Petit Catéchisme*, pp. 281–282; *Novum Testamentum*, John 6 : 37.
84 *Theses*, p. 29.
85 *Quaestiones*, pp. 46–47.
86 *Ibid.*, p. 43.
87 *Ibid.*, pp. 44, 46–47.
88 *Ibid.*, p. 105; *Tractationes*, I, 176, 179.

While it is true that God works *by* evil people, he works in only the righteous.[89] In an especially striking passage Beza employed the analogy of a gigantic clock in which God was the largest wheel. When the reprobate are moved by God, they move in a contrary motion as would some of the smaller wheels. The reprobate are responsible for their evil because they move themselves and also possess reason.[90]

Beza defended his doctrine of reprobation with other arguments as well. He referred to a principle of logic, the law of contraries, and contended that it would force one to move from the proposition that God had predestined the vessels of glory to glory to another proposition: God had predestined the vessels of wrath to death.[91] It may be difficult for us to believe that God would create some for reprobation, but the only other option would be that God did not exercise control over his creation.[92] Furthermore, the justice of God may be seen in that the reprobate are condemned by their own conscience.[93] But in any case one may not call God unrighteous because of reprobation, for 'the will of God is the only rule of righteousness.'[94] The damned cannot complain because God has chosen mercy for some. They should marvel at his goodness.[95]

The destiny of the reprobate has certainly been earned by them. Yet it is impossible to know exactly who belongs to the ranks of the reprobate. For that reason one should attempt to preach the Gospel to all men and try to bring them to a knowledge of Christ.[96]

In this chapter we have shown the way in which Beza pushed beyond the boundaries established by Calvin in considering the issues of the assurance of salvation, the extent of the atonement, and the decree of reprobation. We have argued that Beza's movement was the result of his penchant for systematization, his desire for precision, and his sense of obligation to defend Calvinism from the attacks of its opponents. Next we shall analyze the rationalistic and scholastic elements in Beza's theology that influenced his formulation of this doctrine of predestination.

89 *Quaestiones*, pp. 98–99. Beza accepted the permissive will of God in the sense that God does not work *in* evil people but leaves them to Satan and to their own lusts. He rejected the permissive will if by it one meant that God allowed something to be done that was contrary to his will. In Beza's thinking, for God to 'allow' something would mean that in some fashion God caused it to happen. This would make him the author of evil. See *Quaestiones*, pp. 99–100.
90 *Quaestiones*, pp. 93–98. This is a striking passage, but the logic is not especially persuasive.
91 *Ibid.*, p. 119.
92 *Ibid.*, p. 118.
93 *Tractationes*, I, 196, 205.
94 *Quaestiones*, p. 127.
95 *Sermons sur la Passion*, p. 551.
96 *Tractationes*, I, 204.

CHAPTER VI

RATIONALISM AND SCHOLASTICISM IN BEZA'S TREATMENT OF PREDESTINATION

Scholasticism has been one of the most persistent intellectual movements in the history of European civilization. Although some have identified scholasticism with the medieval period, in point of fact it continued as a strong force through at least the early part of the seventeenth century. Scholasticism has been marked by such vitality and flexibility that, in a very real sense, it succeeded in withstanding the assaults of the magisterial Reformers and emerged triumphant in the form of Protestant scholasticism.

Theodore Beza has been frequently cited as one of those key figures who was responsible for transforming the biblically oriented theology of Calvin into a rigid form of Protestant scholasticism. Many scholars have agreed with the judgment of Amyraut that Beza employed a *'Methode particuliere'* that was not to be found in the works of Calvin.[1]

It is certainly true that predestination became the keystone of Protestant scholasticism.[2] Furthermore, a number of scholars are convinced that Beza's formulation of the doctrine differed significantly from that of Calvin.

If Beza's theology did represent a movement toward Protestant scholasticism then one would expect to find that shift reflected in his doctrine of predestination. The burden of this chapter will be to determine to what degree, if any, one may discover elements of rationalism and scholasticism in his treatment of predestination.

The first portion of this chapter will be devoted to a systematic study of Beza's doctrine of predestination from the perspective of Protestant scholasticism. To what degree was his treatment of predestination marked by traits associated with Protestant orthodoxy? The remainder of the chapter will be devoted to the question of the influences upon Beza that may have propelled him in the direction of scholasticism.

ELEMENTS OF SCHOLASTICISM IN BEZA'S DOCTRINE OF PREDESTINATION

In the Introduction to this study the point was made that it is is extremely

---

1 Amyraut, *Defense de la doctrine de Calvin* (Sauer, 1644), p. 206, cited in Armstrong, *Calvinism and the Amyraut Heresy* (Madison, 1969), p. 159.
2 Johannes Dantine, 'Les Tabelles sur la doctrine de la prédestination par Théodore de Bèze,' *Revue de Théologie et de Philosophie*, XVI (1966), 365.

difficult to generate a precise definition of Protestant scholasticism. Now we shall evaluate Beza's formulation of predestination in terms of the six tendencies that we noted earlier mark Protestant scholasticism. The overlapping of these tendencies will be reflected in our analysis.

The first such tendency is an approach to religious truth which stresses the need to discover basic assumptions or principles on which one may build a logical system of belief that would be capable of rational defense. This approach usually assumed some form of syllogistic reasoning.[3] On the theological level, this first tendency expressed itself in an emphasis upon predestination as the systemic starting point from which a theological system could be built. Although this synthetic, *a priori* bias was to be found in both Lutheran and Reformed scholasticism, it was more clear-cut and obvious in orthodox Calvinism.[4] The emphasis upon a synthetic, deductive starting point in orthodox Calvinism is the reason why some scholars, such as Alexander Schweitzer, came to view predestination as the *Centraldogma* of Calvinism.[5]

The importance of predestination in Beza's theology has already been discussed at length above.[6] A number of scholars would agree with Steinmetz that predestination was Beza's metaphysical starting point.

If one knows the attributes of God, one can deduce from them the whole plan of salvation, including the necessity of atonement by the God-man. The drama of redemption stands from first to last under Beza's speculative doctrine of predestination.[7]

Beza, himself, was partially responsible for the misunderstanding concerning the significance of predestination in his general theology. At times he would make statements concerning the importance of the doctrine far beyond the role that it actually played in his theology. For example, he referred to predestination as 'the principle ground and foundation of our salvation.'[8] For him it had become more basic than justification by faith.[9] Without predestination the doctrine of justification by faith was useless.[10] In the final analysis, the assurance of salvation was also based upon the elective decree. The basis of all redemptive history was to be found in predestination.[11]

3 Edward A. Dowey, Jr., *The Knowledge of God in Calvin's Theology* (New York, 1965), p. 218; Armstrong, *op. cit.*, pp. 121–122, 166.
4 Jürgen Moltmann, 'Prädestination und Heilsgeschichte bei Moyse Amyraut,' *Zeitschrift für Kirchengeschichte* LXV (1954), 287.
5. Alexander Schweitzer. *Die Protestantischen Centraldogmen* (Zurich, 1853–1856); see also Otto Ritschl, *Dogmengeschichte des Protestantismus* (Göttingen, 1926), III, pp. 156, 167.
6 Chapter III above.
7 David C. Steinmetz, *Reformers in the Wings* (Philadelphia, 1971), p. 169. For similar statements by other scholars see Ernst Bizer, *Früorthodoxie und Rationalismus* (Zürich, 1963), pp. 7–10; Walter Kickel, *Vernunft und Offenbarung bei Theodor Beza* (Neukirchen, 1967), p. 169; Dantine, *loc. cit.*, 374.
8 *Tractationes*, I, 199.
9 *Ibid.*, I, 175; *Quaestiones et responsiones*, p. 92.
10 *Tractationes*, III, 412–413;
11 *Tractationes*, I, 173, 177–179, 349; III, 404.

120

And yet, as we concluded in Chapter III, in practice Beza did not use predestination as an organizing center for all of his theology. It is quite clear that the doctrine of predestination did not determine his eucharistic theology, his understanding of salvation history, nor his ecclesiology.

In summary, one may say that when judged by the first basic tendency of Protestant scholasticism, Beza was not a scholastic. Although predestination played an important role in his theology, especially when he felt called upon to defend Calvinism, Beza did not use predestination as a philosophical starting point for his theology.

A second tendency of Protestant scholasticism was a heavy dependence upon the methodology and the philosophy of Aristotle. This was true of both Lutherans and Calvinists.[12] An example of this tendency may be seen in the seventeenth century figure of Pierre du Moulin, who, in his work *Elementa logicae* (Leyden, 1596), not only repeated the categories of Aristotle but even used the examples utilized by Aristotle to illustrate the categories.[13] In some cases the emphasis upon Aristotelianism was reflected in an admiration of Protestants for Thomas Aquinas.[14]

Without a doubt Aristotle had a profound impact upon Beza. One searches his works in vain for the antipathy that Calvin and Luther expressed toward the Aristotelian approach to theology.[15] It was Beza who insisted upon the admission of Aristotle to the curriculum at Geneva as the basis of logic and moral philosophy.[16] His action was paralleled by the work of Melanchthon at Wittenberg.[17] On December 1, 1570, Beza wrote a letter to Ramus in which he insisted upon the importance of Aristotle to the Genevan curriculum.[18] There was no political motivation in Beza's adherence to Aristotle. He had simply become convinced that Aristotelian logic was, in fact, true.[19]

The impact of Aristotle upon Beza and the concomitant proclivity to Aquinas manifested themselves in a variety of ways. On the most basic level, Beza's works are rife with terminology that one would associate with an Aristotelian-Thomistic orientation. His fundamental distinction between primary and secondary cause was clearly scholastic.[20] The same may be said of such terms as 'efficient cause,' 'final cause,' 'material cause,' instrumental cause,' 'formal cause,' and 'end cause'

12 John W. Beardslee III (ed. and trans.), *Reformed Dogmatics* (New York, 1965), p. 12; Robert Scharlemann, *Aquinas and Gerhard* (New Haven, 1964), pp. 3, 22.
13 Armstrong, *op. cit.*, pp. 83–84.
14 *Ibid.*, p. 188.
15 *Ibid.*, p. 32.
16 Borgeaud, *op. cit.*, I, pp. 112–114; Kingdon, *Geneva*, p. 18.
17 For a comparative analysis of Beza and Melanchthon in their attitude toward Aristotle see Kickel, *op. cit.*, pp. 61–68.
18 This letter is quoted by Borgeaud, *op. cit.*, I, pp. 113–114.
19 For a clear statement to this effect see L. Danaeus, *Christiana Isogoge ad Christianorum theologorum locos communes* (Genevae, 1583), Beza's Preface; as cited in Kickel, *op. cit.*, p. 61.
20 Kickel, *op. cit.*, pp. 103–104. This distinction was assumed in most of Beza's systematic works; for representative instances see *Tractationes*, I, 175, 177, 313, 317, 672, 677, 681, 683; III, 402, 404, 411, 417; *Theses*, pp. 17–18.

which Beza utilized in a scholastic fashion to explain causation in salvation.[21] His vocabulary also included 'accidents,' 'substance,' and 'qualities.'[22] The close tie to scholasticism was made explicit in the *Theses.* 'We do, therefore, retain as true and profitable the scholastic distinctions of necessity and compulsion, of natural and voluntary, of absolute and conditional, of forced and ensuing necessity.'[23] Beza also employed terminological distinctions drawn from Aristotle in his attempt to harmonize his statements concerning the will of God with his interpretation of man's will.[24]

We have already indicated that Beza was also impressed by both the force and the truth of Aristotelian logic. He insisted that Aristotle be the basis for logic and moral philosophy as taught in Geneva.[25] In his various works Beza simply assumed that Aristotelian logic was sound and developed his arguments according to its premises. An instance in which this may be seen was his employment of the law of contraries to buttress the case for reprobation.[26]

But the most significant impact that Aristotle had upon Beza was in the areas of ontology and epistemology.[27] For Aristotle, real knowledge was based upon discovering the ultimate cause of events, and that cause of events was, at the same time, its logical foundation. Until one had plumbed the depths of events and discovered the prime cause by which one could describe the logical necessity of events, one had not grasped reality. It was this drive toward the ultimate cause of events and the search for logical relations that pushed Beza beyond the position of Calvin on the question of predestination and resulted in the *Tabula* of 1555. That work may be viewed as a scientific system (in Aristotle's sense of the term) in which God has become the *causa summa* from whose qualities the logical necessity of all events may be drawn. The *causa summa* directs the entire predestination event by means of the middle secondary causes (*causae mediae*).[28] It is for this reason that one finds in the *Tabula* an abundance of terms which connote logical necessity. Even God has been equated to providence and is depicted as 'an unpredictable power.'[29] Within this development Christ has become little more than a logical symbol.[30]

> ... The result of these Aristotelian influences is the removal of Christ and the Word from their place of centrality in theology and the substitution of a rational system of final causation for christocentrism ... It perverts not only all statements of God which are essentially statements of faith, but also removes

21 *Novum Testamentum*, Ephesians 1–2; *Theses*, pp. 43–44.
22 *Quaestiones*, pp. 38–40.
23 *Theses*, p. 18.
24 For a development of this point see Kickel, *op. cit.*, pp. 121–135.
25 Borgeaud, *op. cit.*, I, pp. 112–114; Kingdon, *Geneva*, p. 18.
26 *Quaestiones*, pp. 85, 119, 125, 130–131.
27 For a development of this argument see Kickel, *op. cit.*, pp. 159–166.
28 *Tractationes*, III, 417.
29 Bizer, *op. cit.*, p. 10.
30 Dantine, *loc. cit.*, 376. For a more complete treatment of this question see Johannes Dantine, 'Das christologische Problem im Rahmen der Prädestinationslehre von Theodor Beza,' *Zeitschrift für Kirchengeschichte*, LXXVII (1966), pp. 81–96.

Christ from his place as the foundation stone and criterion of knowledge for theology.[31]

But it should be noted, once again, that the *Tabula*, with its strong polemical orientation, is a poor source for Beza's Christology. In some of Beza's other less polemical works Christ was depicted in very personal terms as Saviour rather than as a logical symbol.[32]

Maruyama has suggested that Beza's Aristotelian inclination may have also been reflected in his ecclesiology. This took such forms as his reluctance to accept such Platonic-Augustinian distinctions as that between the church militant and triumphant and the distinction between the visible and invisible church.[33]

It has been noted that some Protestants who emphasized Aristotelianism also admired Thomas Aquinas.[34] It is uncertain the degree to which Beza was familiar with the work of Aquinas. But one does not find in Beza's works the denunciations of Thomas and his method that one might expect to find in a Protestant reformer. On the contrary, at times there are striking similarities between their concerns and their methodology. Thus the questions that Beza raised concerning the will and the freedom of man were much more closely tied to the issues stressed by Thomas rather than Augustine.[35] Beza's work *De Praedestinationis doctrina* included terms that were clearly Thomistic.[36] Indeed, Beza's most significant original contribution to theology, his distinction between the decree of election and the execution of that decree, may have been suggested to him by Thomas' distinction between providence and the execution of providence.[37]

In summary, one may state that Beza did partake of the second tendency associated with Protestant scholasticism: a heavy dependence upon the methodology and the philosophy of Aristotle. This dependence was much more pronounced in his polemical, systematic works than was the case in his sermons and biblical studies. Even though scholastic terms and methodology intruded increasingly into his works, there is no indication that Beza viewed Aristotle and Thomas as competitors with revelation.[38] But it is probably correct, as Armstrong has observed, that 'as the exigencies of a strong theological program to oppose to Roman Catholicism faced Beza day to day, he resorted more and more to the scholastic type of answer.'[39]

A third mark of Protestant scholasticism was very closely related to the first two characteristics. It took the form of stressing the role of reason and logic in religion at the expense of Scripture. In practice, reason was elevated to a status equal to

31 Kickel, *op. cit.*, pp. 167–168.
32 See Chapter III above.
33 Maruyama, *op. cit.*, p. 346 n. 9.
34 Armstrong, *op. cit.*, p. 188. Donnelly (*op. cit.*, p. 39) has explored Martyr's preference for Thomas.
35 Dantine, 'Les Tabelles . . .,' 372.
36 *Ibid.*, 374.
37 *Ibid.*, 372.
38 *Ibid.*
39 Armstrong, *op. cit.*, p. 129.

that of revelation, even though the scholastics made it a point to pay lip service to the fact of their own intellectual limitations when it came to probing the divine mind. But by the time of du Moulin the orthodox seldom felt it necessary even to pay that lip service.[40] The rationalism of the scholastics was also seen in their extraordinary concern for logical consistency — a concern missing from the works of Calvin.[41] It has been argued by some scholars that it was this very concern for logical consistency that led to the formulation of such doctrines as supra-lapsarianism and limited atonement.[42]

The connections between the view of God and the function of logic in Protestant scholasticism has been lucidly stated by Armstrong.

> . . . No longer was the primary approach the analytic and inductive, but rather the synthetic and deductive. Theology was explained not as experienced by man and from his viewpoint but as determined by God and from the perspective of God. This approach was, then, primarily interested in the logical explication of the source of theology — that is, the counsel of God. It is of course true that even the most scholastic of these divines would, paying lip service to Calvin's principle, caution against excessive speculation concerning the incomprehensible counsel of God. Nevertheless, they would then proceed to discuss theology by taking as their starting point the decrees of God, indeed, in terms of a specific order in these decrees, giving the impression that there was nothing incomprehensible about them.[43]

An examination of Beza's attitude toward reason and logic reveals the same ambivalence that one notes at other points in his thought. Beza was extremely wary concerning the role of reason. The spiritual death of man affected all of his faculties — his reason as well as his will.[44] In man's fallen state his reason does not discern things as it ought.[45] Men think they are reasoning clearly but do not realize that death and damnation hang over their heads.[46] In one sense, man's reason has been so dimmed that Beza could refer to the state as one of blindness.[47] The depths to which man's reason has fallen may be seen when that reason assaults the will and drives it to sin.[48] Fallen man's reason still retains some knowledge of God, but it is not sufficient for salvation and simply renders man inexcusable before God.[49]

These were some of the reasons for Beza's strictures against the speculative use of reason and logic.[50] One must be especially careful concerning this matter in

40 Ibid., p. 194.
41 Dowey, op. cit., p. 241; Armstrong, op. cit., pp. 137, 183–185.
42 Armstrong, op. cit., pp. 136–138.
43 Ibid., p. 136.
44 Quaestiones, pp. 38–42; Theses, pp. 18, 34.
45 Quaestiones, pp. 47–48, 74–75; Theses, p. 18.
46 Tractationes, I, 183.
47 Ibid.
48 Quaestiones, pp. 42–43.
49 Ibid., pp. 41–42; Theses, p. 2.
50 Armand Dückert, Théodore de Bèze: Prédicateur (Genève, 1891), p. 13.

dealing with the doctrine of predestination, for speculation in this area could lead to dangerous consequences.[51] One must not replace the 'pure and simple truth' of God with vain and curious speculation.[52] There is a mystery involved in the hidden decree of God that the mind of man cannot pierce.[53] There is a point beyond which the mind of man cannot go. Man should close his mouth 'and learn that the secrets of God are to be highly reverenced, rather than to be searched into deeply and curiously.'[54] Because God is incomprehensible even in the smallest of his works, it is impossible to know God except as God has revealed himself to man.[55] Consequently, Beza placed two limitations upon articulating the doctrine of predestination. 'The one is that we speak no farther here than God's Word does limit us. The other is that we set forth the same teaching as that of Scripture in a spirit of edification.'[56]

Yet in spite of Beza's strong reservations concerning the limits of reason and the danger of speculation, many scholars would agree with the judgment of Basil Hall that 'Beza re-opened the door to speculative determinism which Calvin had attempted to close.'[57] We have already indicated that the key to this apparent paradox may be found in Beza's most significant original contribution to the question of predestination: his distinction between the decree of election and the execution of that decree. That distinction corresponds to the two layers of statements in Beza's works concerning the function of reason and logic. Reason can tell us nothing about the decree of election itself, but it may be employed by pious men to analyze the secondary means by which God executes the divine decree.

The practical consequences of this distinction had far-reaching significance for Beza's theology. One finds in the systematic works of Beza an increasingly small number of references to the mysterious elements involved in the execution of the decree.[58] His revision of the *Tabula* eliminated the earlier cautious notes concerning the mystery of predestination.[59] He became much bolder in his theological assertions and was willing to take a position on issues that Calvin felt were not clearly resolved in Scripture. A number of these issues became pivotal in the later development of Calvinism. One such issue was the immediate imputation of

---

51 *Tractationes*, I, 203–204.
52 *Ibid.*, I, 197.
53 *Quaestiones*, p. 130.
54 *Commentaries sur Job*, pp. 4–5.
55 Beza, *Sermons sur des Cantiques*, Third sermon, as cited by Dückert, *op. cit.*, p. 36; *Theses*, p. 2; *Ecclesiastes*, p. 44.
56 *Tractationes*, I, 171.
57 Basil Hall, 'Calvin against the Calvinists,' *John Calvin: A Collection of Distinguished Essays*, ed. Gervase E. Duffield (Grand Rapids, 1966), p. 27. For reaffirmations of this judgment see David C. Steinmetz, *Reformers in the Wings* (Philadelphia, 1971), pp. 168–169; E. Wolf, 'Erwählungslehre und Prädestinationsproblem,' *Die Predigt von der Gnadenwahl, Theologische Existenz heute*, Neue Folge XXVIII (1951), 93, cited in Dantine, 'Les Tabelles . . .,' 372–373.
58 Beza's growing confidence in the power of reason distinguished his theological method from that of Calvin; see Dantine, 'Les Tabelles . . .,' 366–367, 375–376.
59 *Ibid.*

Adam's sin. Beza was precise in imputing Adam's sin to all of mankind, but Calvin had avoided the point because of his conviction that it was not clearly taught in Scripture.[60] Beza also took a much stronger stand than had Calvin on the questions of limited atonement and supralapsarianism. So highly did Beza regard reason and logic that eventually the only mysterious realm that remained in the execution of the decree consisted of the distinguishing marks of the reprobate. One could never be certain who belonged to that circle. At this point he and Calvin were in agreement.[61]

Beza's greater respect for the potential of reason and logic was also reflected in his more intensive attempts to justify the activities of God to man by means of logical argumentation. Calvin had been content to state the doctrine as one of the 'inscrutable judgments of God' without attempting to justify it to man via reason and logic.[62] Such was not the case with Beza who constructed technical, precise arguments in his attempt to demonstrate to all men the justice of God's reprobatory activity. Beza went so far as to place the reprobate into neat, discrete groups.[63] Another instance of this rationalistic tendency may be found in the long arguments by which he attempted to harmonize the will of God in election with the will of man.[64] The same thing may be noted in Beza's approach to the question of evil. The tortured argumentation by which he hoped to justify God from the charge of being the author of evil displayed a rationalistic bent foreign to the work of Calvin.[65] In his comments upon this argument Bizer concluded that 'Even in the question of evil, Beza comes finally to a rationalistic result.'[66]

Beza's penchant for logic and rationalism had another impact upon doctrine as well. It led at times to a philosophizing of doctrine in which the religious element in doctrine was replaced by the rational. When applied to the Godhead this led to a depersonalized view of God in which the activities of the various members of the Godhead were to be understood in terms of logical necessity and causation.[67] 'The result . . . is the removal of Christ and the Word from their place of centrality in theology and the substitution of a rational system of final causation for christocentrism.'[68]

The foundation for this rational system may be located in the nature of God – particularly in his desire for self-glorification. The elective decree becomes the vehicle whereby God actualizes his nature.[69] Thus, as Beza expressed it, the final end of God's counsel 'consists of the setting forth of his glory both in saving the

60 Hall, loc. cit., 27.
61 Calvin, Institutes, III, 23, 14; Beza, Tractationes, I, 192, 197, 203–204; III, 439; Novum Testamentum, Romans 11 : 2; Theses, p. 19.
62 Institutes, III, 21, 1; III, 23, 4--5.
63 Tractationes, I, 190–193.
64 This argument has been developed by Kickel, op. cit., pp. 119–135, 155–159.
65 Quaestiones, pp. 93–115.
66 Bizer, op. cit., p. 10. But in keeping with his attempt to demonstrate Beza to be a rationalist, Bizer cited Beza's use of the analogy of a mechanical clock while ignoring his employment of biblical illustrations of the same point; see Quaestiones, pp. 93–98.
67 Bizer, op. cit., pp. 12–13.
68 Kickel, op. cit., p. 167.
69 Bizer, op. cit., pp. 8, 60; Kickel, op. cit., pp. 102, 120, 140.

one by his mercy and in condemning the other by his just judgment.'[70] According to this rational framework, the elect glorify God by showing forth his mercy and goodness; the reprobate also glorify God by demonstrating his wrath and power.[71]

The impersonal quality that this injected in some of Beza's systematic works may be noted in the *Quaestiones* which began with a rational, depersonalized discussion of the nature of God. Nowhere in this discussion was God described in terms of love. Beza then went on to analyze the nature of the person and work of Christ in sterile terms that were dominated by the concept of the justice of God.[72]

In his systematic works Beza has replaced the concept of God the Father with a logical principle of God as the highest cause (*causa summa*) from which follows all middle causes.[73] During this process the omnipotence of God, which Calvin had tied in with God's loving concern for his creatures, has been transmuted into a principle of all-causality that serves as a philosophical starting point for Beza.[74] The immutability of God also received great emphasis by Beza.[75] This doctrine was also transformed into a logical principle of causality.[76]

Similar developments may be noted in Beza's Christology and pneumatology. Christ has assumed a logical dimension in a deterministic system.[77] As such, he has acquired the status of an impersonal symbol.[78] He functions primarily as a mediator whereby the justice of God may be preserved along with his love. It was only through this mediator that the restoration of man could be effected.[79] This may be viewed as both a demonstration of the necessity by which God operates in Beza's theology and also of the fact that Christology has been subordinated to the concept of God's righteousness.[80] Beza has also de-personalized the Holy Spirit and has ascribed to the Spirit a logical function and status not to be duplicated in the works of Calvin.[81]

But, in spite of what has been said above concerning the influence of logic and reason upon Beza's formulation of the function of the Godhead in predestination, one finds, once again, the dualism to which allusion has been made earlier. At other points in Beza's work and activity the biblical categories were dominant and one searches in vain for a logical, philosophical depiction of the Godhead. This was particularly true in Beza's sermons. There one finds virtually no references to God that could be interpreted as scholastic. The main attributes of God that were

70 *Tractationes*, I, 179.
71 *Tractationes*, I, 173, 190; III, 403; *Quaestiones*, pp. 75–76; *Theses*, p. 17.
72 *Quaestiones*, p. 5 ff.
73 *Tractationes*, III, 417.
74 Kickel, *op. cit.*, pp. 152–154.
75 Johannes Dantine, 'Die Prädestinationslehre bei Calvin und Beza' (unpublished Th.D. dissertation, Faculty of Theology, Göttingen University, 1965), pp. 58–60.
76 Kickel, *op. cit.*, pp. 120–122, 153–155.
77 Dantine, 'Les Tabelles . . .,' 376.
78 Dantine, 'Die Prädestinationslehre bei Calvin und Beza,' pp. 88–94.
79 *Tractationes*, I, 180; *Theses*, p. 38.
80 For a clear instance of the subordination of Christ to the logical demands of Beza's system see *Tractationes*, I, 175. In the *Tabula* the work of Christ pertained only to the execution of the decree and was subordinate to the decree itself; see Bizer, *op. cit.*, p. 7.
81 Dantine, 'Die Prädestinationslehre bei Calvin und Beza,' pp. 104–108.

stressed in the sermons were his omnipotence and his goodness. The basic image of God that Beza projected in these sermons was that of a father. His goodness has been poured out upon his creatures in many forms, but especially in his creation of the church and in the death of Christ for our sins.[82] Of the many topics considered in these sermons, the most frequently occurring one was the person and the work of Jesus Christ.[83] Here one finds no hint of Christ as an impersonal, logical symbol whose main value is to support an impersonal process of predestination. Quite to the contrary. In Beza's *Sermons sur la Passion* and his *Sermons sur la Résurrection* the primary image of Christ is that of the suffering savior.[84]

Nor were these personal, more biblically oriented statements restricted to Beza's sermons. One instance may be found in his comments upon Ephesians 1 : 3 where Beza sought to tie in the God of election very specifically with the person of Jesus Christ. 'The efficient cause of our salvation is God — not considered in a confused and general manner, but as the father of our Lord Jesus Christ.'[85] Beza's *Chrestiennes Méditations* abound with a deep sense of the personal as well, and demonstrate that the logical, rationalistic approach to theology did not encompass his entire methodology. The following statement reflects the spirit of the *Méditations.*

If our sins are unnumberable, his mercy is infinite toward those who repent, believe, hope, and pray. What greater proof of this does one need other than the incomprehensible love through which this good father was moved not even to spare his son; than the infinite love of this great shepherd who made himself of no account to enrich us; who has charged himself with all of our sins; who was obedient for his poor Israel, that is, his elect, even to the death of the cross? I embrace you with both of my arms, O Jesus Christ, who has reconciled me to the Father and has assured me by your Spirit of the comfort of my salvation in you. And as I embrace you I receive the pledges of life and everlasting life.[86]

In summary, one may say that Beza's work was definitely influenced by an attitude toward reason and logic that one does not find in Calvin. But, at the same time, Beza was not so enamored with logic and reason that he was willing to forsake biblical categories entirely. And so there was a dualism within Beza's works by which his more polemical, systematic works reflected an attitude toward logic and reason that one would associate with scholasticism, while the sermonic, devotional, less polemical works tended to fall in the biblical tradition favored by Calvin.[87]

82 These generalizations are supported by texts drawn together in Dückert, *op. cit.*, pp. 36–38.
83 *Ibid.*, pp. 24–44.
84 *Ibid.*, pp. 27–28.
85 *Novum Testamentum*, Ephesians 1 : 3.
86 Beza, *Chrestienne Méditations*, p. 92.
87 Logic and reason also had a profound impact upon Beza's approach to Scripture and led him to read philosophical questions into Scripture. In the process, Scripture itself was philosophised. But this issue will be considered below under the fifth criterion of Protestant scholasticism.

A fourth mark of orthodoxy was a strong interest in speculative, metaphysical thought which tended to focus upon questions relating to the will of God.[88] Enough has already been said in this chapter to vindicate the judgment of the majority of scholars who do find this trait in Beza's works. The emphasis that Beza gave to predestination, the process by which the will of God became a metaphysical principle for him — particularly in the *Tabula* — the undue attention that he devoted to questions concerning the will of God, and his forays into the realm of speculation have all been well documented.[89]

But, at the same time, one should note that Beza had very little choice in the matter. As the successor of Calvin, he was called upon to defend Calvin's system against all theological attacks, and many of these attacks focused upon questions relating to the will of God. On many occasions Beza had expressed his own reservations concerning speculation and the folly of attempting to probe the divine mind via reason and logic. Beza's distinction between the decree of election and the execution of that decree was an attempt to recognize the limitations of reason and rational analysis in probing the divine mind. Beza did not advocate speculation, nor did he view himself as engaging in it. Even when he dealt with questions pertaining to the will of God Beza felt that he was simply stating in a clear and logical fashion the teaching of Scripture and the implications thereof.

A fifth tendency of scholasticism was an interpretation of Scripture which tended to define Scripture in an unhistorical fashion as a body of propositions, once and for all delivered by God, the purpose of which was to provide an inerrant, infallible base upon which a solid philosophy could be constructed.[90] Our study does not lend itself very well to an analysis of this trait in Beza, for we have not focused upon works in which this question has been a major consideration. One may only note that Beza did feel free to cite passages of Scripture that substantiated his position, regardless of the historical context within which they were written.

But it is clear that Beza did have a tendency to philosophize Scripture and to exploit it as a base for metaphysical speculations that concerned him. This was especially clear in his *De Praedestinationis doctrina* of 1582 which focused upon Romans 9. In his comments upon Romans 9 : 8-9 Beza used the text as an excuse to draw 'conclusions' concerning predestination that were not clearly supported in the text.[91] His interpretation of Romans 9 : 14-18 emphasized 'middle causes' that were foreign to Paul's work.[92] In Romans 9 : 19-21 Paul quickly dismissed questions of responsibility and guilt by citing the omnipotence of God; Beza, at

---

88 Armstrong, *op. cit.*, pp. 137, 163; Beardslee, *op. cit.*, pp. 18–19; Scharlemann, *op. cit.*, pp. 3, 22.
89 For an instance of the involved argumentation by which Beza hoped to resolve questions pertaining to the will of God see *Quaestiones*, pp. 93–115.
90 Armstrong, *op. cit.*, pp. 120–121; Dowey, *op. cit.*, p. 241.
91 *Tractationes*, III, 415–416.
92 *Ibid.*, III, 423–424. Beza read the same causal material into his annotations upon that passage; see *Novum Testamentum*, Romans 9 : 14–18.

the same point, presented a rationalistic argument which focused upon the spontaneity of man's will.[93] The same rational orientation may be seen in Romans 9 : 14-18 where Beza tried to solve the problem of God's righteousness rationally; whereas Paul had been content to refer to 'the merciful will of God.'[94] The degree to which Beza, at times, read Scripture through metaphysical lenses may be seen in his comments upon the close of Romans 11. Paul had closed this chapter by stating the mystery involved in the final salvation of Israel and by praising God for their salvation. Beza, on the other hand, ended his treatise on predestination by proclaiming the self-glorification of God that was found in his punishment of the reprobate.[95] Beza also managed to work into his exposition his fundamental distinction between the decree of election and the execution of it.[96] Throughout his exposition of Romans 9 Beza assumed that predestination was the fundamental doctrine that dominated Romans.[97] It is impossible to locate a parallel to this type of thing in the works of Calvin.[98]

The last mark of Protestant scholasticism was a new concept of faith in which faith became simply another doctrine that was not necessarily more significant than was any other doctrine. This was a marked departure from the theology of Calvin and Luther for whom faith was a cardinal doctrine.[99] In addition to this, Gründler has argued that for Zanchi the object of faith had become the truth of Scripture rather than a personal bond with Christ through the Holy Spirit.[100] Furthermore, Zanchi returned to a Thomistic understanding of faith in which faith was viewed as 'an infused habit and virtue, a supernatural quality by which we believe.' [101] It was Zanchi's interpretation of faith that became accepted in the ranks of the orthodox.[102] Zanchi's doctrine of faith was a far cry from the position that Calvin had taken in which the only appropriate object for faith was the person of Christ himself, and faith represented a commitment of the total man, rather than a matter of intellectual assent to propositions concerning either Christ or the Scriptures.[103]

Little evidence of a scholastic orientation toward faith may be found in Beza's works. Contrary to Wollebuis, for whom faith was not an important doctrine, Beza spoke of faith often, and it was a crucial doctrine for him.[104] Furthermore, Beza did not equate faith with intellectual assent, as had Zanchi. He viewed faith

---

93 *Tractationes*, III, 428.
94 *Ibid.*, III, 423–424.
95 *Ibid.*, III, 412–413.
96 *Ibid.*
97 *Ibid.*, III, 417. For a summary of the philosophizing by Beza of Romans 9–11 see Kickel, *op. cit.*, pp. 136–146.
98 Armstrong, *op. cit.*, pp. 33–35.
99 Dowey, *op. cit.*, pp. 151–204.
100 Otto Gründler, *Die Gotteslehre Giralmo Zanchis* (Neukirchen, 1965), p. 49.
101 *Ibid.* p. 58.
102 Armstrong, *op. cit.*, p. 139.
103 Gilbert Rist, 'Modernité de la méthode theologique de Calvin,' *Revue de Théologie et Philosophie*, no. 1 (1968), 24–28.
104 For an instance of a work in which faith was relegated to an insignificant position see Wollebuis, *Compendium Theologiae Christianae* (trans. by Beardslee in *Reformed Dogmatics*, pp. 29–262).

as a 'true knowledge' that drives one's person toward a personal commitment to Christ.[105] Beza's relational concept of faith emerged very clearly in the *Petit Catéchisme* where he defined faith as 'A certain persuasion and assurance that every true Christian man ought to have that God the father loves him for the sake of his son Jesus Christ.'[106] The same query in the *Quaestiones* elicited from Beza a more complex answer but one that was marked by the same spirit.

> The faith, or belief, by which the children of light differ from the children of darkness is not just that insight . . . by which a man acknowledges the truth of the writings of the Apostles and Prophets. But, in addition to that, there is a stedfast assent of the mind by which each man applies the promise of everlasting life in Christ to himself as if he were already in full possession of it.[107]

Our attempt to measure Beza against the criteria usually associated with Protestant scholasticism has led us to a qualified conclusion. Although Beza did partake of some of those qualities, he was, in no sense of the word, a full-blown scholastic. It would be more accurate to see within Beza the seeds of scholasticism that were germinating at varying rates.[108] His theology may be viewed as a conflict between a love for logic and systematic clarity on the one hand, and the restraints imposed by biblical categories and the strong traditions of Calvin on the other hand. There may have also been within his breast an unresolved conflict between his earlier humanistic orientation, with its emphasis upon *ad fontes* and its aversion to systematization, and his love for order and precision that could be satisfied by scholasticism. When viewed in this fashion, Beza is seen as a transitional figure bridging the gap between the theology of Calvin and that of Reformed orthodoxy.

But that drives us on to the question of the sources of the rationalism and scholasticism that we have found in Beza. It is to that question that we now turn our attention.

THE SOURCES OF BEZA'S SCHOLASTICISM AND RATIONALISM

There can be little question about the primary source for the rationalism and scholasticism that one finds in Beza. It was Aristotle. Attention has already been directed toward the attraction that Aristotle held for many Protestants in the latter half of the sixteenth century and in the seventeenth century. Beza was no exception to this.

---

105 *Tractationes*, I, 186; *Novum Testamentum*, Romans 10 : 11; *Theses*, pp. 39–40.
106 *Petit Catéchisme*, pp. 281–282.
107 *Quaestiones*, p. 37.
108 This is essentially the same conclusion to which Donnelly came in his study of Peter Martyr: 'Martyr represents a transitional stage between the humanist and biblical orientation of Calvin and the developed scholasticism of the seventeenth century. His thought has many of the characteristics of developed scholasticism, but other traits are either not found in his theology or exist only in a limited and incipient way.' (Donnelly, *op. cit.*, p. 341).

There is good reason to believe that Beza was familiar with the works of both Aristotle and Thomas. Ganoczy found over fifty Aristotelian works entered in the catalog of the library of the Academy for the year 1572.[109] There were eight entries for the works of Thomas Aquinas.[110] Cardinal Cajetan (Thomas de Vio), the neo-thomist, was represented by twelve works.[111]

One must be careful not to draw hasty conclusions concerning the channels through which the concepts of Aristotle and Thomas may have been communicated to Beza because the question has not yet been adequately researched. But it may be helpful at this juncture to indicate the focus of contemporary scholarship.

Althaus had assumed that Melanchthon was the primary channel through which Aristotelianism influenced Reformed theology.[112] But there is a growing body of evidence that the greatest impact of Aristotelianism upon Reformed theology came from Italian sources.[113] The suggestion has been made recently that Beza may have had contacts with Aristotelianism via Girolamo Zanchi and Peter Martyr, both of whom were Italian Aristotelians.[114] There is, indeed, some basis for this conjecture. During the seventeenth century Beza, Martyr, and Zanchi became identified in the minds of du Moulin and other scholastics as harbingers of the scholastic method.[115]

There can be little question about the Aristotelianism of Zanchi.[116] Gründler has argued that Zanchi not only deviated from Calvin in such crucial areas as faith, the knowledge of God, and providence-predestination, but, more significantly, that at each of these points he substituted the teaching of Aquinas for that of Calvin.[117]

The issue has not been so well resolved in the case of Peter Martyr. In a recent scholarly study of Martyr's theology, Joseph McLelland has attempted to acquit Martyr of the charge of scholasticism.[118] And yet, as Armstrong has noted, McLelland has not given due consideration to the fact that Aristotle was Martyr's favorite philosopher during his student days at Padua.[119] Although the work by

109 Alexandre Ganoczy, *La Bibliothèque de l'Académie de Calvin* (Geneva, 1969), p. 123.
110 *Ibid.*, p. 103.
111 *Ibid.*, p. 97.
112 Paul Althaus, *Die Prinzipien der deutschen reformierten Dogmatik im Zeitalter der aristotelischen Scholastik* (Leipzig, 1914), p. 12. The extent of Melanchthon's Aristotelian influence has been evaluated by Kickel, *op. cit.*, pp. 46–68.
113 Donnelly, *op. cit.*, p. 15; Armstrong, *op. cit.*, p. 128. For a recent bibliographical study of Italian Aristotelianism see Charles B. Schmitt, *A Critical Survey and Bibliography of Studies on Renaissance Aristotelianism 1958–1969* (Centro per la Storia della Tradizione Aristotelica nel Veneto. Saggi e testi, XI) (Padua, 1971).
114 Armstrong, *op. cit.*, p. 38 n. 111. In a review of vol. IV of Beza's *Correspondance* Robert Kingdon has suggested that Peter Martyr may have been the source of Beza's Aristotelianism; see *Bibliothèque d'Humanisme et Renaissance*, XXX (1968), 385–387.
115 Armstrong, *op. cit.*, pp. 87, 158.
116 This has been demonstrated by Bizer, *op. cit.*; pp. 50–60 and by Gründler, *op. cit.*, *passim*. A summary of the most significant conclusions of Gründler, as they pertain to our study, may be found in Armstrong, *op. cit.*, pp. 130, 139.
117 Armstrong, *op. cit.*, p. 130.
118 Joseph C. McLelland, *The Visible Words of God: An Exposition of the Sacramental Theology of Peter Martyr Vermiglio, A.D. 1500–1562* (Grand Rapids, 1957), p. 3.
119 Armstrong, *op. cit.*, p. 130.

Philip McNair covered only the early part of Martyr's career, he has demonstrated the importance of scholasticism for Martyr's theological method, and has concluded that 'Peter Martyr was a Thomist before he became a patrist.'[120] McNair did not deal with the career of Martyr as reformer and, consequently, did not answer the question of the role of scholasticism in Martyr's later theology. But he did note that 'Whatever Martyr came to think in later years of the Thomism of the theologians of Padua, he retained to the end of his life a warm regard for the Aristotelianism of the Paduan philosophers.'[121] Additional arguments for a continued scholastic influence upon Martyr's theology have been presented by Armstrong.[122]

But the most helpful analysis of scholastic influence upon Martyr is the recent work by Donnelly in which he has itemized Martyr's references and citations to Aristotle and the Aristotelians.[123] It is clear that Martyr's references to Aristotelians are far more numerous than was the case with Calvin's references.[124] Donnelly has noted that 'again and again his [Martyr's] theological and philosophical writings utilize concepts, terms, and methods of exposition and argument borrowed from the Aristotelian tradition.'[125]

Furthermore, Martyr's basic attitude toward scholastic theology differed radically from Calvin's attitude. The great majority of Calvin's references to the scholastics were critical, but Martyr preferred Thomistic theology and often cited scholastics to support his position.[126] For Martyr, Aristotelian philosophy was 'not even a neutral instrument to be used alike by Catholic and Protestant in the construction of theological argument. Rather, Aristotle was the ally of Protestantism.'[127] In common with Beza, Martyr tended to be more scholastic in his polemical works.[128] There were times when Martyr directed hostile remarks toward the scholastics, but even then he did not object to their method. His objections resulted from their tendency to become involved in too many abstruse questions and also from the fact that Martyr, as a Protestant, disagreed with many scholastics concerning specific theological issues.[129]

Yet, Donnelly is concerned that Martyr not be pigeonholed as a scholastic, and he argues that 'Martyr was at least as much a humanist as a scholastic. The range of humanist literature that Martyr cites and the number of humanist volumes in his library surpass the scholastic.'[130] This juxtaposition of scholastic and humanist elements in a theology has already been noted in the work of Beza. It is obvious that in many ways Beza and Martyr shared a common theological perspective.

---

120 Philip McNair, *Peter Martyr in Italy: An Anatomy of Apostacy* (Oxford, 1967), p. 106.
121 *Ibid.*, p. 107.
122 Armstrong, *op. cit.*, p. 131.
123 Donnelly, *op. cit.*, p. 33.
124 *Ibid.*, pp. 33–34.
125 *Ibid.*, p. 32.
126 *Ibid.*, pp. 39, 42–43.
127 *Ibid.*, p. 315.
128 *Ibid.*, p. 316.
129 *Ibid.*, pp. 43–44.
130 *Ibid.*, p. 44.

Martyr's treatment of the doctrine of predestination was also similar to that of Beza's in many ways.[131] In contrast to Zanchi, who saw predestination as the central dogma in Christian theology,[132] Martyr viewed predestination as a cardinal doctrine that affected his entire theology even though he did not treat it as the central doctrine.[133] Martyr never developed a predestination schema as had Beza in his *Tabula*, but he had great influence upon Beza's *Tabula*.[134] Martyr differed from Beza in distinguishing predestination from providence in a Thomistic fashion, whereas Beza saw predestination as part of providence.[135]

In his work as a theologian Martyr was heavily influenced by Augustine whom he quoted more often than any other non-biblical source.[136] His view of fallen man is essentially Augustinian and places him in the same tradition as Beza, Calvin, Bucer, and Zanchi.[137] Yet at times Martyr was critical of Augustine and read him through scholastic glasses.[138] Bucer also had a strong influence upon Martyr's doctrine of predestination.[139] But part of the genius of Martyr was the ability to weave a coherent theological formulation from these diverse influences. Donnelly has caught this point well.

> What did Martyr borrow from Augustine? In Martyr's view his sacramental theology and his theology of grace, justification, and predestination were derived (after scripture) from Augustine ... Martyr borrowed Augustine's understanding of man's relationship to God and of his path to happiness. In contrast, Martyr's theological method and his manner of exposition owed more to Aristotle and medieval scholasticism than to Augustine. Martyr insisted upon orderly, even rigidly methodical exposition, upon neat technical definitions, upon clarity and precision in theological vocabulary. These are not the hallmarks of Augustine.[140]

In his discussion of predestination Martyr used Aristotelian causes as had Beza.[141] He also employed the argument, rooted in Aristotelianism, that every

---

131 The most comprehensive analysis of Martyr's doctrine of predestination and related questions is to be found in Donnelly, *op. cit.*, pp. 166–258.

132 *Ibid.*, pp. 247–248 n. 88.

133 *Ibid.*, pp. 202–203. Yet Martyr understood predestination to be decisive in the case of those who die in infancy, and he also argued that the incarnation and the death of Christ were the greatest *effects* of predestination; see Donnelly, *op. cit.*, p. 253 n. 115, 117.

134 Meylan, *Correspondance*, I, pp. 153–155.

135 Donnelly, *op. cit.*, p. 252 n. 109.

136 *Ibid.*, p. 51.

137 *Ibid.*, p. 238. Maruyama (*op. cit.*, p. 245 n. 31) has called attention to the similarity between Beza and Augustine in their treatment of the relationship between the church and predestination and has suggested that in his theologizing Beza was more of a traditionalist than a scholastic.

138 Donnelly, *op. cit.*, pp. 51–52.

139 *Ibid.*, p. 208–209. Nor should one overlook the powerful influence of Paul upon Martyr.

140 *Ibid.*, pp. 52–53.

141 *Ibid.*, pp. 305–306.

action of man requires the divine concurrence and he expressed himself very much as Beza had in the *Tabula*.[142] Martyr's analysis of human freedom and necessity was even more scholastic than had been Beza's.[143] Martyr also believed in the doctrine of irresistible grace and eternal security. In teaching them he helped to prepare the way for Dort.[144]

And yet there were ways in which Martyr differed those who are usually viewed as Protestant scholastics. For example, Martyr never dealt with the question of how one may know whether or not one if of the elect.[145] Furthermore, at critical points in his theologizing Martyr would simply quote Scripture rather than argue for his points in a philosophical manner.[146]

It is difficult to determine the precise theological impact that Martyr had upon Beza.[147] But it is clear that Beza viewed Martyr with affection and used such terms in their correspondence as *mi pater* and *alterum meum parentem*.[148] Beza certainly had a high view of Martyr as theologian, and Donnelly has suggested that 'Martyr was one source of the increasingly scholastic tone that Beza's theology took.'[149] Donnelly has substantiated his opinion in the following manner:

He [Beza] urged Bullinger to get Martyr to publish '*thesauros illos suos*,' he first suggested the idea of the *Loci Communes*. In several letters Martyr advises Beza on important theological points: on the Christian's union with Christ, Christ's presence in the Eucharist, and predestination. In 1557 Beza tells Bullinger that he has read Martyr's Corinthians commentary and refers to a particular passage; two years later he writes to Bullinger and refers to passages in both Martyr's *Tractatio* and the Corinthians commentary and says his own views on the Eucharist do not vary a hair's width from Martyr's. When Beza lost his copy of Martyr's *Dialogus*, he wrote Bullinger for another copy; in later letters he tells Bullinger that he has three times devoured . . . the *Dialogus*. In his attack upon Brenz Beza cites the *Dialogus* over a dozen times. Charles Schmidt has described the *Dialogus* as a very scholastic discussion of an essentially scholastic question.[150]

Although there has not been any definitive research concerning this question, the work of Donnelly and others provides some basis for viewing Martyr as a scholastic influence upon Beza. This is particularly the case with Martyr's doctrine of predestination. Thus Donnelly notes that 'there is . . . a line running from

---

142 *Ibid.*, pp. 119 ff.
143 For a discussion of the relationship between human freedom and predestination see Donnelly, *op. cit.*, pp. 223–230.
144 *Ibid.*, p. 220.
145 *Ibid.*, p. 253 n. 120.
146 , *Ibid.*, p. 226.
147 This is a question that has not yet been carefully researched. The most comprehensive summary that we have thus far is the work by Donnelly (*op. cit.*, pp. 349–350), and my comments below draw heavily upon that source.
148 Meylan, *Correspondance*, I, p. 148; II, p. 172.
149 Donnelly, *op. cit.*, p. 350.
150 *Ibid.*

Martyr through Ursinus and Zanchi to the Synod of Dort in 1619 which made the extreme interpretation of predestination normative for Reformed orthodoxy.'[151]

In addition to the possible scholastic influence that may have been exerted upon Beza by Martyr and Zanchi, recent scholarship has called attention to another potential source: Pomponazzi. Volume IV of Beza's correspondence contains a letter in which Beza requested a work by the Italian Aristotelian Pietro Pomponazzi.[152] In a recent article Martin Pine has argued that Pomponazzi's primary concern was with reason rather than with faith, and, as such, his work should be viewed as a 'turning point in the history of European rationalism.'[153] It was this logic which motivated the editors of Beza's correspondence to interpret his request for Pomponazzi's work as evidence for the claim that Beza was a Protestant scholastic.[154]

---

151 *Ibid.*, p. 311.
152 Meylan, *Correspondance*, IV, pp. 182–183. Donnelly (*op. cit.*, p. 22 n. 33) has made the following observations concerning this request: 'Strangely the editors seem to have overlooked an earlier letter in their own edition (II, 155) from Beza to Grataroli which indicated that Beza already had a copy of Grataroli's edition of Pomponazzi's *De Incantationibus*. This raises a further possibility. The editors assume that Beza's request on August 4, 1563, for "illum tuum Pomponatium" refers to the *De Incantationibus*, but Beza had had a copy of that book for six years and had almost certainly read Grataroli's statement in its preface that he had a second Pomponazzi manuscript which he hoped to publish. In 1567 he did publish at Basel *Libri Quinque de Fato, de Libro Arbitrio, et de Praedestinatione*. For Protestant theologians this surely must have been the most suggestive of all of Pomponazzi's writings. Could Beza's request, which the editors consider so important, refer to the *De Fato?* Probably not, since Beza would probably have been more specific than "illum tuum Pomponatium" if he wanted a manuscript. But the *possibility* cannot be discounted. In either event, the fact that Beza was seeking a copy of Pomponazzi for a *second* time in 1563 strengthens the point the editors were making and the Bizer-Kickel thesis.'
153 Martin Pine, 'Pomponazzi and "Double Truth," ' *Journal of the History of Ideas*, XXIX (1968), 176.
154 Meylan, *Correspondance*, IV, pp. 9, 183 n. 5.

CHAPTER VII

SUMMARY AND CONCLUSION

The basic goal of this study has been to shed some new light on the rise of the theological movement known as Protestant scholasticism by a detailed examination of a central dogma developed by a key figure in systematic theology. Our focus has been upon the scholastic developments within the Reformed tradition with particular attention given to the figure of Theodore Beza. We have concentrated upon Beza's doctrine of predestination because that doctrine became the keystone of the theological structure erected by scholasticism. We have sought to ascertain the role that Beza may have played in the gradual transformation of Calvin's biblically oriented theology into the rigid scholasticism that characterized Reformed orthodoxy.

No adequate, precise definition of Protestant scholasticism has emerged from the critical literature surrounding that topic. Therefore we have followed the lead of Armstrong in pointing to certain 'basic tendencies' that marked scholasticism.[1] The first such tendency was an approach to religious truth that stressed the need to discover basic assumptions or principles upon which one might build a logical system of belief that would be capable of rational defense. That approach usually assumed some form of syllogistic reasoning. On the theological level, this tendency expressed itself in an emphasis upon predestination as the synthetic, deductive starting point from which a theological system could be built. A second tendency of Protestant scholasticism was a heavy dependency upon the methodology and the philosophy of Aristotle. In some instances the admiration for Aristotle was accompanied by a new respect for Thomas Aquinas. Another mark of scholasticism was an emphasis upon the role of reason and logic in religion. In practice that meant the elevation of reason to a status equal to that of revelation. As a consequence, less emphasis was placed upon Scripture in the theology of the scholastics. One also finds in their works a growing concern for logical consistency. A fourth tendency of orthodoxy was a strong interest in speculative, metaphysical thought which would frequently focus upon questions relating to the will of God. The fifth mark of scholasticism was an interpretation of Scripture which tended to define Scripture in an unhistorical fashion as a body of propositions, once and for all delivered by God, the purpose of which was to provide an inerrant, infallible base upon which a solid philosophy could be constructed. The last tendency of scholasticism was an attitude toward faith which minimized the theological role and importance of faith. In this process faith was

---

1 Brian Armstrong, *Calvinism and the Amyraut Heresy* (Madison, 1969), p. 32.

also transmuted into intellectual assent to the truth of Scripture, rather than commitment to the person of Christ.

In order to place the work of Beza within its appropriate historical context, it was then necessary to compare and to contrast the theology of John Calvin with that of the later Reformed scholastics. Particular attention was given to Calvin's doctrine of predestination.

The conclusion reached was that there was little, if any, scholastic element in Calvin's mature theology. There was an enormous gap between Calvin's theology, which Dowey has correctly designated as a 'theology of the Word,' and the theology of Reformed scholasticism. [2] Contrary to the opinion of some scholars, predestination was not the central dogma in Calvin's theology from which everything else could be derived. In a very real sense, there was no central dogma — at least not as the scholastics would have developed one. As a theologian of the Word, Calvin simply attempted to expound the Word in its fullness. He was generally successful in rejecting the influence of Aristotle upon his theologizing. There has been a growing emphasis in contemporary scholarship upon the Christological orientation of Calvin's theology.[3] Calvin also placed a great deal of emphasis upon faith, for he viewed faith as that which linked the believer experientially to Christ. The basic distinction between the theology of Calvin and that of the scholastics has been expressed well by Armstrong.

> ... Indeed, if there is a persistent theme in Calvin it is that God's ways and thoughts are incomprehensible to man without special revelation. His theology then is an expression of faith and complete trust in God, written by a man of faith to encourage and aid the faithful of God. As such the rational dimension is clearly subordinated to the religious. In this program theology is designed not to meet the demands of a rationally acceptable and defensible system but to assist the faithful in understanding God's revelation.[4]

Calvin's biblical and Christological orientation emerged in our analysis of his doctrine of predestination. He refused to deal with the doctrine in a speculative fashion and insisted that it be considered Christologically and soteriologically. This was the reason why Calvin dealt with predestination within soteriology, not under the doctrine of God, in the 1559 edition of the *Institutes*. Calvin feared the speculative employment of predestination and cautioned that one should not go beyond the bounds of Scripture in considering the question. All that the believer had to know concerning the doctrine was to be found there. Calvin's fear of violating the limits of Scripture was seen in his refusal to speak on the question of

---

2 Edward A. Dowey, Jr., *The Knowledge of God in Calvin's Theology* (New York, 1965), p. 3.
3 For ready examples of this emphasis see Dowey, *op. cit.*; *Paul Jacobs, Prädestination und Verantwortlichkeit bei Calvin* (Neukirchen, 1937); Wilhelm Niesel, *The Theology of Calvin*, trans. Harold Knight (Philadelphia, 1956); François Wendel, *Calvin: The Origins and Development of His Religious Thought*, trans. Philip Mairet (London, 1963); Thomas F. Torrance, *Kingdom and Church* (Edinburgh, 1956); Armstrong, *op. cit.*
4 Armstrong, *op. cit.*, pp. 34–35.

the order of the decrees and his caution concerning the immediate imputation of Adam's sin to mankind. Nor did he feel that logic compelled him to assume the position of limited (specific) atonement. His belief in the accommodated character of our knowledge of God entailed a need for humility concerning the limits of rational inquiry. Although Calvin firmly believed in predestination, the result of these reservations was that he seldom dealt with the topic in his preaching.

Calvin also believed in the negative dimension of election — reprobation. In contrast to Augustine, who had taken the position that God simply abandoned those who were not elect and allowed them to feel the consequences of their sin, Calvin argued that reprobation took place as a result of the counsel of God. But Calvin refused to speculate concerning the reasons for reprobation as some of the scholastics would do later. He was convinced that he should not deal with this question because of the silence of Scripture at this point. Nor did Calvin attempt to employ reason and logic in such a manner as to convince men of the justice of God in choosing some for reprobation. Because of the danger of misunderstanding a doctrine concerning which Scripture said so little, Calvin concluded that reprobation was not an appropriate topic for preaching. Our analysis also concurred with the judgment of Dowey that reprobation was not so integral to Calvin's theology as was his doctrine of predestination.[5]

The above conclusions lead then to the next question: what was the process by which the biblically oriented theology of Calvin became transmuted into a new scholasticism? This has been the major consideration of our study. Our attempt to answer that question has led us to the figure of Theodore Beza in the hope that an analysis of his doctrine of predestination might shed some light on the rise of Reformed scholasticism.

The selection of Beza was not fortuitous. There were a number of considerations that would compel one to scrutinize his role in this process. The most obvious factor was the prominence that Beza held in the development of Calvinism for over forty years. As Calvin's successor in Geneva, Beza wielded more influence than any other single person — even though he strove to minimize the cult of personality. It would be very difficult to envisage significant changes in the development of Calvinistic theology without Beza being involved at some point in the process. After all, it was Beza who had been responsible for establishing the tone and the character of the new Academy in which so many Calvinist pastors had been trained. As the Rector of the Academy and as the successor to Calvin as Professor of Theology, Beza was viewed as the outstanding Calvinist dogmatician. And there is good evidence that Beza viewed himself as continuing the work of Calvin and as being responsible for the doctrinal purity of the Reformed cause. His post as moderator of the Company of Pastors gave him added leverage in the theological developments at Geneva.

Another reason for our selection of Beza as the object of this study is the clear evidence that in some areas Beza did, in fact, alter the practice and the teaching of Calvin. This was particularly the case in ecclesiology.

5 Dowey, *op. cit.*, pp. 212—220.

A third clue that would direct one to Beza as perhaps being instrumental in shifting the theology of Calvin into a scholastic mode is the fact that established seventeenth century scholastics, such as Pierre du Moulin, cited Beza as a harbinger of their own scholastic methodology. Was there any substance to that claim?

Our study of Beza's doctrine of predestination has led us to the conclusion that there was, indeed, some substance to that claim. His theological formulation exhibited scholastic traits not to be found in the work of Calvin, and those formulations then became normative in the development of Calvinism. Yet, at the same time, there were many ways in which Beza's theology differed from that of scholasticism, and it would be quite misleading to label him as a Protestant scholastic. This became clear when we analyzed Beza's theology in terms of the emphases usually found in scholasticism.

The scholastics exploited predestination as a basic doctrine upon which a theological system could be built. In a number of his works Beza did present predestination as the foundation of all doctrine and spoke of it as being more important than justification by faith and as providing the basis for assurance of salvation.

But, at the same time, Beza warned specifically that one should not employ predestination as a metaphysical principle which would be used to explain all phenomena of belief and unbelief. He sought to be biblical and stressed the need to explain those phenomena in such biblical categories as the result of faith and sin. It was never Beza's intention to use predestination as an organizing principle for a total theological system. His most comprehensive work, the *Confession*, did not build upon predestination as a theological foundation. The doctrine of predestination played a minor role in Beza's ecclesiology, eucharistic theology, and concept of salvation history. This was not the case with the later Protestant scholastics.

It is true that predestination played a greater role in Beza's theology than had been the case with Calvin. But part of this may have reflected the fact that Beza, as the successor of Calvin, felt the need to defend Calvin's system against the attacks of his antagonists. Many of the attacks were directed against Calvin's doctrine of predestination. Hence Beza devoted more attention to that doctrine than would have ordinarily been the case.

The basic difference between Beza and Calvin in their treatment of predestination was that Beza was more of a systematizer than was Calvin. It does appear that Beza's systematic treatment of predestination was an important step toward the rigid systems that marked the work of the Protestant scholastics.

There was also reflected in Beza's doctrine of predestination an inclination toward Aristotle and Aquinas for which there was no parallel in Calvin. This proclivity manifested itself in a variety of ways. On the simplest level, we discovered an abundance of terminology that one would associate with a scholastic orientation. There were also striking similarities between the theological concerns of Beza and Aquinas. Even Beza's most significant original contribution to theology, his distinction between the decree of election and the execution of that decree, may have been suggested to him by Thomas.

140

Although it appears that Beza was quite enamored of Aristotle and Aquinas, he was also cautious about employing non-biblical terminology and categories in presenting biblical doctrine. Our analysis of Beza's works led us to the conclusion that he resolved the conflict by restricting the influence of Aristotle and Aquinas primarily to his polemical, systematic works in which they were of great service to him. One finds little trace of their influence in Beza's works that were primarily devotional, biblical, or sermonic.

Beza's theology was also characterized by another mark of scholasticism: an emphasis upon the role of reason and logic in religion. Calvin's strictures concerning the limitations of man's reason and Beza's own reservations at that point were effectively nullified by Beza's distinction between the decree of election and the execution of that decree. Man's reason could not pierce the decree itself, but it could be employed to analyze the secondary means by which God effected that decree.

The practical impact of this was a much greater confidence on the part of Beza concerning man's ability to reason and to employ logic in the solution of theological problems. Beza's references to the mysterious elements involved in the execution of predestination became minimal. He also became much bolder in his theological assertions and was willing to take a position on issues that Calvin felt had not been clearly resolved in Scripture. Some of these issues that became pivotal in the later development of Calvinism were the immediate imputation of Adam's sin, supralapsarianism, and the extent of the atonement. Beza's greater respect for the potential of reason and logic was also reflected in his more intensive attempts to justify the activities of God to man by means of logical argumentation. But a consequence of this was that Beza's theology became so philosophised that even the actions of God were viewed in terms of logical, rational necessity.

But here, once again, we noted the same type of dualism that was observed earlier in Beza's attitude toward Thomas and Aristotle. In his systematic and polemical works Beza stressed the role of reason and logic far beyond anything to be found in Calvin. But he was not willing to forsake biblical categories entirely and tended to employ them in his nonpolemical works. Nor did Beza even view reason or logic as a substitute for revelation.

Beza's orientation toward faith was not at all scholastic. Contrary to the practice of the scholastics, Beza viewed faith as a crucial doctrine, and he spoke of it often. He did not equate faith with intellectual assent, but he followed Calvin in viewing it as a true knowledge that drove one toward a personal commitment to Christ.

Beza's theology shared with scholasticism a strong interest in speculative, metaphysical thought which tended to focus upon questions relating to the will of God. This was clearly seen in the undue attention that he devoted to the question of predestination and to issues which focused upon harmonizing the will of man with the will of God. But, once again, Beza's theological agenda was, to some degree, dictated for him by his opponents, and they were the ones who stressed questions pertaining to predestination.

Therefore we have concluded that Beza was, in no sense of the word, a full-blown scholastic. Many of the emphases found in scholasticism are absent

141

from his work, and Beza denounced the very methodology into which he was partially drawn. Bizer, Kickel, and Dantine have overemphasized the scholastic element in Beza's theology and have underplayed the biblical component. This may have been the result of their neglect of Beza's non-systematic works in favor of his systematic studies.

The precise channels through which scholastic elements were transmitted to Beza are not yet clearly understood. The most promising leads would suggest Zanchi, Martyr, and Pomponazzi as possible sources for those elements of scholasticism that have been discovered in Beza's work.

Theodore Beza was not a Protestant scholastic. It would be more accurate to view him as a transitional figure who bridged the gap between Calvin's biblical theology and the rationalistic approach of Reformed orthodoxy. Although his theological methodology included scholastic elements, it was also subject to the restraints imposed by the tradition of Calvin's biblicism and Christocentrism. There may have also been a congruent conflict between Beza's earlier humanistic orientation, with its emphasis upon the principle of returning *ad fontes* and its aversion to systematization, and Beza's love for order and precision that could be satisfied by scholasticism.

Nor was Beza responsible for the rise of Protestant scholasticism. That development was tied in with medieval scholasticism and with sixteenth century Aristotelianism. By the time that Beza wrote the *Tabula* the polemic had evolved to such a point that it demanded a new method. The following statements by Donnelly concerning the work of Peter Martyr are equally applicable to Beza.

> To be fresh and telling, polemics had to take new directions by 1550. One direction was a more extensive use of the church fathers ... Another direction was greater rigor, subtlety, sophistication, and elaboration in argument. Since scripture alone had in fact settled few arguments, it became important to show that the opposite doctrine contained logical flaws or led to philosophical absurdities and contradictions ... A variation on this is to show that the opponent's doctrine logically implies an ancient heretical teaching repudiated by the early Church ... The use of these arguments inevitably involved a more scholastic theology.[6]

Beza, with his penchant for systematization, was unusually well equipped for the theological demands of his era. He did move beyond Calvin and, in a very real sense, established a precedent for the rigid systems of the Reformed scholastics. His use of scholastic terminology and, at times, methodology, in his role as Calvin's successor resulted in granting to scholasticism a respectability in the Reformed tradition that would later be eagerly seized by others.

If it is true, as suggested by Armstrong and Hall, that Beza turned to predestination as a weapon in his polemic against Roman Catholicism, then this would be

6 John P. Donnelly, 'Peter Martyr on Fallen Man: A Protestant Scholastic View' (Unpublished Ph.D. dissertation, Department of History, University of Wisconsin, 1972), pp. 317–318.

142

evidence for the theory concerning the rise of Protestant scholasticism that has been advocated by Hornius, Weber, and Beardslee.[7] But, at the same time, the doctrine of predestination once employed, did exert a coercive, logical force upon the total body of theology. This insight, exploited by Bizer, Kickel, and Dantine in their analyses of Beza's theology, would lend support to the other theory concerning the rise of Protestant scholasticism that has been associated with the figure of Troeltsch, Tiedemann, Gass, Althaus, and Petersen. The rise of scholasticism was such a complex phenomen that, in all probability, no single theory is sufficient to encompass all of its dimensions.

7 Armstrong, *op. cit.*, p. 129; Basil Hall, 'Calvin Against the Calvinists,' *John Calvin: A Collection of Distinguished Essays*, ed. Gervase E. Duffield (Grand Rapids, 1966), p. 27.

143

BIBLIOGRAPHY

BEZA'S WORKS
COLLECTIONS OF HIS WORKS

Beza, Theodore. *Volumen primum (-tertium) Tractationum Theologicarum, in quibus pleraque Christianae Religionis dogmata adversus haereses nostris temporibus renovatas solide ex Verbo Dei defenduntur, Editio secunda ad ipso Auctore recognita.* Genevae, 1582. This collection contains most of Beza's important systematic works.
– –. *Correspondance de Théodore de Bèze.* Collected by Hippolyte Aubert. Edited by Fernand Aubert, Henri Meylan, Alain Dufour, Arnaud Tripet, and Alexandre de Henseler. 6 vols. to date. Geneva, 1960.

INDIVIDUAL WORKS ARRANGED IN CHRONOLOGICAL ORDER

Beza, Theodore. *Theodori Bezae Vezelii Poemata.* Lutetiae, 1548.
For a recent edition of this work see *Un premier recueil de Poesies Latines de Théodore de Bèze.* Edited by Fernand Aubert, Jacques Boussard, and Henri Meylan. Geneva, 1954.
– –. *Brevis et utilis zographia Joannis Cochleae.* Basel, 1549.
This work has been reprinted in Beza's *Correspondance*, I, pp. 49–55.
– –. *Abraham sacrifiant.* Genève, 1550.
A recent critical edition has been edited by Keith Cameron, Kathleen M. Hall, and Francis Higman. Geneva, 1967.
– –. *Epistola magistri Benedicti Passavantii responsiva ad commissionem sibi datam a venerabili D. Petro Lyseto, nupex curiae pariensis praesidente, nunc vero abbate sancti Victoris, prope muros.* Genevae, 1553.
– –. *Response à la confession du feu duc Jean de Northumberlande, n'aguères décapité en Angleterre.* Genève, 1554.
A recent edition of this work with an historical introduction has been prepared by A.H. Chaubard. Lyon, 1959.
– –. *De haereticis a civili Magistratu puniendis libellus adversus Martini Belii farraginem et novorum Academicorum sectam Theodore Beza Vezelii auctore.* Geneve, 1554.
– –. *Alphabetum Graecum: Addita sunt Theodori Bezae Scholia, in quibus de germana Graecae linguae pronuntiatione differitur.* Genève, 1554.
– –. *Summa totius Christianismi, sive descriptio et distributio causarum salutis electorum et exitii reproborum ex sacris literis collecta et explicata.* Genevae, 1555.
– –. *Novum D.N. Jesu Christi Testamentum, Latine jam olim a veteri interprete, nunc denuo a Theodoro Beza versum: cum ejusdem annotationibus, in quibus ratio interpretationis redditur.* Genevae, 1556.
– –. *Ad sycophantarum quorumdam calumnias, quibus unicum salutis nostrae fundamentum, id est aeternam Dei predestinationem evertere nituntur, responsio Theodori Beze Vezelii.* Genevae, 1558.
– –. *Confession de la foy chrestienne, contenant la confirmation d'icelle, et la refutation des superstitions contraires.* Genève, 1558.
A modernized text of this confession with introduction and notes has been prepared by Michel Réveillaud in *La Revue réformée*, VI (1955).
– –. *Discours du Recteur Th. de Bèze prononcé à l'inauguration de l'Académie dans le Temple de Sainte-Pierre à Genève le 5 juin 1559.* Geneve, 1559.

A new French edition of this work has been prepared by Henri Delarue. Geneva, 1959.

– –. *Altera brevis fidei confessio.* Genève, 1559.

This work was usually attached to the *Confession* of 1559.

– –. *Summa doctrinae de re sacramentaria.* Genevae, 1561.

– –. *Vie de J. Calvin.* Genève, 1564.

The weight of opinion is that the first edition of this work was written by Beza, and that subsequent editions were heavily dependent upon him.

– –. *Ad D. Jo. Brentii argumenta quibus carnis Christi omnipraesentiam nititur confirmare, Theodori Bezae Vezelii placidum et modestum responsum.* Genevae, 1565.

– –. *Defensio et Sacramentalis coniunctionis corporis et sanguinis Christi cum sacris symbolis adversus Mathaei Flacii Illyrici falsissimas demonstrationes et eiusdem Apologiam.* Genevae, 1565.

– –. *Grammaire Grecque.* Genève, 1568.

– –. *Quaestionum et responsionum Christianarum libellus, in quo praecipua Christianae Religionis capita* κατ᾽ επιτομὴ *proponunter.* Genevae, 1570.

– –. *Ad D. Nicolai Selnecceri et theologorum Jenensium calumnias, brevis et necessaria Theodori Bezae responsio.* Genevae, 1571.

– –. *Theodori Bezae modesta et christiana defensio ad Nicolai Selnecceri maledicam et virulentam responsionem.* Genevae, 1572.

– –. *Epistolarum theologicarum Theodori Bezae Vezelii, liber unus.* Genevae, 1573.

– –. *Du Droit des magistrats sur leurs subiets.* Lyon, 1574.

The best critical Latin edition, based on the text of 1580, is that by Klaus Sturm. Neukirchen-Vluyn, 1965. A new French edition of this work has been prepared by Robert M. Kingdon. Geneva, 1970. A complete, literal translation based upon the Latin text of 1595 has been done by Henri-Louis Gonin. Capetown, 1956.

– –. *Petit Catéchisme.* Genève, 1575.

This work was usually attached as an appendix to Calvin's catechism.

– –. *Quaestionum et responsionum christianarum pars altera, quae est de Sacramentis.* Genevae, 1576.

– –. *Lex Dei moralis, ceremonialis et politics, ex libris Mosis excerpta.* Genevae, 1577.

– –. *Theodori Bezae ad repetitas Jacobi Andreae et Nicolai Selnecceri calumnias responsio.* Genevae, 1578.

– –. *De veri et visibilibus ecclesiae catholicae notis tractatio.* Genevae, 1579.

– –. *Icones.* Genevae, 1580.

– –. *L'Harmonia confessionum fidei . . .* Genevae, 1581.

It is probable that Beza was the chief author of this work.

– –. *Chrestiennes méditations sur huict Psaumes du prophète David. Composées et nouvellement mises en lumiere par Theodore de Besze.* Geneva, 1582.

This work has recently been edited and translated into French by Mario Richter. Geneva, 1964.

– –. *De Predestinationis doctrina et vero usu tractatio absolutissima. Ex Th. Bezae praelectionibus in nonum Epistolae ad Romanos caput a Raphaele Eglino Tigurino Theologiae studioso in schola Genevensi recens excepta.* Genevae, 1582.

– –. *De francicae linguae recta pronuntiatione tractatus.* Genevae, 1584.

– –. *Sermons sur les trois premiers chapitres du Cantique des Cantiques, de Salomon, par Theodore de Bèze, ministre de la Parole de Dieu en l'Eglise de Genève.* Geneve, 1586.

– –. *Acta Colloquii Montis Belligartensis.* Tübingen, 1587.

– –. *Réponse aux actes de la conférence de Montbéliard.* Genève, 1587.

– –. *Ecclesiastes.* Genevae, 1588.

– –. *Iobvs. Theodore Bezae partim commentariis partim paraphrasi illustratus.* Genevae, 1589.

– –. *Sermons sur l'Histoire de la Passion et Sepulture de nostre Seigneur Jesus Christ.* Geneve, 1592.

– –. *Sermons sur l'Histoire de la Résurrection de nostre Seigneur Jesus Christ.* Geneve, 1593.

THESES COMPLETED UNDER BEZA

Beza, Theodore, and Fayus Antonius. *Theses theologicae in Schola Genevensi ab aliquot Sacrarum literarum studiosis sub DD Theod. Beza & Antonio Fayo SS Theologiae professoribus propositae & disputatae. In quibus methodica locorum communium S.S. Theologiae epitome continentur.* Genevae, 1586.

BOOKS

Althaus, Paul. *Die Prinzipien der deutschen reformierten Dogmatik im Zeitalter der aristotelischen Scholastik.* Leipzig, 1914.

Amyraut, Moise. *Defense de la doctrine de Calvin.* Saumur, 1644.

Armstrong, Brian G. *Calvinism and the Amyraut Heresy: Protestant Scholasticism and Humanism in Seventeenth-Century France.* Madison, 1969.

Aubert, Fernand, and Meylan, Henri. *Correspondence de Th. de Bèze, 1539–1564: Inventaire.* Genève, 1950.

Aymon, Jean. *Tous les synodes nationaux des églises réformées de France.* 2 vols. The Hague, 1710.

Baird, Henry Martyn. *Theodore Beza: The Counseller of the French Reformation, 1519–1605.* New York and London, 1899.

Bangs, Carl. *Arminius: A Study in the Dutch Reformation.* Nashville and New York, 1971.

Barnikol, Hermann. *Die Lehre Calvins vom unfreien Willen und ihr Verhältnis zur Lehre der übrigen Reformatoren und Augustins.* Neuwied, 1927.

Barth, Karl. *Church Dogmatics.* Vol. II/2. Translated by Geoffrey W. Bromiley *et al.* Edinburgh, 1957.

Bauke, Hermann. *Die Probleme der Theologie Calvins.* Leipzig, 1922.

Baum, Johann Wilhelm. *Theodor Beza nach handschriftlichen Quellen dargestellt.* 2 vols. Leipzig, 1843–52.

Beard, Charles. *The Reformation of the 16th Century.* Ann Arbor, 1962.

Beardslee, John W. III (ed. and trans.). *Reformed Dogmatics: J. Wollebuis, G. Voetius, F. Turretin.* New York, 1965.

Berkouwer, G.C. *Divine Election.* Translated by Hugo Bekker. Grand Rapids, Michigan, 1960.

Bernus, Auguste. *Théodore de Bèze à Lausanne.* Lausanne, 1900.

Beyerhaus, Gisbert. *Studien zur Staatsanschauung Calvins, mit besonderer Berücksichtigung seiner Souveränitatsbegriffs.* Berlin, 1910.

Bizer, Ernst. *Frühorthodoxie und Rationalismus. Theologische Studien.* Vol. LXXI. Zürich, 1963.

Boisset, Jean. *Calvin et le souveraineté de Dieu: Choix de textes, biographie.* Paris, 1964.

Bolsec, Jerome. *Histoire de la vie, moeurs, doctrine et deportements de Théodore de Bèze.* Paris, 1582.

Borgeaud, Charles. *Histoire de l'Université de Genève.* 2 vols. Genève, 1900.

Breen, Quirinus. *John Calvin: A Study in French Humanism.* Grand Rapids, 1931.

Buisson, Ferdinand. *Sébastien Castellion.* 2 vols. Paris, 1892.

Calvin, John. *Calvini opera selecta.* Edited by Peter Barth and Wilhelm Niesel. 5 vols. Munich, 1926–1936.

– –. *Calvin's New Testament Commentaries.* Edited by D.W. and T.T. Torrance. 12 vols. Grand Rapids, 1959–68.

– –. *Concerning the Eternal Predestination of God.* Translated by J.K.S. Reid. London, 1961.

– –. *Institutes of the Christian Religion.* Edited by J.T. McNeill, translated and indexed by F.L. Battles. 2 vols. *The Library of Christian Classics,* Vol. XX, XXI.

– –. *Institution de la religion chrestienne.* Edited by Jean-Daniel Benoit. 5 vols. Paris, 1957–63.

– –. *Joannis Calvini opera quae supersunt omnia.* Edited by G. Baum, E. Cunitz, and E. Reuss. 59 vols. *Corpus Reformatorum,* Vols XXIX–L. Brunswick, 1863–1900.

‒ ‒. *Predigten über das 2. Buch Samuelis.* Edited by Hans Rückert. Neukirchen, 1936–1961.

Cartier, Alfred. *Les idées politiques de Th. de Bèze, d'après le traité: Du droit des magistrats.* Genève, 1900.

Cassirer, Ernst. *The Individual and the Cosmos in Renaissance Philosophy.* Translated from the German by Mario Domandi. New York, 1963.

Chemnitz, Martin. *The Two Natures in Christ.* Translated from the Latin by Jacob Preus. St. Louis, 1970.

Choisy, Eugene. *La théocratie a Geneve au temps de Calvin.* Genève, 1897.

‒ ‒. *L'état chrétien calviniste à Genève au temps de Théodore de Bèze.* Genève, 1902.

Clavier, Henri. *Théodore de Bèze: Un apercú de sa vie aventureuse, de ses travaux, de sa personnalité.* Cahors, 1960.

Cochrane, Arthur C. (ed.). *Reformed Confessions of the 16th Century.* Philadelphia, 1966.

Collinson, Patrick. *The Elizabethan Puritan Movement.* Berkeley and Los Angeles, 1967.

Compte rendu de 3ᵉ centenaire de la mort de Théodore de Bèze. Genève, 1906.

Copleston, F.C. *A History of Philosophy.* Vol. III/ii. Garden City, 1963.

Costello, William T. *The Scholastic Curriculum at Early Seventeenth Century Cambridge.* Cambridge, 1958.

Cremeans, Charles David. *Reception of Calvinistic Thought in England.* Urbana, 1949.

Daane, James. *A Theology of Grace.* Grand Rapids, 1954.

Danaeus, L. *Christiana Isagoge ad Christianorum theologorum locos communes.* Genevae, 1583.

De La Faye, Antoine. *Bref discours de la vie et mort de M.Th. de Bèze.* Geneve, 1610.

De Vries [de Heekelingen], Herman. *Genève: Pépiniere du Calvinisme Hollandaise.* 2 vols. Vol. I: *Les Etudiants des Pays-Bas à Genève au Temps de Théodore de Bèze.* Fribourg, 1918. Vol. II: *Correspondânce des Elèves de Théodore de Bèze après leur Départ de Genève.* The Hague, 1924.

Dibon, Paul. *La Philosophie néerlandaise au siècle d'or: L'Enseignement philosophique dans les universités a l'epoque précartésienne, 1575–1650.* Paris, 1954.

Douen, Emmanuel-Oretin. *Clément Marot et le psautier huguenot.* 2 vols. Paris, 1878.

Doumergue, Emile. *Jean Calvin, les hommes et les choses de son temps.* 7 vols. Lausanne, 1899–1917.

Dowey, Edward A., Jr. *The Knowledge of God in Calvin's Theology.* 2nd printing. New York, 1965.

Dückert, Armand. *Théodore de Bèze: Prédicateur.* Genève, 1891.

Du Moulin, Pierre. *Elementa logicae.* Leyden, 1596.

Du Plessis-Mornay, Philippe. *Vindiciae contra Tyrannos.* Basel, 1579.

Elliott, J.H. *Europe Divided, 1559–1598.* New York and Evanston, 1968.

Evennett, H. Outram. *The Cardinal of Lorraine and the Council of Trent.* Cambridge, 1930.

Faguet, Emile. *La Tragédie française au XVIᵉ siècle.* Paris, 1883.

Forstman, H. Jackson. *Word and Spirit in Calvin.* Stanford, 1962.

Franklin, Julian H. *Constitutionalism and Resistance in the Sixteenth Century: Three Treatises by Hotman, Beza, and Mornay.* New York, 1969.

Ganoczy, Alexandre. *Calvin théologien de l'église et du ministère.* Unam Sanctam, no. 48. Paris, 1964.

‒ ‒. *La Bibliothèque de l'Academie de Calvin.* Geneva, 1969.

‒ ‒. *Le jeune Calvin: Genèse et évolution de sa vocation réformatrice.* Wiesbaden, 1966.

Gardy, Frédéric, and Dufour, Alain (eds.). *Bibliographie des oeuvres théologiques, littéraires, historiques et juridiques de Théodore de Bèze.* Genève, 1960.

Geisendorf, Paul F. *Bibliographie raisonée de l'Histoire de Genève: Des Origines à 1798. Mémoires et documents,* vol. XLIII. Geneve, 1966.

‒ ‒. *Théodore de Bèze.* Geneva and Paris, 1949.

Gerrish, Brian. *Reformers in Profile.* Philadelphia, 1967.

Giran, Etienne. *Sébastien Castellion et la Réforme calviniste.* Paris, 1914.

Gohler, Alfred. *Calvins Lehre von der Heiligung.* Munich, 1934.

Gooszen, M.A. *Heinrich Bullinger en de strijd over de Praedestinatie.* Rotterdam, 1909.

147

Greenslade, S.L. (ed.). *The Cambridge History of the Bible.* Vol. III: *The West from the Reformation to the Present Day.* Cambridge, 1963.

Gründler, Otto. *Die Gotteslehre Giralmo Zanchis.* Neukirchen, 1965.

Hägglund, Bengt. *History of Theology.* Translated by Gene L. Lund. St. Louis, 1968.

Hauck, Wilhelm A. *Die Erwählten: Prädestination und Heilsgewissheit bei Calvin.* Gütersloh, 1950.

– –. *Sünde und Erbsünde nach Calvin.* Heidelberg, 1938.

Heppe, Heinrich. *Die Dogmatik der evangelisch-reformierten Kirche.* Edited and revised by Ernst Bizer. Neukirchen, 1958.

– –. *Theodore Beza: Leben und ausgewählte Schriften.* Elberfeld, 1861.

Herminijard, Aimé Louis. *Correspondance des Réformateurs dans les pays de langue française.* 9 vols. Geneva, 1878–97.

Heyer, Henri. *Catalogue des thèses de théologie soutenues à l'Académie de Genève pendant les XVIᵉ, XVIIᵉ et XVIIIᵉ siècles.* Genève, 1898.

Histoire ecclésiastique des églises réformées au royaume de France. Geneva, 1580. *Edition nouvelle avec commentaire, notice bibliographique et table des faits et des noms propres par feu G. Baum et par Ed. Cunitz.* 3 vols. Paris, 1883–89.

This work has been often ascribed to Beza who provided most of the materials for it and supervised its actual composition. But Beza spoke of it as an anonymous work, and most contemporary scholars discount his authorship.

Holl, Fritz. *Das Politische und Religiöse Tendenzdrama des 16. Jahrhunderts in Frankreich.* Leipzig, 1903.

Hollweg, Walter. *Neue Untersuchungen zur Geschichte und Lehre des Heidelberger Katechismus.* Neukirchen, 1961.

Jacobs, Paul. *Prädestination und Verantwortlichkeit bei Calvin.* Neukirchen, 1937.

Kampschulte, J.W. *Johann Calvin: Seine Kirche und sein Staat in Genf.* 2 vols. Leipzig, 1869–1899.

Keller, J.J.E. *Dieu et l'Homme d'après Calvin et d'après Arminius.* Lausannc, 1860.

Kickel, Walter. *Vernunft und Offenbarung bei Theodor Beza: Zum Problem des Verhältnisses von Theologie, Philosophie und Staat. Beiträge zur Geschichte und Lehre der Reformierten Kirche,* vol. XXV. Neukirchen, 1967.

Kingdon, Robert M. *Geneva and the Consolidation of the French Protestant Movement, 1564–1572.* Madison, 1967.

Kingdon, Robert M., and Bergier, Jean-François (eds.). *Registres de la Compagnie des Pasteurs de Genève au temps de Calvin.* 3 vols. Geneva, 1962, 1964, 1969.

Klooster, Fred. H. *Calvin's Doctrine of Predestination. Calvin Theological Seminary Monograph Series,* vol. III. Grand Rapids, n.d.

Knappen, Marshall. *Tudor Puritanism.* Chicago, 1939.

Kristeller, Paul O. *Eight Philosophers of the Italian Renaissance.* Stanford, 1964.

– –. *Renaissance Thought: The Classic, Scholastic and Humanist Strains.* New York, 1961.

– –. *Renaissance Thought II: Papers on Humanism and the Arts.* New York, 1965.

– –. *The School of Padua and the Emergence of Modern Science.* Padua, 1961.

Krusche, Werner. *Das Wirken des Heiligen Geistes nach Calvin.* Göttingen, 1957.

Laingaeus, Jacob. *De vita et moribus Th. Bezae omnium haereticorum nostri temporis facile principis.* Parisii, 1585.

Laplanche, François. *Orthodoxie et prédication: L'oeuvre d'Amyraut et la querelle de la grâce universelle.* Paris, 1965.

Lebrègue, Raymond. *La tragédie religieuse en France: Les Débuts, 1514–1573.* Paris, 1929.

Léonard, Emile G. *A History of Protestantism.* 2 vols. Edited by H.H. Rowley. Vol. I: *The Reformation.* Translated from the French by Joyce M.H. Reid. London, 1965. Vol. II: *The Establishment.* Translated from the French by R.M. Bethell. London, 1967.

Lobstein, P. *Peter Ramus als Theologe.* Strassburg, 1878.

McDonnell, Kilian. *John Calvin, the Church, and the Eucharist.* Princeton, 1967.

Mackinnon, James. *Calvin and the Reformation.* 2nd printing. New York, 1962.

McLelland, Joseph C. *The Visible Words of God: An Exposition of the Sacramental Theology of Peter Martyr Vermiglio, A.D. 1500–1562.* Grand Rapids, 1957.

McNair, Philip. *Peter Martyr in Italy: An Anatomy of Apostacy.* Oxford, 1967.
McNeill, John T. *The History and Character of Calvinism.* Oxford, 1954.
Marmelstein, J. *Etude comparative des textes latins et français de l'"Institution de la religion chrestienne' par Jean Calvin.* Groningue, 1925.
Martin, P.E. *Histoire de Genève.* 2 vols. Genève, 1951–1956.
Mealy, Paul F.-M. *Origine des idées politiques libérales en France: Les publicistes de la Réforme sous François II en Charles IX.* Paris, 1903.
Mehl, Roger. *Explication de la Confession de Foi de La Rochelle.* Paris, 1959.
Mesnard, Pierre. *L'essor de la philosophie politique au XVIe siècle.* 2nd edition. Paris, 1952.
Milner, Benjamin C., Jr. *Calvin's Doctrine of the Church.* Leiden, 1970.
Moltmann, Jürgen. *Prädestination und Perseveranz: Geschichte und Bedeutung der reformierten Lehre 'de perseverantia sanctorum.'* Neukirchen, 1961.
Monnier, Marc. *Genève et ses poetes.* Paris, 1874.
Monter, E. William. *Calvin's Geneva.* New York, 1967.
Morison, Samuel Eliot. *Harvard College in the Seventeenth Century.* 2 vols. Cambridge, 1936.
Müller, E.F. Karl. *Die Bekenntnisschriften der reformierten.* Leipzig, 1903.
Naef, Henri. *La Conjuration d'Amboise et Genève.* Geneva and Paris, 1922.
Neander, J.A. *Vitae quattuor.* Berlin, 1841.
Niesel, Wilhelm. *Calvin – bibliographie, 1901–1959.* Munich, 1961.
– –. *The Theology of Calvin.* Translated from the German by Harold Knight. Philadelphia, 1956.
Oechsli, Wilhelm. *History of Switzerland, 1499–1914.* New York, 1922.
Otten, Heinz. *Calvins theologische Anschauung von der Prädestination.* München, 1938.
Pannier, Jacques. *Calvin et l'épiscopat: l'épiscopat élément organique de l'Eglise dans le Calvinisme intégral.* Strasbourg and Paris, 1927.
Pelikan, Jaroslav. *From Luther to Kierkegaard.* St. Louis, 1950.
Petersen, Peter. *Geschichte der aristotelischen Philosophie im protestantischen Deutschland.* Leipzig, 1921.
Pfister, P. *Le colloque de Montbéliard.* Geneva, 1873.
Picard, A. *Théodore de Bèze: ses idées sur le droit d'insurrection et son rôle pendant la première guerre de religion.* Cahors, 1906.
Polman, Andries Der Rietema. *De Praedestinatieleer van Augustinus, Thomas van Aquino en Calvin.* Franeker, 1936.
Polman, Pontien. *L'Elément historique dans la controverse religieuse du XVIe siècle.* Gembloux, 1932.
Popkin, Richard H. *The History of Scepticism from Erasmus to Descartes.* Assen, 1960.
Preus, Robert D. *The Inspiration of Scripture: A Study of the Theology of the 17th Century Lutheran Dogmaticians.* Mankato, Minn., 1955.
– –. *The Theology of Post-Reformation Lutheranism: A Study of Theological Prolegomena.* St. Louis, 1970.
Quistorp, Heinrich. *Calvin's Doctrine of the Last Things.* Richmond, 1955.
Raitt, Jill. *The Eucharistic Theology of Theodore Beza: Development of the Reformed Doctrine.* American Academy of Religion Studies in Religion 4. Chambersburg, Pennsylvania, 1972.
Ritschl, Otto. *Dogmengeschichte des Protestantismus.* Vol. III., Göttingen, 1926.
Romier, Lucien. *Catholiques et Huguenots à la cour de Charles IX.* Paris, 1924.
Rossel, Virgile. *Histoire littéraire de la Suisse romande.* Neuchâtel, 1903.
Rost, Gerhard. *Der Prädestinationsgedanke in der Theologie Martin Luthers.* Berlin, 1966.
Scheibe, Max. *Calvins Prädestinationslehre.* Halle, 1897.
Scharlemann, Robert. *Aquinas and Gerhard: Theological Controversy and Construction in Medieval and Protestant Scholasticism.* New Haven, 1964.
Schlosser, Friedrich Christophe. *Leben des Th. de Beza.* Heidelberg, 1809.
Schmidt, Albert-Marie. *Calvin and the Calvinistic Tradition.* Translated from the French by Ronald Wallace. New York, 1960.
Schmitt, Charles B. *A Critical Survey and Bibliography of Studies on Renaissance Aristotelianism 1958–1969.* Padua, 1971.

149

Schwarzenau, Paul. *Der Wandel im theologischen Ansatz bei Melanchthon von 1525–1535.* Gütersloh, 1956.

Schweitzer, Alexander. *Die Protestantischen Centraldogmen in ihrer Entwicklung innerhalb der reformierten Kirche.* 2 vols. Zürich, 1854–56.

Simon, Richard. *Histoire critique des versions du Nouveau Testament.* Rotterdam, 1690.

Smits, Luchesius. *Saint Augustin dans l'oeuvre de Jean Calvin.* 2 vols. Translated from the Dutch by Egbert von Laethem. Assen, 1957.

Stauffer, Richard. *L'Humanité de Calvin.* Neuchâtel, 1964.

Steinmetz, David C. *Reformers in the Wings.* Philadelphia, 1971.

Stéphan, Raoul. *Histoire du protestantisme français.* Paris, 1961.

Stone, Donald, Jr. (ed.). *Four Renaissance Tragédies.* Cambridge, Mass., 1966.

Tonkin, J.M. *The Church and the Secular Order in Reformation Thought.* New York and London, 1971.

Torrance, Thomas F. *Calvin's Doctrine of Man.* London, 1949.

– –. *Kingdom and Church.* Edinburgh, 1956.

Trinterud, Leonard J. (ed.) *Elizabethan Puritanism.* New York, 1971.

Troeltsch, Ernst. *Vernunft und Offenbarung bei Johann Gerhard und Melanchthon.* Göttingen, 1891.

Van Buren, Paul. *Christ in our Place.* Grand Rapids, 1957.

Van Til, Cornelius. *The Defense of the Faith.* Philadelphia, 1955.

Vuilleumier, Henri. *Histoire de l'Eglise Réformée du Pays de Vaud sous le Régime bernois.* 4 vols. Lausanne, 1927–1933.

Wallace, Ronald S. *The Doctrine of the Christian Life.* Grand Rapids, 1959.

Weber, Emil. *Der Einfluss der protestantischen Schulphilosophie auf die orthodoxlutherische Dogmatik.* Leipzig, 1908.

– –. *Die analytische Methode der lutherische Orthodoxie.* Naumburg, 1907.

– –. *Die philosophische Scholastik des deutschen Protestantismus im Zeitalter der Orthodoxie.* Leipzig, 1907.

Weber, Hans Emil. *Reformation, Orthodoxie und Rationalismus. Beiträge zur Forderung Christlicher Theologie,* vols. XXXVII and LI. Gütersloh, 1937 and 1951.

Weber, Otto. *Grundlagen der Dogmatik.* 2 vols. Neukirchen, 1955 and 1962.

Wendel, François. *Calvin: The Origins and Development of His Religious Thought.* Translated from the French by Philip Mairet. London, 1963.

Wundt, Max. *Die Deutsche Schulmetaphysik des 17. Jahrhunderts.* Tübingen, 1939.

Zeller, Walther (ed.) *Der Protestantismus des 17. Jahrhunderts.* Marburg, 1963.

ARTICLES, PERIODICALS, AND UNPUBLISHED MANUSCRIPTS

Aubert, Fernand. 'Une manifestation internationale en l'honneur de Théodore de Bèze, enfant de Vézelay.' Genève, 1926. 8 pp. (Extracted from *La Tribune de Genève.*)

Aubert, Hippolyte. 'La conversion de Théodore de Bèze a la Réforme: Théodore de Bèze et sa famille d'après des extraits de la correspondance de Bèze,' *Bulletin de la Société de l'histoire protestant français,* LII (1904), 533–548.

Barnaud, J. 'La confession de foi de Théodore de Bèze,' *Bulletin de la Société de l'Histoire protestant français,* XLVIII (1899), 617–633.

Barth, Peter. 'Die Erwählungslehre in Calvins Institutio von 1536,' in *Theologische Aufsätze, Karl Barth zum 50. Geburtstag* (München, 1936), 432–442.

Benoit, Jean-Daniel. 'D'une édition à l'autre de l'Institution; comment Calvin travaillait,' *La revue réformée,* XI (1960–61), 39–51.

Bost, Ch. 'Théodore de Bèze, Rabelais et le "passavant,"' *Revue du XVIe Siècle,* XIX (1932–33), 282–290.

Carbonnier, J. 'Le Colloque de Poissy,' *Foi et Vie,* new series, LX (1961) 43–52.

Cartier, Alfred. 'Les idées politiques de Theodore de Bèze d'après le traité: "Du droit des magistrats sur leurs sujets,"' *Bulletin de la Société d'histoire et d'archéologie de Genève,* II (1900), 187–206.

150

Choisy, Eugene. 'Beza,' in *Realencyklopädie für protestantische Theologie und Kirche*. Edited by J.J. Herzog. Vol. II (Leipzig, 1897), 677–686.

Dantine, Johannes. 'Das christologische Problem in Rahmen der Prädestinationslehre von Theodor Beza,' *Zeitschrift fur Kirchengeschichte*, LXXVII (1966), 81–96.

– –. 'Die prädestinationslehre bei Calvin und Beza,' Doctoral dissertation, Faculty of Theology, Göttingen University, 1965.

– –. 'Les Tabelles sur la doctrine de la prédestination par Théodor de Bèze,' *Revue de Théologie et de Philosophie* XVI (1966), 365–377.

Davis, Natalie Z. 'Peletier and Beza part company,' *Studies in the Renaissance*, XI (1964), 188–222.

D'Eszlary, Charles. 'Jean Calvin, Théodore de Bèze et leurs amis hongrois,' *Bulletin de la Société de l'histoire du protestantisme français*, CX (1964), 74–99.

Donnelly, John Patrick. 'Peter Martyr on Fallen Man: A Protestant Scholastic View,' Ph.D. dissertation, Department of History, University of Wisconsin, 1972.

Doumergue, Emile. 'Les Théories Politiques de Théodore de Bèze,' in *Compe rendu du 3e centenaire de la mort de Théodore de Bèze* (Genève, 1906), 12–16.

Droz, Eugénie. 'Fausses addresses typographiques,' *Bibliothèque d'Humanisme et Renaissance*, XXIII (1961), 379–384.

– –. 'Les débuts de Théodore de Bèze à Genève,' *Geneva*, XIII (1965), 59–72.

– –. 'L'imprimeur de L'Histoire ecclésiastique (1580),' *Bibliothèque d'Humanisme et Renaissance*, XXII (1960), 371–376.

– –. 'Notes sur Théodore de Bèze,' *Bibliothèque d'Humanisme et Renaissance*, XXIV (1962), 392, 589.

Dufour, Alain. 'L'affaire de Maligny (Lyon, 4–5 septembre 1560) vue à travers la correspondence de Calvin et de Bèze,' *Cahiers d'histoire*, VIII (1963), 269–280.

– –. 'Le Colloque de Poissy,' *Mélanges d'histoire du xvie siècle offerts à Henri Meylan*. Lausanne, 1970, 127–137.

Giesey, Ralph E. 'The Monarchomach Triumvirs: Hotman, Beza and Mornay,' *Bibliothèque d'Humanisme et Renaissance*, XXXII (1970), 41–56.

– –. 'Why and When Hotman wrote the Francogallia,' *Bibliothèque d'Humanisme et Renaissance*, XXIX (1967), 583–611.

Gray, Hanna. 'Renaissance Humanism: The Pursuit of Eloquence,' *Journal of the History of Ideas*, XXIV (1963), 497–514.

Hall, Basil. 'Calvin against the Calvinists,' in *John Calvin: A Collection of Distinguished Essays*, edited by Gervase E. Duffield (Grand Rapids, 1966), 19–37.

– –. 'The Calvin Legend,' *John Calvin: A Collection of Distinguished Essays*, edited by Gervase E. Duffield (Grand Rapids, 1966), 1–18.

Hoss, Irmgard, 'Zur Genesis der Widerstandlehre Bezas,' *Archiv für Reformationsgeschichte*, LIV (1963), 198–213.

Kingdon, Robert M. 'The First Expression of Theodore Beza's Political Ideas,' *Archiv für Reformationsgeschichte*, LV (1955), 88–100.

– –. 'Les idées politiques de Bèze d'après son traitté de l'autorité du magistrat en la punition des hérétiques,' *Bibliothèque d'Humanisme et Renaissance*, XXII (1960), 566–569.

Labarthe, Olivier. 'Le changement du mode de presidence de la Compagnie des Pasteurs de Genève (1578–1580),' *Zeitschrift für schweizerische Kirchengeschichte*, LXVII (1972), 160–186.

LaVallee, Armand A. 'Calvin's Criticism of Scholastic Theology,' Ph.D. dissertation, Harvard University, 1967.

Lods, A. 'Les Actes du colloque de Montbéliard, 1586: Une polémique entre Théodore de Bèze et Jacques Andreae,' *Bulletin de la Société de l'histoire du protestantisme français*, XXXXVI (1897), 192–215.

McNeill, John T. 'The Doctrine of the Ministry in Reformed Theology,' *Church History*, XII (1943), 78–86.

– –. 'The Significance of the word of God for Calvin,' *Church History*, XXVIII (1959), 131–146.

151

Marsden, George M. 'Perry Miller's Rehabilitation of the Puritans: A Critique,' *Church History*, XXXIX (1970), 91–105.

Maruyama, Tadataka. 'The Reform of the True Church: The Ecclesiology of Theodore Beza,' Th.D. dissertation, Princeton Theological Seminary, 1973.

Mercier, Charles. 'Les théories politiques des calvinistes en France au cours des guerres de religion,' *Bulletin de la Société de l'histoire du protestantisme français*, LXXXIII (1934), 243–248.

Meylan, Henri. 'Bèze et les Italiens de Lyon,' *Bibliothèque d'Humanisme et Renaissance*, XIV (1952), 235–249.

– –. 'La conversion de Bèze ou les longues hésitations d'un humaniste chrétien,' *Geneva*, VII (1959), 103–125.

Molard, Francis. 'Quand Théodore de Bèze a-t-il rompu avec l'Eglise romaine?,' *Bulletin de la Société des sciences historiques et naturelles de l'Yonne*, 1888, 201–204.

Moltmann, Jürgen. 'Prädestination und Heilsgeschichte bei Moyse Amyraut,' *Zeitschrift für Kirchengeschichte*, LXV (1954), 270–303.

Niesel, Wilhelm. 'Syllogismus practicus?,' *Aus Theologie und Geschichte der reformierte Kirche; Festgabe für E.F.K. Muller.* Neukirchen, 1933, 158–179.

Nugent, Donald G. 'The Colloquy of Poissy: A Study in Sixteenth Century Ecumenism,' Ph.D. dissertation, Department of History, University of Iowa, 1965.

Pannier, Jacques. 'Comment Calvin a revisé les éditions successives de l'Institution,' *Bulletin de la Société de l'histoire du protestantisme française*, LXXIX (1930), 79–81.

Partee, Charles B., Jr. 'Calvin and Classical Philosophy: A Study in the Doctrine of Providence,' Th.D. dissertation, Princeton Theological Seminary, 1971.

– –. 'Calvin and Experience,' *Scottish Journal of Theology*, XXVI (1973), 169–181.

Pine, Martin. 'Pomponazzi and the "Double Truth," ' *Journal of the History of Ideas*, XXIX (1968), 163–176.

Pirotti, Umberto. 'Aristotelian Philosophy and the Popularization of Learning: Benedetto Varchi and Renaissance Aristotelianism,' in *The Late Italian Renaissance*, edited by Eric Cochrane (New York, 1970), 168–208.

Popkin, Richard H. 'Skepticism and the Counter-Reformation in France,' *Archiv für Reformationsgeschichte*, LI (1960), 58–86.

Quistrop, Heinrich. 'Sichtbare und unsichtbare Kirche bei Calvin,' *Evangelische Theologie*, IX (1949–50), 83–101.

Raitt, Jill. 'Roman Catholic New Wine in Reformed Old Bottles? The Conversion of the Elements in the Eucharistic Doctrines of Theodore Beza and Edward Schillebeeckx,' *Journal of Ecumenical Studies.* VIII (1971), 581–604.

Réveillaud, Michel. 'L'autorité de la tradition chez Calvin,' *La revue réformée*, IX (1958), 25–44.

Rist, Gilbert. 'Modernité de la méthode théologique de Calvin,' *Revue de théologie et philosophie*, no. 1 (1968), 19–33.

Shepherd, Norman. 'Zanchius on Saving Faith,' *The Westminster Theological Journal*, XXXVI (1973), 31–47.

Smid, T.D. 'Beza en Nederland,' *Nederlands archief voor Kerkgeschiedenis*, XLVI (1963–64), 169–191.

Tedeschi, John A., and Willis, E. David. 'Two Italian translations of Beza and Calvin,' *Archiv für Reformationsgeschichte*, LV (1964), 70–74.

Thonnard, F.-J. 'La prédestination augustinienne,' *Revue des études augustiniennes*, X (1964), 97–123.

Van Schelven, A.A. 'Beza's "De jure magistratum in subditos," ' *Archiv für Reformationsgeschichte*, LIV (1954), 62–83.

Vuilleumier, Henri. 'Th. de Bèze à Lausanne,' in *Compte rendu du 3ᵉ centaire de la mort de Théodore de Bèze* (Genève, 1906), 22–28.

Walty, J.N. 'Bulletin d'histoire des doctrines modernes Calvin et le calvinisme,' *Revue des sciences philosophiques et théologiques*, XLIX (1965), 245–287.

Weiss, N. 'Le procès de Bèze au Parlement de Paris,' *Bulletin de la Société de l'histoire du protestantisme français*, XXXVII (1888), 530–537.

– –. 'Le role de Th. de Bèze en France au XVIe siècle,' in *Compte rendu du 3e centaire de la mort de Théodore de Bèze* (Genève, 1906), 35–61.

Wiley, David N. 'Calvin's Doctrine of Predestination: His Principal Soteriological and Polemical Doctrine,' Ph.D. dissertation, Duke University, 1971.

Wolf, Ernst. 'Erwählungslehre und Prädestinationsproblem,' *Theologische Existenz heute*, Neue Folge, XXVIII (1951), 63–94.